THE NEW CULTURAL ATLAS OF

THE GREEK WORLD

Edited by Tim Cooke

This edition first published in 2010 in the United States of America by Marshall Cavendish.

Marshall Cavendish
99 White Plains Road
Tarrytown, New York 10591-9001

Library of Congress Cataloging-in-Publication Data

Marshall Cavendish Corporation
The new cultural atlas of the Greek world.
    p. cm.
Includes bibliographical references and index.
ISBN 978-0-7614-7878-2 (alk. paper)
1. Greece--Civilization--Maps. 2. Greece--History--Maps.
3. Greece--Antiquities--Maps. I. Title.
G2001.E6M3 2009
911'.38--dc22
                    2009008611

Printed and bound in Singapore

Picture credits

Front Cover:
Bridgeman Art Library: Staatiche Museum.

Corbis: Alinari Archives 177, Art Archive 170, Atlantide Phototravel 21, Bettmann 28, Kristi J. Black 47, Walter Bibikow 87, Kevin Flemming 22, 34, 51, Gallery Collection 25, Rainer Hackenberg 63, Robert Harding World Imagery 159, Chris Hollier 121, Eric & David Hosking 137, Hanan Isachar 9, 135, Richard List 147, Araldo de Luca 52, 53, Gail Mooney 3, Gianni Dagli Orti 41, 141, Robert Patrick 157, Paul A. Souders 107, Kevin Schafer 75, Grafton Smith 135, Jon Sparks 150, Sandro Vannini 173, Roger Wood 57; **Getty Images:** Bridgeman Art Library 131, De Agostini 175, Hulton Achive 27, National Geographic 15, Robert Harding World Imagery 163, Roger Viollet 37; **iStockphoto:** 10–11, Beni 67, DenGuy 65; **Shutterstock:** Florin Cirstoc 68, Mark Higgins 81, Juha-Pekka Kervinen 99, Nick Koumans 81, Timothy R. Nichols 44, Scion 102, D. Martin Vonka 82, Yan Zverev 105.

Artworks: Brown Reference Group Ltd.

For the Brown Reference Group Ltd:
Editorial Director: Lindsey Lowe
Senior Managing Editor: Tim Cooke
Design Manager: David Poole
Designer: Kim Browne
Indexer: Christine Michaud
Picture Manager: Sophie Mortimer
Production Director: Alastair Gourlay

Text adapted from the *Atlas of the Greek World*, revised edition, 1990, Checkmark Books (Facts On File), New York. Original text by Peter Levi.

E NEW CULTURAL ATLAS OF

THE GREEK WORLD

Edited by Tim Cooke

Marshall Cavendish
Reference
New York

500 BCE	400 BCE	300 BCE	200 BCE	1 CE	500 CE

Classical period	Hellenistic period		Roman Empire	Byzantine Empire

Persian invasions

Athens dominates Delian League

Age of Perikles

Peloponnesian War

Athenian revival

Rise of Macedon

Fall of Sparta

Campaigns of Alexander

Rise to power of Achaean and Aetolian leagues

Macedonian wars

Macedonia becomes Roman province

Achaea becomes Roman province

Greece remains cultural and intellectual center of Mediterranean

The Venus de Milo, a second-century BCE marble statue from Melos.

Alexander the Great at the battle of Issos. Detail from the "Alexander mosaic" found at Pompeii, copy of a Greek painting c.300 BCE

Roman coin of Hadrian, second century CE.

The Parthenon at Athens, completed 441–432 BCE

Athenian Red Figure

Temple of Zeus at Olympia

Parthenon, Erechtheion

Pheidias and Polykleitos (sculptors)

Polygnotos (painter)

South Italian painters

Praxiteles (sculptor)

Mausoleum at Halikarnassos

Hellenistic baroque

Altar of Zeus, Pergamon

Winged Victory of Samothrace

Venus de Milo

Roman copying of Greek sculpture and architecture

Santa Sophia built Constantinople (Istanbul)

Fifth-century BCE vase with archaic poets, Sappho and Alkaios.

Silver coin from Athens, c.440 BCE

Painted terracotta, women gossiping, c.320 BCE

Bust of philosopher, possibly Bion.

Aischylos, Pindar, Sophokles, Herodotos, Euripides, Sokrates, Hippokrates, Thucydides, Aristophanes

Plato, Aristotle, Epicurus, Theokritos, Euclid, Archimedes

Creation of library at Alexandria

Pausanias

Darius crosses Hellespont and invades Greece

Alexander conquers Asia Minor, Egypt, Persia, NW India

Successor kingdoms, Ptolemaic, Seleukid dynasties

Gauls settle in Galatia (modern Turkey)

Parthian Empire founded

Rome defeats Antiochos of Syria

Pergamon becomes Roman province

Egypt becomes Roman province

Sasanian Empire founded in Persia

Byzantion refounded by Romans (Constantinople)

Introduction

The history of humankind had a crisis in the 5th century BCE, an explosion of light that affected everything and still does so today. Europe is the result and Greece is the key. What happened in Greece in the 5th century was part of a long process.

It is impossible to understand Greek history or art or poetry at all well without a strong sense of the prehistory, of the landscape, the climate, the mountains and the rivers, and the conditions of life. For this understanding it is necessary to have some acquaintance with the ruins and places of the Greeks; and getting to know them is an attractive process, even in the pages of a book. This book is an attempt to make sense of the ancient Greeks, of their spiritual and mental world, as well as the physical world of their experiences, of their history, and their travels and expansion, as well as their arts and their achievements. Those include philosophy, medicine, natural science, the theatrical arts, marble architecture, a new economic system, and the rule of law.

For this simple-sounding but in fact rather vast enterprise of making sense of the Greeks, pictures and plans as well as maps and a continuous text are not a luxury, they are actually necessary. The medium of an atlas is ideal; but even so it is not possible to include everything. No one has visited all the Greek ruins in the world. Very few scholars have seen all the antiquities even of Greece itself, inside and outside the museums. Certainly no book includes them all. No attempt to make sense of this mass of material, and of the many hundreds of years of Greek history, can have absolute authority. Although this cultural atlas is a reliable guide within its limitations, it is meant, at a deeper level, to excite, engage, and amuse.

Contents

Timeline

	2000 BCE	1500 BCE	1000 BCE	800 BCE	600 BCE
CULTURAL PERIOD	Bronze age		Dark age	Archaic period	

AEGEAN AND GREEK MAINLAND

Cretan palace civilization

Shaft graves at Mycenae

Iron introduced from East then return to bronze

Rise of aristocratic families

Population increases in Greece

First Greek coins

Beginnings of democracy at Athens

Explosion at Santorini

Fall of Knossos

Fall of Mycenaeans

Chief period of colonization to E and W

Sparta dominates Peloponnese

International festivals established

Tyrants in control of many cities

Invention of hoplite fighting

So-called mask of Agamemnon from Mycenae, 1550–1500 BCE

The "warrior vase" from Mycenae, early 12th century BCE

Geometric amphora from Athens, c.750 BCE

The "peplos kore" from the Athenian Akropolis, c.530 BCE

POTTERY STYLE ART AND ARCHITECTURE

Great palaces in Crete

Santorini frescoes

Great beehive tombs

Sub-Mycenaean protogeometric

Geometric

Orientalizing

Archaic (Athenian Black Figure)

Kouroi and korai

Figurines, fine working in gold and semiprecious stones (e.g. sealstones)

Monumental vases

Olympia tripods

First stone temples

Octopus flask from eastern Crete, 1350 BCE

13th-century BCE carved ivory from Mycenae.

Bronze statue of hoplite, Dodone.

LITERATURE, PHILOSOPHY, AND SCIENCE

Linear A tablets

Linear B tablets

Phoenician alphabet

Greek alphabet

Homer

Hesiod

Lyric poets

Beginnings of tragedy and comedy

Pythagoras

Sappho

EGYPT, ASIA MINOR, AND THE EAST

Egyptian New Kingdom

Great temples

Tutankhamon

Hittite Empire in Anatolia

Babylonian Empire

Greek colonies in Ionia, then around Black Sea

Assyrian Empire at most powerful

Assyrians lose power to Medes and Babylonians

Darius founds Persian Empire

Persians conquer Egypt

Evening light falls on the Temple of Poseidon at Cape Sounion, near Athens, built in the mid–5th century BCE to honor the Greek sea god.

The Geography of Ancient Greece

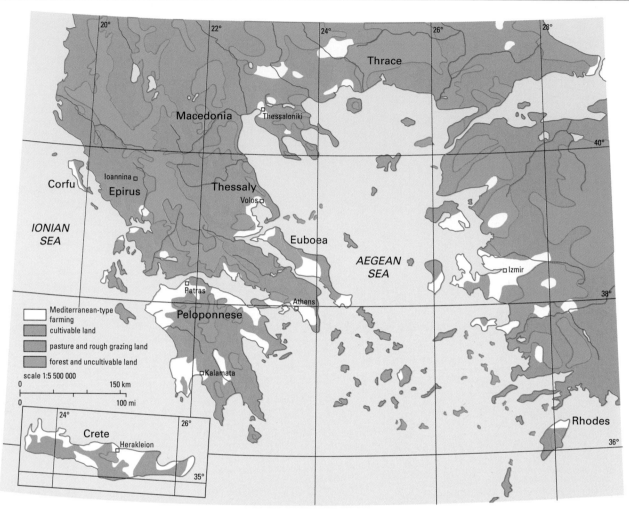

▲ *This map shows the vegetation of the Greek world today. Forests were more extensive in antiquity, especially in Crete and the Pindos mountains, and there was a great deal more game.*

The map labels:
Thrace, Macedonia, Thessaloniki, Ioannina, Corfu, Epirus, Thessaly, Volos, IONIAN SEA, Euboea, AEGEAN SEA, Izmir, Patras, Athens, Peloponnese, Rhodes, Kalamata, Crete, Herakleion

Mediterranean-type farming
cultivable land
pasture and rough grazing land
forest and uncultivable land
scale 1:5 500 000
0   150 km
0   100 mi

◄ *(previous pages) According to myth, the rocky summit of Mount Olympos was home to the chief gods of ancient Greece.*

The geography of ancient Greece could be isolating. Thrace and Macedonia in the northeast were wild; Epirus was wild and isolated; and Arcadia was the remotest part of the Peloponnese. Within the last century there were villages in the Peloponnese where a foreign traveler would be greeted as an explorer or arrested as a spy. Toward the Albanian frontier, or high in the Cretan mountains, some shadow has lingered of the isolation of ancient times. The isolation of the mountains has not altered much. The Pindos, the rocky backbone of northern Greece, is still crossed by only three roads.

Climate, calendar, and farming

Three-quarters of Greece is mountainous, and only one fifth of the land can be farmed; but the coastal plains and some inland areas are very rich. The olive and the vine have long flourished, but not everywhere. It has been said that the Greeks spread as far afield as the olive will grow, and the Romans as far afield as the vine. That may be true, but it should be remembered that even mainland Greece was not fully colonized. Wheatfields in mainland Greece were never very big. Small wonder that the population struggled over the riches between rock and rock.

The average temperature differs from one part of Greece to another, with hot summers and mild winters in coastal and southern areas but cold winters in Macedonia and the mountainous interior. Rainfall is high in the west (up to 50 in/130 cm per year) but much lower on the eastern plains (15 in/38 cm in Thessaly and Athens). The differences between seasons are dramatic. Winter is shorter than in northern Europe, but in the mountains winter is very hard and summer is stupefying. All this has affected human societies, from the festivals of the gods and the moving of herds to questions of war and peace and the details of colonization.

Until recently Greece was full of herds of sheep and goats that moved twice a year to have summer grazing in the mountains and winter grazing well below the snowline. This pattern of movement is very ancient all over the world. Transhumance involves a complete way of life, and it nourishes a system of values and a social organization of great interest to scholars of the ancient world.

Greek mythology is full of stories of cattle raids, as is history down to the first campaigns of the Peloponnesian war. The cattle sacrificed at Athens in the 5th and 4th centuries must have been immensely numerous. Later still, we know from inscriptions that on island after island sheep farming was annihilated by huge flocks of goats: Overgrazing by goats is destructive of the landscape, and has done more to shape

▼ *From ancient times Greek farmers have threshed their grain by covering the floor of a threshing circle with harvested straw and walking a mule over it in circles. The grain is then winnowed.*

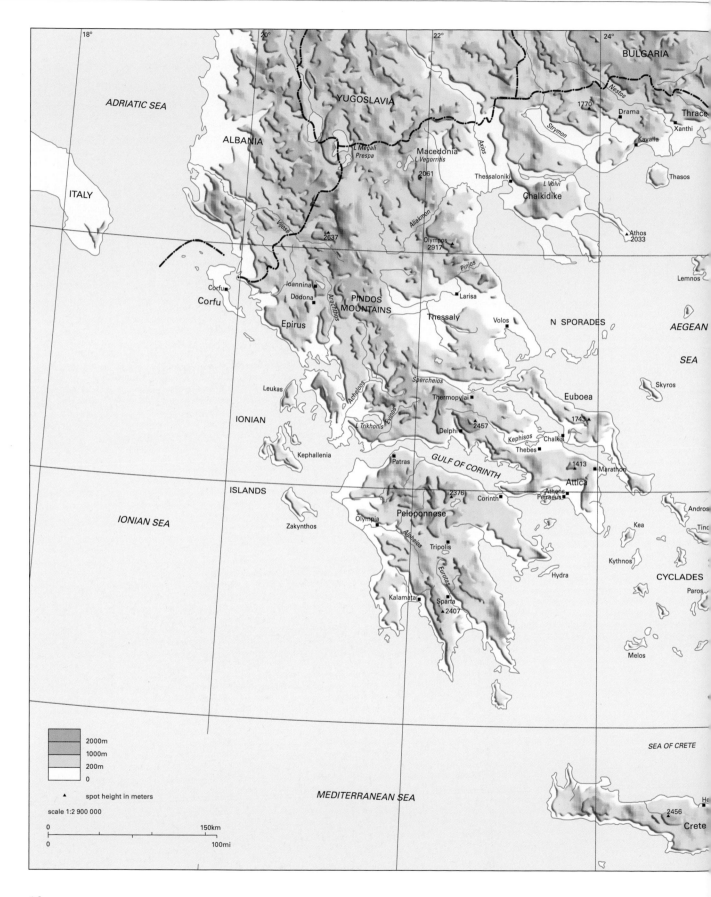

ADRIATIC SEA

BULGARIA

YUGOSLAVIA

Thrace

ALBANIA

Drama

Xanthi

Strymon

1770

Nestos

Kavalla

ITALY

L Megali
Prespa

Macedonia

L Vegorritis

2061

Thessaloniki

L Volvi

Chalkidike

Thasos

Vijosa

Axios

Aliakmon

2637

Olympos
2917

▲Athos
2033

Pinjos

Lemnos

Corfu

Ioannina

Dodona

PINDOS
MOUNTAINS

Larisa

Corfu

Epirus

Arachthos

Thessaly

Volos

N SPORADES

AEGEAN

SEA

Skyros

Spercheios

Leukas

Achelous

Euboea

IONIAN

L Trikhonis

Thermopylai

1743▲

Evinos

2457

Delphi

Kephisos

Chalkis

Kephallenia

Thebes

Patras

GULF OF CORINTH

1413

Marathon

ISLANDS

2376

Attica

Olympia

Corinth

Athens

Pejraeus

Andros

Peloponnese

Alpheios

Kea

Tino

Zakynthos

Tripolis

Hydra

Kythnos

IONIAN SEA

Eurotas

CYCLADES

Paros

Kalamata

Sparta

▲2407

Melos

2000m
1000m
200m
0

▲ spot height in meters

scale 1:2 900 000

0   150km

0   100mi

SEA OF CRETE

MEDITERRANEAN SEA

2456

Crete

the eastern Mediterranean, than even earthquakes or forest fires.

Caves, springs, and rivers

Springs, caverns, and rivers were important. Rivers were boundaries, because each side grazed its flocks and watered them to the same limit. Caves were mysterious, religious places, associated with fertility cults. Springs of pure water had powerful influences; sanctuaries of healing and oracles of worldly help would center on a spring.

The principal way in which the physical geography of tall rocks and misty seas affected the ancient Greeks was economic. For a Greek in the 5th century, what romantic scholarship now sees as the sacred landscape of Vergil, or of Pausanias, or of a Roman wall painting, was the difficult earth where he made a hard living, and most of its gods were equally difficult gods. At the popular level, Greek religion was fearful, envious, and desperate.

Serfs and slaves

The ancient Greek economy was limited not only by its material resources, but also by lack of knowledge. The silver mines that made Athens rich in the 5th century had been

◀ Mountains cover three-quarters of Greece. Although only one fifth of the land can be cultivated, the coastal plains and some inland areas are very fertile.

▶ *The temperature in centigrade in January and the prevailing winds. Winters in Macedonia and the mountainous interior are very hard.*

known to the Mycenaeans, but their techniques of recovering silver were poor. Lake Kopais, north of Thebes in Boeotia was drained at least partially by the Mycenaeans. It went back to water, reeds, and eels after the fall of Mycenae. No attempt to cut the Corinth canal was successful in antiquity. At least until the 5th century, the Greeks were unable to attempt any huge disturbances of nature. To raise a stone temple was for them a colossal project. The great temples of the 6th century were even more impressive to the Greeks than they are to us.

Patterns of settlement

Cities rose and fell. Corinth was rich because it was nearly impregnable, and because of its position, commanding the Isthmus and the trade of the eastern and the western seas. The Romans destroyed Corinth (146 BCE) and built up Patras instead, but in late antiquity Corinth again overshadowed Patras. Another repeated pattern is the alternating movement of towns uphill to defensive sites in bad times, and downhill to trading positions in periods of peace.

The growth of modern towns on ancient sites is not always a matter of continuity. Modern Corinth, for example, is 3 miles (5 km) from the village of Palaia-Korinthos, which covers part of the ancient site. There are ancient sites without a village, and some modern towns, like Pyrgos in Eleia,

▶ *This map shows the temperature in centigrade in July and the prevailing winds. Coastal areas have hot summers and mild winters.*

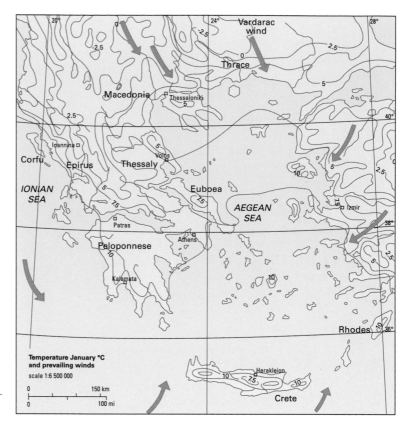

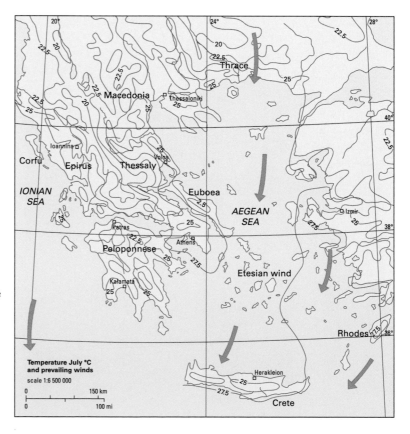

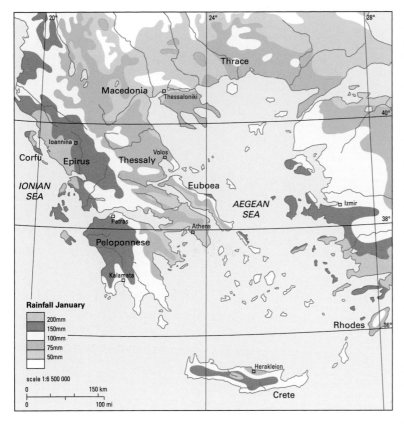

which are not built on ancient sites. But the position of Corinth, the harbors of Athens and of Corfu (Kerkyra), the site of Kalamata, where the Messenian plain meets the sea, and the positions of certain islands make it inevitable that human settlements will occur there.

The place of Greece in Europe

From time to time in history Greece has seemed to belong to the east; from the 7th century BCE until the 1920s the western coast of Asia was predominantly Greek. At other times Greece has seemed to be the frontier of Europe against the Persian or the Turkish world. It can be said that Greece both is and is not part of the Balkans. Athenian relations with Thrace in the northeast were essential in the culture and consciousness of both peoples in the 5th century, even though in Classical Athens the Thracians were considered to be barbarians.

The relation of Classical Greeks to their northern neighbors needs to be seen through the relation of Greece with the north as well as with the east. The paradox that best illustrates this is the treasure of Vix in central France, whose prize item is a vast 6th-century bronze vessel, made perhaps in south Italy, by a Spartan. The interpenetration of the Greek with other worlds in the archaic age was often more productive than in later times of more aggressive relationships.

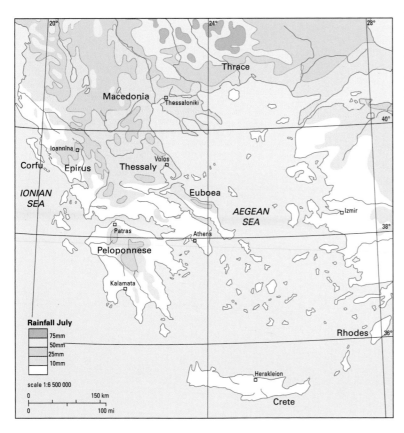

◄ *Mediterranean crops such as wheat, barley, olives, grapes, figs, and pomegranates thrive on winter rainfall and need no summer rain.*

▶ *Rainfall is highest in the west (over 50 inches/127 cm per year) but much lower on the eastern plains (15 inches/38 cm in Thessaly and Athens).*

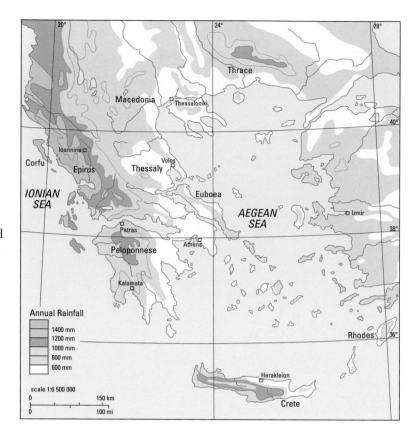

Around the year 2000 BCE, when identifiably Greek people become visible to archaeology, the same social and economic system seems to have prevailed across Europe: the tribes were ruled by a heroic warrior class living by the values celebrated later in epic poems, and buried in state. As a class system, with a fighting and hunting gentry living in great houses, that lasted nearly 4,000 years, perhaps until 1914. The houses that went with it, with their porches, great halls, and inner rooms, existed before 2000 BCE, in Anatolia and in eastern Europe as well as in Greece, but it was in Greece that the great halls of this kind of house became the impressive centers of palaces. Yet Greek architecture at that time was not the most ambitious in Europe, and Troy was smaller than Stonehenge.

What happened in Greece was a special, but never quite an isolated development. The Mycenaeans of the late 17th century BCE took their treasures of gold and silver, and the sacredness and perhaps also the use of horses, from the east, ornaments of amber from the north, weapons from Crete or the Levant. Weapons spread swiftly, and it was a Mycenaean helmet copied in Germany that became the standard battle helmet of the west. The Mycenaeans measured their wealth in weapons; 90 bronze swords were found with only three bodies in one of the shaft graves at Mycenae. As far away as Brittany at the same time the rich and powerful were buried with bronze

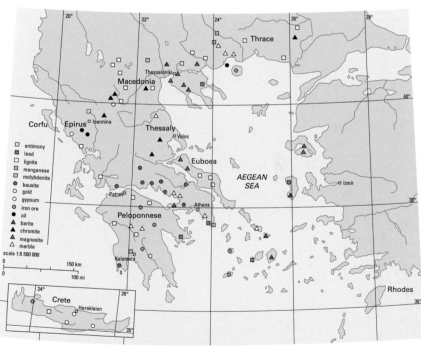

▲ *This map shows the mineral resources of modern Greece. In antiquity silver was the one ore with which the area was well supplied. The Athenians struck it rich at their own mines in Laurion in the 5th century.*

daggers in the same extravagant numbers. Although no palaces have been found in the rest of Europe like those of Greece, the warrior graves are equally rich in many places. The similarity of grave goods suggests that the trade of the world ran in a sense uninterrupted from Britain to Mongolia.

That the Greece of the Mycenaeans had such formidably wide horizons is due to the physical position of Greece. In both ancient and modern times Greece has been doomed by its place on the map to be a doorstep between Europe and Asia. At the beginning of the 5th century BCE Greece was almost but not quite swallowed up by the Persian empire, a situation that Alexander reversed. From the west the Romans overwhelmed

Greece for a time; but Greece revived and, as part of the Byzantine empire, became subject to Oriental influences, while its own cultural tentacles reached Anglo-Saxon England. The comparative obscurity of Greek relations with the barbarian north is equally the effect of geography, of mountains and of forests. Influences moved more swiftly by sea, and there is no time except perhaps immediately after the fall of the Mycenaeans when Greek ships were not fingering the surface of the western Mediterranean.

From the general pattern of human geography within which the ancient Greeks must be studied, it is fascinating how prehistory repeated itself in Greece. Shortly before 1000 BCE, when the level of material

▼ *The sun sets over Santorini's caldera, which was formed around 1500 BCE by one of the largest volcanic eruptions known. The island's settlements were buried under volcanic debris.*

▲ *Donkeys have long played a vital role in Greek agriculture, for transportation as well as a means of threshing grain and drawing water.*

from the achievements of the Celts to claim something special for the Greeks in the 1,000 years before Christ.

It is interesting that the Iron Age started earlier in Greece, at the end of the Mycenaean period, than in Celtic Europe. The reasons for the introduction of iron are uncertain. If it was smelted from meteorites, as sometimes it was, it may have had a magical value. Once the technique of forging was mastered, not an easy step, iron was cheaper and more abundant than bronze. It seems likely that the beginnings of the Iron Age in Greece were connected with a failure in the supplies of bronze from the east, together with the arrival of the necessary techniques, from the same direction. The skill to temper an iron blade was certainly available in Greece before the 5th century BCE, since swords of that date have shown under analysis a tempered steel cutting edge applied to a bronze weapon. An early iron ax head with bronze rivets from the start of the Greek Iron Age suggests that, independent of the shortage of bronze, iron was preferred to bronze for some purposes.

In that dark age, when Greece was as poor as the rest of Europe or poorer, light came from the east. The closeness of the Phoenicians and the Egyptians, the Syrians and the Hebrews, constitutes an influence sufficient in itself, if there were no other, to account for the development of the Greeks. From the Phoenicians came the alphabet, from the Egyptians came sculpture, and from the whole Levant architecture. Even the individuality of what grew up in Greece— the insistence on interpreting every foreign influence in Greek terms—is due to the physical nature of Greece, the not quite complete isolation of so many vigorous communities, the mountains, and the islands.

culture in Greece had sunk to the level of the rest of Europe, something like a new beginning occurred again in the Aegean, which prepared that explosion into form and light we call Classical. It is no derogation

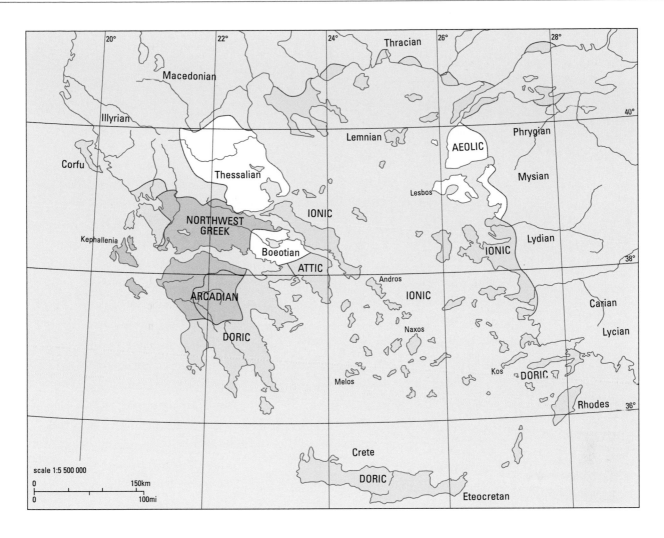

The Classical Greeks used Mycenaean roads: the only great Roman road in Greece ran east across the far north. The diversity of Greek provincial styles is a product of this trickling system of communications; so perhaps are the wars between city-states, and so may be the racial theories of the Greeks. The chauvinistic division of humankind, into Hellenes and barbarians, is not specially Greek; such divisions are almost universal. But the Greeks of the Classical period developed a mythical history of racial conflicts of Greek against Greek, Dorians and Ionians and Achaeans, following roughly the evidences of ancestry and dialect.

These racial theories may have been entirely false. It is at least not contrary to our evidence of Mycenaean and later Greeks to suggest that the growth of dialects was post-Mycenaean. They may be the product of the mountainous divisions and isolation of the dark age. If so, the racial consciousness of Dorians and Ionians was a false consciousness. One should remember that the whole Peloponnese was not divided into states even in the 5th century. The southernmost towns were independent until the time of Augustus, Arcadia itself was hardly unified, and between Sparta and Argos there were semi-independent tribes. Even to have sailed a few times around the stormy southern point of Greece was an achievement worth recording on a gravestone as late as the Roman empire.

▲ *This map shows the dialects of ancient Greece. They may partly have been the product of the mountainous divisions of the country and the isolation of some communities.*

23

The Study of Ancient Greece

The study of the Greeks is an inseparable part of European cultural history, and even the archaeology of Greece has a history of its own. The long process of discovery has left traces on what we think of today as the available or the most important knowledge of the ancient world.

Greece and Rome

Even after the Greeks were swallowed up into the Roman empire, their prestige remained immense. The Rome that swallowed them was itself partly Greek. The literature, the philosophy, all the fine arts, even most of the religious mythology that the Romans valued were Greek. The Greek language had the highest prestige. The Romans were overawed by Greek athletics, by the notion of Greek liberty, even by idyllic notions of Greek peasants and shepherds. The Romans even seem to have believed that Greek personal, physical beauty was greater than theirs. The foundation of our own attitude to the Greeks rests heavily on Roman literature and romantic Roman understanding. Politically, the Romans both despised and admired Greece extravagantly, and in most other ways they idealized the Greeks. Eduard Fraenkel, one of the greatest scholars of Roman literature, has observed that the deeper any Roman writer was as a man, the more deeply he was penetrated by what was Greek; but the Roman feeling for, and conception of, the Greek world are not embodied only in deep humanity or in great literature.

Already in the Roman period there were nostalgic historians like Plutarch; there were accepted notions of art history, which in writers like Pliny the elder, author of the famous sentence "art at this time ceased to exist," had an immense influence; and there were even archaeologists, of a kind, like the Asian Greek Pausanias, whose *Guide to Greece* is a comprehensive description of the cities and monuments of religion and art that survived in mainland Greece in the 2nd century CE. But down to the Renaissance, it was through literature, and chiefly Roman literature, that western Europeans understood the Greeks. Pausanias was seldom copied and little read. When by chance he came to light in the 15th century, one Italian scholar remarked to another how this text showed that only through the power of literature could monuments survive.

Archaeology began in Rome, and Greek archaeology began and long continued as an extended version of Roman treasure hunting. The first great collectors of Greek antiquities took their inspiration from Italy. As late as the end of the 18th century Athenian painted pottery, because it was first known in Italy, was thought to be Etruscan. It was in Italy, in the 17th century, that Milton took a notion to visit Delphi, and in the 18th, that Johann Joachim Winckelmann planned to excavate Olympia. It was from Rome that the British Society of Dilettanti sent out in 1764 its first Greek expedition. Giovanni Battista Piranesi's drawings of the ruins of Paestum, made in the year of his death in 1778, and James Stuart and Nicholas Revett's *The Antiquities of Athens* (1762–1816) are extensions of a conventional Roman taste.

Travelers and despoilers

The first recorded serious survey of ancient monuments in Greece after Pausanias was by that intrepid traveler, merchant, diplomat, scholar, and eccentric, Cyriaco of Ancona (1391–1455). Already in court circles and in learned monasteries in Greece, there was some interest in identifying the ancient cities named by Pausanias and in the accounts of Strabo (c. 63 BCE–after 21 CE) and Ptolemy (2nd century CE) with modern villages. Few if any names had survived unmangled, and most cities were the merest ruins. Some sanctuaries had become fortresses: part of the temple of Zeus at Olympia had become a castle, the rotunda of Asklepios at Epidauros had been a keep, the Parthenon a church and the rest of the acropolis at Athens an Italian palace. By the time of Cyriaco's journeys, most of the reused monuments had again

been abandoned and lay in ruins. The acropolis of Athens was in use, but it had still to face the worst part of its history. Cyriaco drew what he saw, recorded ancient inscriptions, hoarded information, and annotated the manuscripts he owned. But he had no followers.

The first learned travelers and despoilers appeared before the end of the 17th century, from France and from England. The Venetian expedition against the Turks at the end of that century did appalling damage in Athens, and it was still true down to 1700 that the artists and amateurs who recorded Greece saw almost exclusively what they expected to see. The first great change occurred in the 1760s, when architectural drawings and

▼ *The temple of Athena, later known as the Parthenon, was built in the 5th century BCE. It was badly damaged in 1687 and in the 19th century Lord Elgin removed much of the remaining sculpture and sold it to the British Museum.*

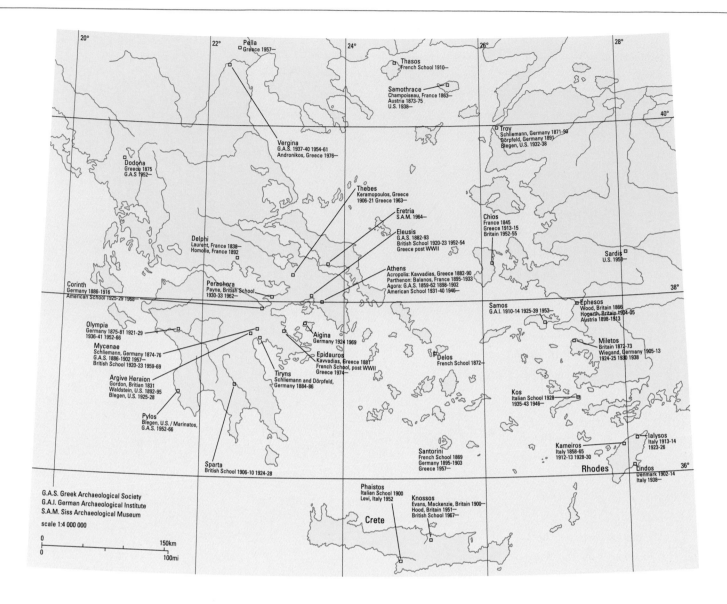

20°　　　　22°　Pella　　　　　24°　　　　26°　　　　28°
　　　　　　　　Greece 1957—

Thasos
French School 1910—

Samothrace
Champoiseau, France 1863—
Austria 1873-75
U.S. 1938—

40°

Troy
Schliemann, Germany 1871-90
Dörpfeld, Germany 1891
Blegen, U.S. 1932-38

Vergina
G.A.S. 1937-40 1954-61
Andronikos, Greece 1976—

Dodona
Greece 1875
G.A.S 1952—

Thebes
Keramopoulos, Greece
1906-21 Greece 1963—

Eretria
S.A.M. 1964—

Chios
France 1845
Greece 1913-15
Britain 1952-55

Delphi
Laurent, France 1838—
Homolle, France 1892

Eleusis
G.A.S. 1882-93
British School 1920-23 1952-54
Greece post WWII

Sardis
U.S. 1958—

Athens
Acropolis: Kavvadias, Greece 1882-90
Parthenon: Balanos, France 1895-1933
Agora: G.A.S. 1859-62 1898-1902
American School 1931-40 1946—

Corinth
Germany 1886-1916
American School 1925-29 1968—

Perachora
Payne, British School
1930-33 1962—

38°

Samos
G.A.I. 1910-14 1925-39 1953—

Ephesos
Wood, Britain 1866
Hogarth, Britain 1904-05
Austria 1898-1913

Olympia
Germany 1875-81 1921-29
1936-41 1952-66

Aigina
Germany 1924 1969

Mycenae
Schliemann, Germany 1874-76
G.A.S. 1886-1902 1957
British School 1920-23 1959-69

Epidauros
Kavvadias, Greece 1881
French School, post WWII
Greece 1974—

Delos
French School 1872—

Miletos
Britain 1872-73
Wiegand, Germany 1905-13
1924-25 1930 1938

Argive Heraion
Gordon, Britian 1831
Waldstein, U.S. 1892-95
Blegen, U.S. 1925-28

Tiryns
Schliemann and Dörpfeld,
Germany 1884-86

Kos
Italian School 1928
1935-43 1946—

Pylos
Blegen, U.S. / Marinatos,
G.A.S. 1952-66

Santorini
French School 1869
Germany 1895-1903
Greece 1957—

Kameiros
Italy 1858-65
1912-13 1928-30

Ialysos
Italy 1913-14
1923-26

Sparta
British School 1906-10 1924-28

Rhodes

Lindos
Denmark 1902-14
Italy 1938—

36°

G.A.S. Greek Archaeological Society
G.A.I. German Archaeological Institute
S.A.M. Siss Archaeological Museum

scale 1:4 000 000

0　　　　　　　　150km
0　　　　　　　　100mi

Phaistos
Italian School 1900
Levi, Italy 1952

Knossos
Evans, Mackenzie, Britain 1900—
Hood, Britain 1951—
British School 1967—

Crete

▲ *This map details
the excavations
carried out on
classical sites in
the 19th and
20th centuries.*

exact landscape records taught Europe for the first time to see Greek realities without Italian spectacles, although a romantic preoccupation with oppressed peasants and a rococo interest in the Turks did color the attitudes of travelers. Nor had the Roman influence died out; when Lord Elgin sold the spoils of the Parthenon to the British state, in 1816, the established connoisseurs still argued down their value in comparison with the Roman work for which they felt a more familiar affection.

It may be that today we define Greek originals too sharply against Roman copies,

that we neglect those warmer and easier qualities to which both Greek and Roman art aspired from time to time, exaggerating starkness and strength. It takes a lifetime to disentangle the past within one's limits.

Modern perceptions of Greece

In 1804 William M. Leake, an English officer who had been given secret orders to intrigue against the French in this way and that, was lent to the Turks to study the defenses of southern Greece. In the course of this task he made what was the first and still the most sympathetic survey of Greek ruins and sites. The slightly later French scientific expedition to the area did excellent work of the same kind.

During the 19th century, eagerness for the physical details of antiquity increased. Archaeology, however incompetent it remained in its own techniques, began to overwhelm art history with the variety of its examples. By the end of the century, the new and immense prestige of prehistoric archaeology had begun to be felt. Heinrich Schliemann had been digging in the 1860s to 1880s for Homer's Troy and Homer's Mycenae, but Sir Arthur Evans dug at Knossos in 1900 for a world which to the Greeks themselves had been merely fabulous, for a pre-Greek script and a pre-Greek language.

Evans found the evidence he was looking for of an early script within a fortnight, but it was more than 50 years before the language was deciphered as an early form of Greek. In the meantime, Mycenaean and Cretan excavations have spread, and we know by now enough about the Cretan palace civilization, about the Mycenaeans, and even about much earlier stages of Greek prehistory, to be more careful in our estimates of the admittedly unique arts and graces of the 5th century BCE.

There have been other changes. First, the idea of a Classical education as aristocratic has withered in Europe. It is no longer specially usual for a Classical scholar to be a "gentleman" or a "lady." There is more anthropological questioning of ancient societies, a more active criticism of Plato, of the historians, even of the epic heroes and the dramatic poets. Excavation is more precise, more probing, and more concerned with the analysis of information than the recovery of objects. Even art history has

settled among minute details of stylistic change and the attribution of complex works. There has been only a gradual shift of focus, backward in time from the 5th century toward the 8th, as new generations of scholars grow up who are familiar with more and more of the early material, particularly sculpture, which began to appear in the 1890s in Greece itself, and is still appearing. It was only between the two world wars that the first adequate studies of archaic Greek sculpture were published. One should remember also, so far as the wider public taste is concerned, that it was a luxury and an adventure to visit Greece until the 1950s, nor has it always been easy even for scholars to gain access to study the vast collections for which the Greek archaeological service is responsible.

▲ *Sir Arthur Evans uncovered evidence of a sophisticated Bronze Age civilization in Crete. He named it Minoan, convinced that the ancient legends about King Minos and the labyrinth at Knossos were based in fact.*

▲ *Heinrich Schliemann sketching the ruins of Troy. His discoveries at Troy and Mycenae contributed greatly to prehistoric archaeology in Greek lands.*

As a result, archaeology has become bewildering. Works of art which, if they had been recovered 100 or 200 years ago, would have had immense influence, and would have modified the idea of ancient Greece, are nowadays neglected. Greek religion and mythology have lost their definition in a welter of comparative studies. History is argued in learned journals, but there has been no single convincing exposition of the whole history of the ancient Greeks since the last century, and there was never anything about the Greeks to touch Mommsen's *History of Rome* (1854-56) or Gibbon's *Decline and Fall of the Roman Empire* (1776-88). Archaeology today is making its greatest intellectual efforts in an area in which no one showed interest until the late 20th century: the darkness between the end of the Mycenaeans and the first glimmer of archaic Greece.

Inevitably, we know a great deal more about certain types of problem, the centers of great cities, and the extent of fortifications, than our predecessors. Easier travel has brought comparative studies of colonial and trading sites, of architecture, town planning, and so on. Ancient machinery has its experts. On any great site one should remember that archaeology has been forced to deal with some things simply because they were there. A hundred years ago those who excavated were more aristocratic, they dug where they chose, and neglected what they scorned.

They were often precious and falsely aesthetic in their choice, and no doubt the modern fault is more on the right side. Opportunities once neglected will not recur. There is plenty about Olympia we shall now never know, and there are very few places, if any, where the field system of an ancient town can be found intact. Such excavation would have been a simpler job in the 19th century than it is today, for many sites then intact are now disturbed or hidden.

There is still a prejudice in favor of cities with known names, that are historically famous. This has affected prehistorians in the past as badly as it still affects classicists. It is pleasant to dig in a place mentioned by Homer, and almost everywhere is mentioned by Pausanias. The word "city" may be a misleading description of what was sometimes smaller than a modern village, and we grossly mislead ourselves by using the same word both for the tiny fortified villages of the Peloponnese and for Athens. In other ways, we exaggerate the importance of Athens, largely because it is the modern capital, and many archaeologists and scholars prefer it to the provinces. At least the sites are known of most of the smaller towns of ancient Attica; the rest of Greece was not so comparatively underpopulated as it is today underexcavated.

Prehistorians, because they have always been forced to depend less on literature, are technically sharper than classicists, and more committed to the proper disciplines of archaeology. In this century they have finally rid themselves of the incubus of Homer and are losing interest in mythology. Only when the results of archaeology began to emerge in some quantity, independent of any suggestion in the text of Homer, did it become possible to see in what way Homer and prehistoric Greece are related. While one was studied by means of the other, confusion prevailed. It is likely that Classical archaeology has still to undergo a similar process, some shrugging off of famous names and associations, a concentration on physical evidence, on what the stones themselves want to tell us. It needs to be more sociological than it has sometimes been.

Some of the things we still do not know after so many centuries will surprise the non-specialist. There is still no complete study of the use of Greek marbles. The ancient sources of bronze, and even of gold, are still largely a matter of conjecture. We have almost no statistical studies of any kind. The physical history of nearly every great sanctuary in Greece, in one or other of its crucial phases, is in doubt. The only near exceptions to that generalization are the Athenian acropolis and perhaps Delphi.

Successive generations of scholars have made different aesthetic mistakes. The Minoan restorations that Sir Arthur Evans commissioned in the 1900s have, to put it politely, an Edwardian air. His draftsman Piet de Jong's reconstruction drawing of the throne room in a Mycenaean palace is like a rejected design for the foyer of a 19th-century railroad hotel.

To consider the aesthetic misjudgments in our own time, much of the recent photography of archaic Greek sculpture has made it look indecently pretty. It is only now, when it is almost too late, that Pindar and his values are coming into focus, and at a time when we are telling ourselves to value ancient poems as poetry, comparable with other poetry, translation, at least in English, is frequently weak and berserk, though it is better in French, and in Italian it is often excellent.

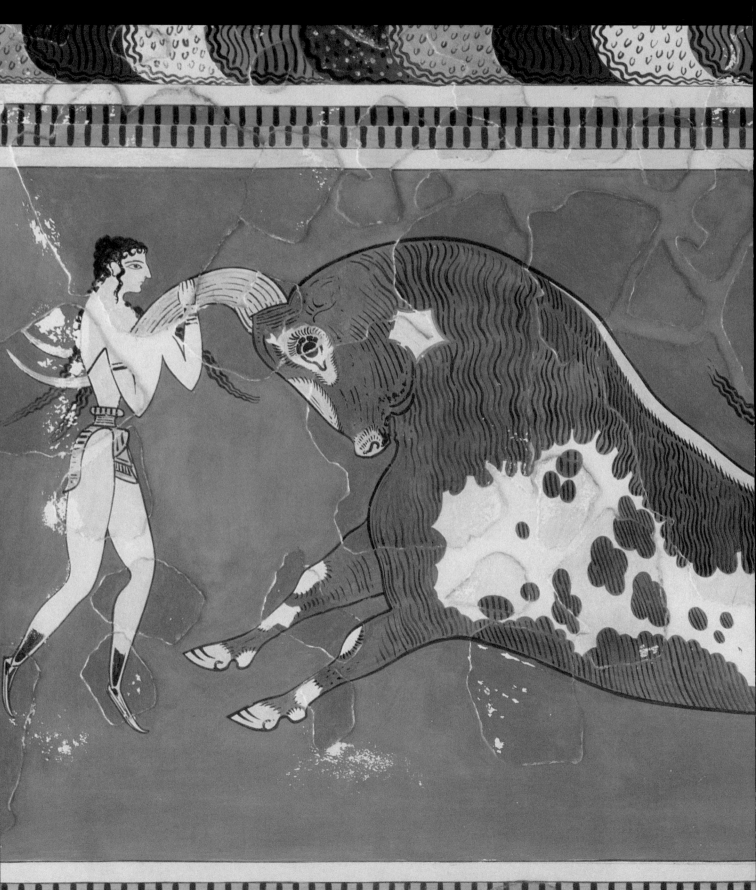

The Palace Civilizations of Crete and Mycenae

◄ *(previous pages) Boys leap over a bull in a restored mural from the Minoan palace at Knossos.*

▼ *Archaeological finds have indicated the spread and variety of the Mycenaean culture. Pottery was exported to Italy and to the Levant.*

The accumulation of archaeological evidence has made clear many details of life between 2100 and 1100 BCE when Knossos and Mycenae flourished. There were Indo-Europeans in Greece well before 2000 BCE. But some of the obvious questions are still unanswered. Embittered controversy on some subjetcs, and the spreading thin over others of evidence that is suggestive rather than conclusive, have made events in those 1,000 years even harder to interpret. The timescale which archaeologists have used differs slightly for Crete, for the others islands, and for the mainland. But by the end of the period the time scale of development in all the Greek lands had become unified, and much of Greece begins to have a single history.

In the southern mainland, the first dynasty of the Mycenaeans, the first people we know to have spoken Greek, appeared comparatively late, about 1700 BCE. By then the palace civilization of Crete already existed and Cretan influence had been

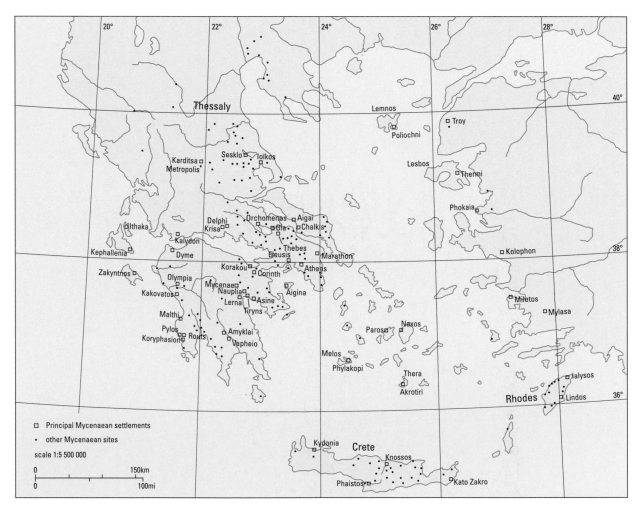

Principal Mycenaean settlements

other Mycenaean sites

scale 1:5 500 000

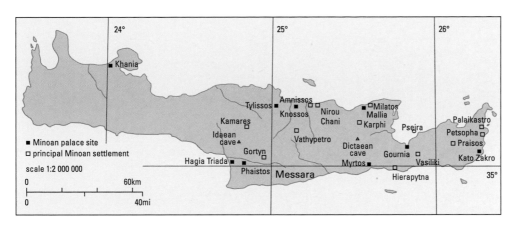

◀ Knossos was the grandest of the Minoan palaces on Crete. After its destruction in about 1450 BCE, it was occupied by the Mycenaens in the same tradition of grandeur.

widespread in the Aegean for a thousand years. At Knossos on Crete a settlement grew slowly and the palace, unlike the later one at Mycenae, stands on the deep debris of earlier human settlements. The Cretans came originally from somewhere in the Levant, possibly as refugees from Egypt, possibly from further east, but the site at Knossos had been inhabited for some 4,000 years before the Cretans who laid out the palace in about 1900 BCE.

The context of the great palaces

The earliest examples of writing in Crete date from 1900 BCE. They are hieroglyphic or pictographic. The script, the art of working stone vessels, and the engraving of stone seals probably came to Crete from Syria. The arts seem to have been carried by refugees. The majority of surviving examples of written language from this period—the Minoan Linear A script—are administrative records, and only the slightly later Mycenaean Linear B script has been deciphered. Among the Mycenaeans after 1450 BCE there may have been a written literature in Greek. At the same time the visual arts emerged in greater quantity in Crete (and in the islands Crete dominated). The artists were intensely conscious of stone and its colors, of shells, and of everything to do with the sea.

The great palaces of the heyday of Crete—between 2000 and 1400—were at Knossos, Phaistos, Mallia, and Khania. Knossos and Phaistos were destroyed about 1700 BCE and both were rebuilt. Knossos in its most flourishing period was about 175 yards square (160 m square), the size of a small Oxford or Cambridge college.

In the mid-16th century BCE, at the height of Crete's palace civilization, the nearest of the Cyclades, the volcanic island of Santorini (Thera), exploded. On Santorini devastation was complete. In Crete the crops suffered severely, there were other earthquakes, and at some time in the following years Zakro and Mallia were destroyed and Knossos damaged. But the exact order and connection of events remains doubtful. Starvation, disease, and revolution may have played a part. It now appears certain that there was a Mycenaean occupation of Knossos around 1400 BCE, but it is not clear in what circumstances.

The Cretan economy

An archive discovered at Knossos tells us about the economy of a Cretan palace. The clay tablets are inscribed in Linear B, which occurs in Crete only at Knossos at the time of Mycenaean domination.

The tablets show that agriculture underlay all riches. The ruler was a king, but there

Mycenae

The great city of Mycenae has yielded royal burials of extraordinary grandeur. The earliest graves, of the 17th and 16th centuries BCE, were deep shafts in the ground. Later in the Bronze Age the massive architecture of the city, including a circuit wall built in the 13th century, matched the awe-inspiring ambition of the vaulted tombs, among them two known today as the treasury of Atreus and the tomb of Klytaimnestra.

The influence and power of the Mycenaeans spread to Crete, to the Asian coast, to Sicily, and some way north of Rome. Their possessions were luxurious; but the Mycenaeans were a military people, and it is characteristic that the most glorious decorations should appear on an inlaid dagger hilt of lapis lazuli, crystal and gold. The dagger, which came from a shaft grave, dates from the 16th century.

1 grave circle A
2 grave circle B
3 tomb of Klytaimnestra
4 tomb of Aigisthos
5 tomb of the lions
6 house of the wine merchant
7 house of the oil merchant
8 lion gate
9 palace
10 treasury of Atreus

▲ *Archaeological excavations have revealed grave goods of astonishing quality and magnificence.*

▲ *The palace-citadel at Mycenae was sited on the summit of a low hill between two ravines and protected by a thick wall of large, unworked, closely fitting stones.*

▼ *The palace-citadel is surrounded by large private houses, tholos (beehive tombs) and shaft graves. All are protected by the encircling wall.*

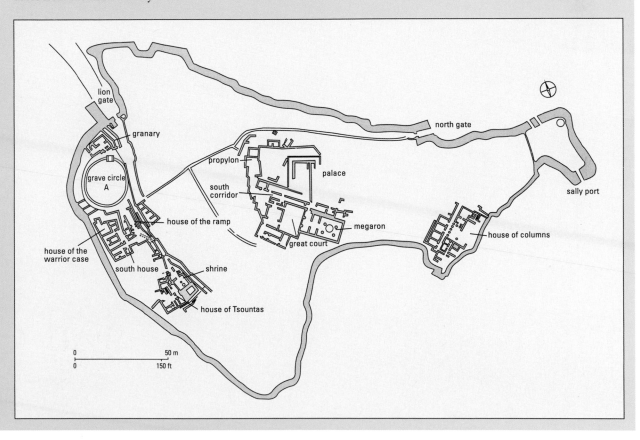

Knossos

Knossos was the greatest of the Cretan palaces and, later, the greatest city in Crete in the Classical period. It was excavated principally by Sir Arthur Evans, and its history is central to that of Bronze Age civilization in Greek lands. It was here that Evans first found evidence of a written language in the Greek Bronze Age. The clay tablet archives that he discovered have enabled later scholars to build up a rather comprehensive picture of many aspects of Cretan society and economy. But the first impression of Knossos' princely culture remains, that it was very rich, but almost finer than it was rich, and also that it had its sinister aspect.

The site of Knossos itself continues to be excavated. Indeed it has been the focus of such concentrated work over generations that it is hard today for an amateur to control all the evidence and all the arguments that have accumulated. The palace was laid out about 1900 BCE on a low mound comprising the debris of thousands of years of habitation. Knossos was more than once ruined, and in its last flourishing period toward 1400 BCE it was under Mycenaean control. But even after the collapse of palace civilization, there was another Knossos, a town of about a square kilometer, that grew up just to the north of the ruins. Knossos in Classical Greek legends was the palace of King Minos, a king far greater than Agamemnon of Argos.

▶ *The palace of Knossos has a central courtyard surrounded by public and private rooms, kitchens, bathrooms, storerooms and cult rooms.*

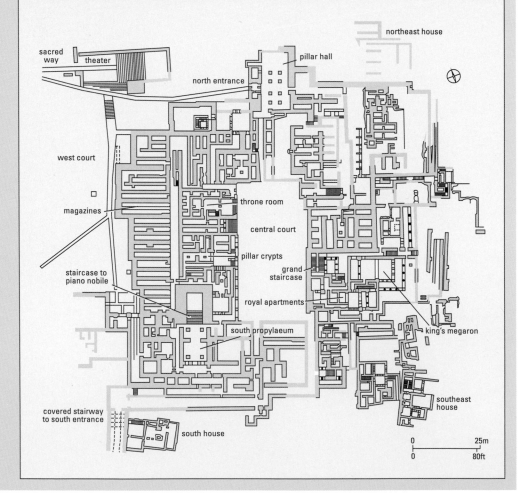

masks of gold, which were the destiny of the rich dead, suggest serious views about life after death. Altars have survived, as have a number of sacred symbols, such as the double ax, which probably belonged to the sky god, and the representations of a pillar cult, of which the most famous example is the lion gate of Mycenae. The lion gate may well have been a griffin gate, but whatever they were before they lost their heads, these

◄ The Hall of the Royal Guard at Knossos was partially restored by Sir Arthur Evans. Light shafts open to the sky illuminate the lower floors of the palace, two of which were below ground.

heraldic beasts rest their forepaws on twin altars on either side of a single pillar.

Some gods mentioned in Linear B tablets prefigure Greek deities. The gods received offerings and owned possessions. They also sanctioned kingship, as illustrated by the throne room at Knossos, where a freestanding throne is flanked by griffins on the walls behind it.

Mycenaean secular art

We can obtain a better taste of Cretan palace life from such objects as a games board inlaid with ivory and lapis lazuli. There was only one source of lapis in the known world, in Afghanistan; ivory must also have traveled from a distance, usually from North Africa. Crete was not isolated, it existed in a vast international context, just as Knossos existed in a landscape.

were other high-ranking officials. There were several lesser ranks or functions, and a number of specialized services: shepherds, goatherds, huntsmen, woodcutters, masons, shipbuilders, carpenters, and so on. Women ground and measured grain, but men baked. Bread, oil, and wine were common and the ordinary animals were kept. We know of a wide variety of condiments, including mint, and that Mycenaeans at Knossos ate cheese. Knossos shepherds and goatherds grazed their flocks at a distance from the palace, and special collectors took from each herd its quota of animals and wool. There were very few horses, and not many cattle. Pigs were herded, and fat ones specially listed.

Mycenaean religion

By contrast, we know little for certain about Mycenaean religion. Tomb offerings and

Santorini

Santorini is the ancient Thera, a picturesque volcanic island not very far from Crete. The volcano exploded with great violence during the Bronze Age, preserving a palace in lava as wonderfully as Pompeii and Herculaneum were preserved by the explosion of Vesuvius. Excavation of the buildings under the lava, at Akrotiri in the south of the island, was begun in 1967, erosion by rainwater having revealed painted plaster.

The Classical city of Thera lies to the east, on a rocky promontory. It was occupied before the 9th century, and there are 7th- and 6th-century remains. But most of the ruins are from the time of the Ptolemies and later.

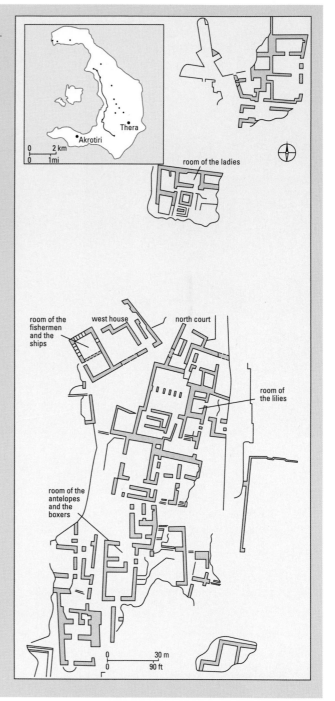

▶ *The buildings that have been excavated at Akrotiri have been named for the Bronze Age frescoes that decorated their walls.*

It was surely the brilliance of the Cretan palaces that attracted and perhaps civilized the Mycenaeans. The Cretans' spectacular objects of luxury—gems, bronze, terracotta, small sculpture, fescoes, gold and silver, glass and lapis lazuli—could match for quality anything in the whole world.

Late Mycenaean civilization

As the Bronze Age drew to a close, the surviving palaces of the Mycenaeans became an exchange place and storehouse of goods and services. We are unable to describe the decline accurately. Early in the 14th century, Knossos burned in Crete, and Thebes in

mainland Greece; neither was rebuilt. At the end of the 13th century several great fortresses were attacked. In the 12th century Mycenae was destroyed, Tiryns and Pylos perished by fire, and many smaller centers were abandoned. At Pylos the archive baked hard in the final fire; it records an emergency distribution of rations to divided sections of the coastal defense force.

The Mycenaeans had attained to a life of intellectual sophistication and great luxury. The massive architecture of their tombs makes these the most memorable of all Greek prehistoric monuments, and the size and weight of their fortifying walls are reminders of what their power must have been like. Their trade extended beyond Sicily and Lipari to Spain. Art and craft were more or less unified, and the whole Greek world had begun to have a single history:

such a unification of the world implies a metropolis. The bearded barbarians with the gold death masks and the interest in horses had founded a powerful people.

Spiritually, what bridges the age of the early palaces and their glitter to the world centuries later, yet more remote, in which epic poetry germinated, is a certain hard Mycenaean gaiety which is splendid rather than graceful. The riches of their palace decorations, the pillars of their graves, and the elaborate styling of their body armor give some sense of a coherent taste, the projection of a society that can be understood. What brings early Mycenaean society to life for us are the inlaid daggers, the sihouetted battles and lion hunts, the leopards and wild geese.

Although it was not dominant, Mycenaean trade and influence penetrated much of western Europe and the Levant. Mycenaean

▲ *Thera, the modern capital of Santorini, is situated on the edge of the ancient volanic caldera. The eruption may have contributed to the collapse of the Minoan civilization.*

Pylos

The Mycenaean palace of Pylos lies in almost the furthest southwestern corner of mainland Greece, above a natural harbor and in rich, hilly country. One of the last outposts of the Mycenaeans, it survived the fall of Mycenae. The palace was luxurious, but not huge.

The palace has yielded Linear B tablets, frescoes, and quantities of pottery. One fine fresco of warriors in battle—some in helmets, others in animal furs—is probably a variation on a North African original, but in its context in the last days of the palace it must have seemed to its viewers to show a battle of Mycenaeans against barbarians.

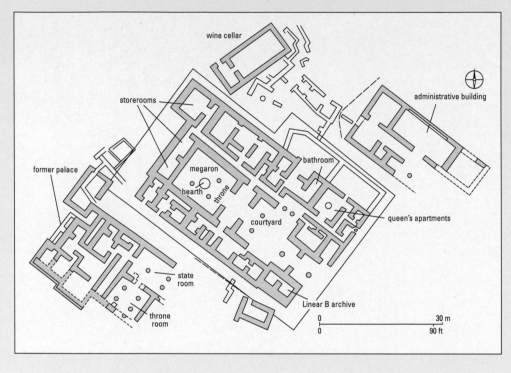

► *Aside from the steep sides of the hill itself the palace at Pylos had no external protection. Like other Minoan palaces it had a central courtyard, staircases, storerooms, frescoes and painted floors.*

pottery has been recovered from Sicily, south Italy, and Spain, and from many sites in Asia Minor. It is hard to know how that world system collapsed, but it seems likely that political changes in West Asia determined other power changes, that there were raids, or a great raid, from the north, and that there was internal unrest in Greece. Nowhere is there evidence of anything so simple as mere dynastic change or the mere pushing out of one people by another.

It would be mistaken to underestimate the luxurious grandeur of even a small provincial palace like Pylos in its last days around 1250

► *The massive stones of the Mycenean citadel at Tiryns gave rise to the legend that it was built by the Cyclopes—giants with a round eye in the middle of their foreheads.*

BCE or soon after. The frescoes and the objects of fine stone, and the location of the palace, which seems not untypically to have been chosen on aesthetic grounds, speak of a society which has not surrendered. It is no longer the best workmanship in the world, but the tribute of the villages is still coming in; the palace bath is not as fine as the finest Knossos bath, but still fine; ivory is still being inlaid into wood, and we hear of lions' heads of ivory, and of a ewer belonging to the queen which was designed like a bull's head decorated with seashells, although that may have been an heirloom.

Mycenaean Survivals

The flourishing Bronze Age society of roughly 1,000 years from 2100 BCE left a contrast of bright illuminated points and areas of darkness. Now, for some 300 years, the darkness becomes more uniform. We know little of the populations of most of Greece after the fall of the Mycenaeans. Agriculture did not cease, of course, and the dead were buried; the levels of luxury sank lower, but we know little of the levels of social organization, and nothing of those of happiness.

Population movements

About 1190 BCE the Egyptians recorded that "the northerners were disturbed in their isles." New Mycenaean colonists arrived at this time in Achaea in the north Peloponnese, and on the Ionian island of Kephallenia, where they settled peacefully, side by side with the old Kephallenians. Handmade native pottery and Mycenaean pottery continued together there for some time. In Cyprus there had already been colonizers, probably invaders, from the Argolid. But the rebuilding of the capital, Enkomi, was followed by another destruction, depopulation, and a partial desertion of the site. At the same time the Mycenaeans who had nested much further east at Tarsus, in Cilicia on the Anatolian coast, died out. Other Mycenaeans—or perhaps the Mycenaeans of Enkomi—seem to have melted away among the Philistines, and ended enrolled into the tribe of Dan, as Jews.

If anywhere, the Mycenaeans seem to have survived at Iolkos near modern Volos in Thessaly. There, even the old domed tombs continued to be built. The survival of other Myceaeans in what are more like refuge sites, for example at Grotta on the island of Naxos, is easier to understand. But it is surely on Naxos that we must search for the mysterious trickle of worshipers who seem to have kept open a Mycenaean religious center on nearby Delos down to the 8th century. Mycenaean life may well have survived longer in the islands than it did on the mainland, though archaeological evidence of a violent catastrophe does exist in a chain of eastern islands. The fall of Miletos seems to mark the end of that story.

The style of painted vessels found at Miletos indicates a reoccupation from Attica in the first half of the 11th century BCE. The movements of peoples in the Aegean at this time were like the disturbed movement of waves. However, the Greek language of the Mycenaeans remained the same and even extended its territory during the dark age.

This is the period when what we know of as Greek mythology took form. A very few elements have genuine Mycenaean touches: the Minotaur, the labyrinth, the name of Hyakinthos, some part of the cult of Iphigeneia, perhaps the connection of honey with immortality. But the supposed historic legends, the lists of mythical kings and wars and invasions are mostly too late and too confused to be useful as historical evidence. That is true also of accounts of the early kings of Sparta and the mythical division of the Peloponnese. Greek mythology never ceased to be alive, or to alter. For us the darkest aspect of the Greek dark age is that it was illiterate. A story retold was a new story, so that consciousness of the past became an amazing jumble.

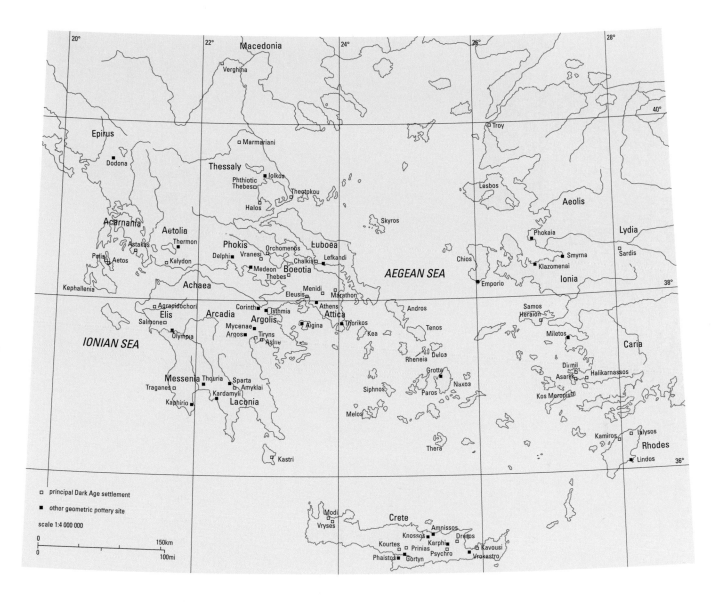

Map legend:
- □ principal Dark Age settlement
- ■ other geometric pottery site

scale 1:4 000 000

| 0 | | 150km |
| 0 | | 100mi |

Kea, Delos, Cretan caves

The survivals of the Mycenaeans sometimes took strange forms. On the island of Kea, for example, just south of Attica, a small Mycenaean palace occupied a headland. In one of the rooms were a number of religious statues of goddesses or priestesses, the furniture of a late Mycenaean palace shrine. The palace perished, and the rooms filled up with rubble. No earlier than the 9th century BCE, the decapitated head of one of the statues came to light, and someone set it up in a circle of stones. No attempt was made to

excavate in the loose stones to find other statues or the rest of this one. The head went on being worshiped until the 5th century BCE when an inscription on an offering gives us the name of the goddess. She was apparently being worshiped as Dionysos, the beardless god. The sex change remains unexplained, though there is probably some connection with a nearby waterspring, Dionysos being often found among nymphs.

At Delos, on a late Classical wall, we have a number of graffiti of ships. One of them is almost exactly like the Mycenaean ship on a

▲ Little is known about the dark ages around the Aegean. However, tomb remains and votive offerings have yielded geometric pottery in nearly all regions except Lesbos and Aeolis.

▶ *Excavations at the Minoan site of Akrotiri on Santorini have revealed remarkably preserved frescoes, such as this depiction of two boys boxing.*

gold ring from Mochlos. On the wall at Delos, a tall lady stands on the ship, shedding light or influence with her right hand. She is Brizo, a birth goddess, worshiped in Crete as Britomartis. Brizo was an alternative name of Leto, the mother of Artemis and Apollo. We know that Brizo liked offerings in the shape of ships. Her skirt in the graffito is surely the ancient Cretan skirt. How the construction of her ship was transmitted is a mystery.

The case of this graffito is so paradoxical that we might prefer to ignore it, if it were not for the sacred deposit buried in the 8th century behind what became the temple of Artemis on Delos. The deposit is of very mixed material of various dates, and the pottery and small finds do not completely bridge the gap from the Bronze Age. The sacred deposit includes some Orientalizing ivories, perhaps from Cyprus, a curious gold plaque of a sphinx-like creature which is apparently Hittite, a bronze double ax, fragments of pottery, some possibly (in my view probably) sub-Mycenaean terracottas, and a 13th-century bronze statue of a naked god with a round shield and a crooked weapon. Figures of this last kind seem to have a Hittite origin; they turn up not only at shrines in Asia and Greece, but as far afield as Schernen in East Prussia. I am inclined to credit the continuous use of the temple on Delos, but the argument is not complete.

The places where continuity of worship is most often claimed are cave sanctuaries, particularly in Crete, although the lack of a detailed archaeological context leaves much room for doubt. One exceptional site is the so-called Dictaean cave at Psychro on the high plain of Lassithi in Crete. It was surely a Zeus cave of some sort. Its two main periods of activity are Bronze Age and 8th–7th centuries BCE, which would fit the chronology of the Idaean cave. From the 6th century onward it was neglected, and that too is not uncommon for archaic religious sites in Crete. There is no doubt about its being used in the post-Minoan period.

Artifacts and visual arts

When the palaces disappeared, there was a discontinuity in visual narrative art. It is however suggestive that so much of the beginnings of narrative art, when it starts up again in the period of the geometric pottery style (about 1050 to about 700 BCE), seems to adapt a new repertory of images from the Levant. One of the most startling images of this period, in terracotta, appears to be a domed Mycenaean tomb with a divine figure revealed inside, being discovered from above by shepherds with their dog. That is a persuasive interpretation; there is no convincing alternative.

The emergence, or rather reemergence, of figure painting took a long time. By the early 9th century, sphinxes and lions glared, and wild-haired hunters pursued animals with spears across the shoulders of an early geometric pot. A series of pairs of men fighting with long daggers or short swords, arms crossed and holding one another by the hair, recalls the two boy boxers, if that is what they are, painted in Santorini 700 years earlier. But the problem of transmission of the image has no obvious solution. In what medium was it transmitted? The repertory of horse, bird, and man was largely transmitted from the late Bronze Age to the 8th century in the conservative tradition of funerary art, where changes were slower and less frequent than one might expect.

Early physical objects undoubtedly survived; Minoan engraved gems and heirlooms were treasured as late as the 6th century BCE, and early figurines were discovered and reburied. On the island of Skyros, Mycenaean gold disks have been found in early geometric graves, and a Mycenaean jar in a grave of similar date at Athens. Ancient patterns lingered on textiles. The necklace of green beads which was kept at Delphi, was to judge from its description Mycenaean. The evidence of later worship in Mycenaean tombs is conclusive.

At one site, the sanctuary of Hera on the plain of Argos, groups of late offerings have been found in 15 out of 50 Mycenaean chamber tombs. There was worship at the domed tomb of Klytaimnestra at Mycenae in the 8th century, and a full religious cult at a tomb at Menidi in Attica.

Continuity and discontinuity

The signs of the break between Mycenaean and later societies include the disturbance of human settlements, the corruption not only of the decorative patterns but also of the shapes of pottery, followed by the transition to a new style, and other evidences of a new way of life. The pottery sequence developed slowly: the development of geometric pottery took some 400 years.

The one clear material change is supposed to have been the adoption of iron for swords, knives, and plowshares. It is clear that by the time iron inlay had come to decorate bronze, when parts of iron completed parts of bronze, and when iron was used to repair bronze, the change was complete. But no such examples can be found in Greece until the 10th or 9th century, and inlay never. In fact, the detail of what occurred is complicated. It is certain that in most of the earliest geometric period, that is from about 1050 to 900 BCE, in most places iron was in use for nearly everything. Attica seems to have set the pace of technology in metalwork as it did in pottery. A gradual reaction then took place in favor of bronze.

Craft skills may have been lost due to depopulation or to the comparative poverty of at least the 11th century, but if that did happen, then it seems only a short time before communities recovered. By the 10th century their painted decoration is splendid, the finest in the Mediterranean. By 800 BCE

▶ *Minoan pottery was made on a hand-turned wheel and was often decorated with plant and marine motifs. In the 15th century BCE pots were buff colored and painted with dark shapes.*

a necklace of gold appears in Crete with serpents' heads and a lunar shape of rock crystal, decorated with crystal and amber, brilliant and fine enough for a Mycenaean though not perhaps for a Minoan princess. Throughout this period Crete is rich, and more influential than is usually realized.

In Crete, the skills that survived were directly related to what had existed there long before. At 12th-century Karphi and Kavousi there were still builders working in a Minoan tradition. The rebuilders at Phaistos and the builders of Gortyn in the 12th century worked in the same tradition. Such a craft can survive a long time: at Iolkos on the mainland, one of the few settlements where any comparable survival of skills has been recognized, a mason's mark from the Linear B script was still in use in the 9th century BCE. Shipbuilding must also have survived; there was even some mining of silver. These survivals do not mean that the Greeks in the 11th century were not few and poor. The small treasures they valued, and carried to the grave, confirm that they were so.

One suggestion is that the earlier, essential Greece was a peasant community living from agriculture, and that in its burial customs, its pottery, and its habit of life it reasserted its existence in the dark age. The Mycenaeans with their huge buildings, herds of animals, and pomp, were aliens who vanished. To some degree this must be right: but the argument for an essential underlying Greece is confused enough to throw darkness on any significance it may have. What emerges at the end of the dark age is quite different from anything the Mycenaeans would lead one to expect. We are confronted in the 8th century not only with economic, social, and technical recovery, but with an achievement as tall as Olympos itself: the poems of Homer.

continuous reworking. Genuine classical and folk epic poetry is transmitted by memory and adaptation, from singer to singer. It flourishes in an illiterate society, and its moral rules and traditions reflect a world in which honor is paramount, and wealth is almost equivalent to honorable prestige. The prince protects his people, and he risks his life. The rules of society, for example the duty of blood vengeance and the supremacy of physical courage, are absolute; it is unthinkable that society should be otherwise. Magnanimity is a rule in conflict with other rules. But of course societies are always altering, they are never quite stable. The end of the *Iliad*, where Achilles gives up Hektor's body to his father, is immensely strong,

because compassion is felt to have overcome conflicting rules of the world. The power of the *Iliad* comes from just this tension. Homer knows clearly that the world of the Trojan war is appalling; but nevertheless the poem proceeds remorselessly.

Oral epic poetry uses a vast repertory of set phrases; a study of how they reappear tells us something about how the mind of Homer worked. The Greek prince Agamemnon says, "There shall come a day when sacred Troy shall perish." Homer reuses this sentence later. He puts it into the mouth of Hektor, who is going out to fight, knowing that in the end he has to die. Even Achilles, the greatest hero, who survives the *Iliad*, has to know that he will die. He has

◀ *Many artists have depicted Homer, but little is known about him aside from his name and the probability that he played a major part in shaping the Iliad and the Odyssey.*

chosen to be famous and to die young in battle. Without that darker tone, and without the compassion an avenging Homeric hero can hardly show, Achilles would be intolerable. It is in order for Achilles to show compassion that the dead body of Hektor has to be begged back by his father, Priam. The *Iliad* ends not with the triumph of the Greeks, but with the burial of Hektor.

Small wonder we do not know the origins of many Homeric conventions. Every retelling is for a different audience, and is a new attempt to make sense of given material. We are not even sure when Homeric poetry was first written down—it may have been when the tradition of epic composition and oral transmission was still in its fullest vigor.

Yet it is not being written down that destroys epic poetry, at least not in the ourse of one generation. It is rather written law, new social organization, and the widespread transformations of a whole society to which the spread of literacy is linked. Homer's world is cloudy to us. He stands on the edge of a great darkness. His poetry has a crispness and a purity we associate with beginnings rather than endings; yet if we are to do justice to the dark age, we should think of the *Iliad* as its evening star, not as the morning star of a later age.

The Eighth-Century Renaissance

Greek colonization of Asia Minor was well established in the 8th century BCE. Al Mina at the mouth of the Orontes was a trading station, founded from Euboea before the end of the 9th century, and exploited by Corinth. Styles in the east intermingled, and what reached mainland Greece arrived in an adapted form. The penetration of Greek art by these new influences transformed it utterly. The increase of representational art in Greek lands is inseparable from the expansion.

The styles we first detect as early as the 10th century roughly mark out what were to emerge as regional states: some by the dominance of one city, Argos or Thebes; some by aggressive policy ending in imperial adventures, Sparta for instance; some in leagues of cities like the 12 Ionian cities of the east, which combined in the 8th century; some by loose aggregation without a central city, like Elis. The great international sanctuaries of Dodona, Delos, and Olympia were already oracular shrines or centers of common worship, implying and perhaps imposing a degree of common law and common language. Before the mid-8th century we know that Olympia was hosting the first of the four great international athletic festivals. Month, year, and festival were to some extent synchronized all over Greece.

Visual arts

Painted decorations in the dark age in principle followed regional styles, but did not differ greatly. In mainland Greece, the painting and making of pottery became by the 8th century a monumental art. The huge pots made at that time for Athenian graveyards stood as high as a man or higher. Their decorations of alternating tan-colored areas and black paint were executed in bold schemes. Greek painting never quite lost sight of the formal and geometric organization of the 10th and 9th centuries. Within its formal limits, Greek art had an astonishing vigor in the 8th century.

This is the period of the first figure sculptures we know after the Bronze Age: not only small cult-images in bone or ivory or wood, but powerful bronzes. The decoration of the heavy bronze tripods of the gods at Olympia appears in a dashing contrast to the heavy material, but it shows a strong feeling for the depth of the bronze. The earliest Olympian warrior figures show an Oriental influence, and a number of direct Oriental bronze imports have been found at the sanctuary. In fact the refreshed and reviving arts of Greece begin by Orientalizing. Still to come were the influence of Levantine stone-carving, the adoption of marble decorations for public building, and the laborious adaptation of Egyptian human sculpture via eastern imitations. But already the new repertory of images was mostly Oriental.

There was also a revival of architecture. The long apsidal or elliptical huts of earlier settlements gave way for sacred use to a rectangular style with a columned porch. Houses began to be square, built around a hearth, although apsidal houses and houses with curved walls did not die out at once.

There are unsolved questions about the increase of population and of wealth, and about foreign relationships. The quantity of objects and styles that are recognizably Greek increases dramatically in relatively few years. At first one has the sense that in

◄ The theater at Dodona, built in the 3rd century BCE, has one of the most spectacular locations of any Greek theater. The cavea is partially recessed into the acropolis hill and originally seated over 14,000 spectators. The theater has been restored for use in the annual festival of drama.

every bronze statuette the balance of lines and masses is being worked out as if for the first time. The same is true of terracottas, though only of types, hardly of individual figures. In the course of a generation that situation had altered. The variations within a received style are considerable, and they are sometimes rewarding. In the visual arts in Greece a remarkable period of adaptations came from 750 to 650 BCE for bronzes, and from 650 to 550 for the figures in heavy marble. Their cumbersome grace took longer than a century to go out of fashion, and that was still not the end of development; the strongest development of representational painting was from 550 to 450.

▲ *The palaestra at Olympia was built in the 3rd century BCE as a school and exercise area for wrestlers. It consisted of an open square surrounded by Doric colonnades. Next door was the covered gymnasium.*

Dodona

Dodona is the site of an ancient (reputedly the oldest) and mysterious oracle of Zeus on the northwestern edge of the Classical Greek world, toward the modern border with Albania. The remote site lies some miles inland in a cranny beneath the Pindos mountains.

According to Homer, the priests at Dodona had unwashed feet and slept on the ground. The priests interpreted the noise of the wind in a great oak tree. There is plenty of evidence of late Bronze Age activity, but none of continuity of cult. Perhaps we ought to expect none. In Homer's lifetime Zeus was enthroned here with a goddess called Dione. There was some cult of an underground goddess, and some unusual beliefs about sacred pigs. Dione may be closely related to Demeter, the evidence suggests.

Dodona's buildings were poor and few until Hellenistic times, and most of the ruins visible today, which are very beautiful, have a late origin. Most prominent is the theater, built after the death of Alexander the Great, in the time of Pyrrhos of Epirus (297–272 BCE), and recently restored. Above the theater lies the walled acropolis; below it was a stadium.

Odysseus is supposed to have visited Dodona, but he was a famous traveler. Most of the clients of the oracle seem to have been simple people; pottery finds suggest that they came more often from nearby or from the remote northern Balkans than from the center of the Greek world. The core of the sanctuary was the holy tree itself. Only the foundations of the sanctuary buildings now survive.

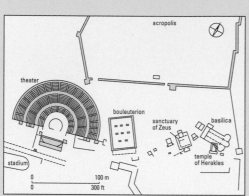

▲ *Until Hellenistic times Dodona had few buildings. The most prominent building is the theater. Above it is the walled acropolis; below it is a stadium.*

The big stone statues are grave monuments to individuals or dedications to the gods. The naked athlete statues that crowded the open-air sanctuaries where games were held were both portraits and dedications. The huge painted pottery of the ripe geometric period, the 8th century, represents the grave monuments of rich and powerful Athenians.

Mainland Greece

At the same time certain great families, in Athens and elsewhere, were claiming mythical, half-divine ancestry. With the coming of wealth, the politics of colonial expeditions, and the emergence of a literate state with written laws, the conflicts of family interests must have taken on a new importance. We know that the distribution of wealth in Attica was more uneven than elsewhere. Athenian history in the 8th century was not a success. Population increased, but overseas Athenian commercial influence decreased. At home, the Oriental luxuries in graves were no longer imports, but local adaptations. Riches were as great in the countryside as in Athens itself, but the contrast of wealth and poverty between rich and poor graves was dire in the 8th century, and it became worse in the 7th.

The foreign aspect of this situation would be explained by defeat at sea, and Herodotos, three centuries later, does mention such a war and such a defeat. The interior situation of Attica is clear. The big baronial families squatted on the riches of the countryside, presumably in rivalry to one another, and certainly to the detriment of the poor. The worship of the heroic dead in the Mycenaean tombs, which began all over Greece about 725 BCE, is another aspect. Every clan venerated the bones of legendary ancestors. The epic poetry and the legends, the grave monuments and the hero-cults, the claims of the great families and their position in the countryside, at Menidi or Spata or Koropi or Anavyssos, are all parts of one situation.

The Argolid, the plain dominated by Argos, by contrast was powerful and outward-looking. At the end of the 8th century the fortress of Asine was utterly destroyed by King Eratos; the grave of a soldier of that time reveals a splendid conical helmet copied from the east, and a bell-shaped corselet copied from central Europe. Most of the bronze cauldrons ornamented with bulls' heads that have been found in Greece are copies made in Greece itself or in Cyprus of Syrian originals, which were copies in their turn of the work of Urartu. The painting of vases at Argos was grand and monumental, as it was at Athens, with the same exception of cheap, mass-produced wares for the local peasants. The only center to produce fine wares for small shapes and everyday uses was Corinth, which produced also for export. Argive pottery did travel, at least as far as

Eleusis

Eleusis, the home of the sanctuary of Demeter, lies on the seacoast west of Athens in what used to be idyllic countryside, now utterly swallowed up by industry. It was a Mycenaean, and an early archaic site; continuity of worship is perfectly possible, even perhaps likely. But we know nothing of any Mycenaean Demeter. Most of her shrines are in the country all over Greece, outside town walls. Demeter was the goddess of grain, and the religion of Eleusis was based on the mysteries of the natural cycle of resurrection and rebirth. The laws of agriculture, of sex, of nature, and of the gods were to the early Greeks one interwoven code. The Homeric *Hymn to Demeter*, which centers on Eleusis, is one of the most important documents we have for ancient religion.

Athens took over Eleusis in early historical times. The Telesterion, or temple of Demeter, is somewhat representative of building on the site, with a complex history of rebuilding from Mycenaean to Roman times. Eleusis has its own extremely rich museum.

▼ *The buildings at Eleusis have been modified and rebuilt at various times as shown in this plan of the area around the Telesterion.*

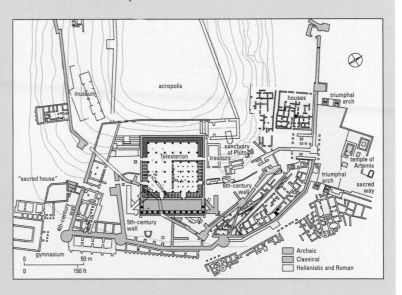

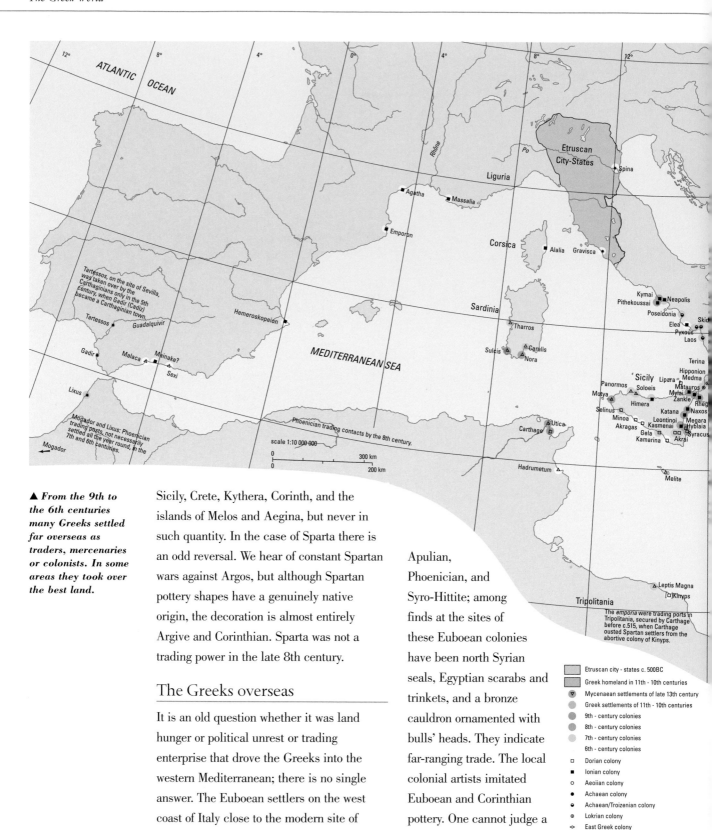

The map shows labels including: ATLANTIC OCEAN, Liguria, Etruscan City-States, Spina, Po, Rhône, Agatha, Massalia, Emporon, Corsica, Alalia, Gravisca, Kymai, Pithekoussai, Neapolis, Poseidonia, Elea, Skid, Pyxous, Laos, Sardinia, Tharros, Terina, Hipponion, Medma, Sicily, Lipara, Mataurus, Panormos, Soloeis, Mylai, Zankle, Rheg, Motya, Himera, Katana, Naxos, Selinus, Minoa, Leontinoi, Megara, Akragas, Kasmenai, Hyblaia, Gela, Akrai, Syracus, Kamarina, Carthage, Utica, Tartessos, Guadalquivir, Gadir, Malaca, Mainake?, Sexi, Lixus, Mogador, Hemeroskopeion, MEDITERRANEAN SEA, Hadrumetum, Leptis Magna, Kinyps, Tripolitania, Melite, Sulcis, Nora, Caralis

Tartessos, on the site of Sevilla, was taken over by the Carthaginians only in the 5th century, when Gadir (Cadiz) became a Carthaginian town.

Mogador and Lixus: Phoenician trading posts, not necessarily settled all the year round, in the 7th and 6th centuries.

Phoenician trading contacts by the 8th century.

scale 1:10 000 000

0 — 300 km
0 — 200 km

The emporia *were trading ports in Tripolitania, secured by Carthage before c.515, when Carthage ousted Spartan settlers from the abortive colony of Kinyps.*

Etruscan city - states c. 500BC
Greek homeland in 11th - 10th centuries
Mycenaean settlements of late 13th century
Greek settlements of 11th - 10th centuries
9th - century colonies
8th - century colonies
7th - century colonies
6th - century colonies
□ Dorian colony
■ Ionian colony
○ Aeoiian colony
● Achaean colony
◓ Achaean/Troizenian colony
◉ Lokrian colony
◇ East Greek colony
• Greek trading post
△ Phoenician colony
▲ Phoenician trading post
[□] temporary settlement

▲ *From the 9th to the 6th centuries many Greeks settled far overseas as traders, mercenaries or colonists. In some areas they took over the best land.*

Sicily, Crete, Kythera, Corinth, and the islands of Melos and Aegina, but never in such quantity. In the case of Sparta there is an odd reversal. We hear of constant Spartan wars against Argos, but although Spartan pottery shapes have a genuinely native origin, the decoration is almost entirely Argive and Corinthian. Sparta was not a trading power in the late 8th century.

The Greeks overseas

It is an old question whether it was land hunger or political unrest or trading enterprise that drove the Greeks into the western Mediterranean; there is no single answer. The Euboean settlers on the west coast of Italy close to the modern site of Naples were traders. The pottery they handled had a variety of sources: Euboea, Athens, Corinth, Rhodes, Crete, Etruscan, Apulian, Phoenician, and Syro-Hittite; among finds at the sites of these Euboean colonies have been north Syrian seals, Egyptian scarabs and trinkets, and a bronze cauldron ornamented with bulls' heads. They indicate far-ranging trade. The local colonial artists imitated Euboean and Corinthian pottery. One cannot judge a human society by the commercial success of its painted pottery, but the

process of Greek expansion, which was underway in the 8th century, and in which eastern products reached the western borders, was internationally important.

Troy, close to the entry of the Black Sea, had been occupied by Greeks before 700 BCE. We know little about this early Troy, because it was destroyed to build a great sanctuary 300 years later. We do know that it had long been virtually deserted.

In the east the Greeks were in contact with Lydia and Phrygia in west and northwest Asia Minor. The evidence of decorated pottery at Sardis in Lydia suggests not only an east Greek presence from 750 to 725 BCE, but perhaps also a local style imitating Greek pottery in the 9th century or the early 8th. The Phrygians were culturally in advance of the Greeks; it was their bronze bowls and bronze pins that stirred the imagination of the Greeks in western Asia. It may be that Gordion, the capital city of the Phrygians, was a great trading center. At the end of the 8th century conditions were easy for such a long-range trade. Around the year 700 BCE Phrygian pottery influenced the outline birds and animals that decorated amphorae on Paros and the nearby islands.

Adoption of an alphabetic script

Meanwhile, before we have any literary versions of most of them, we can begin to make out familiar stories or story-patterns among the decorations of painted pottery. Is the helmeted soldier handling a woman on a Cretan pot of around 700 BCE Paris carrying off Helen? We can recognize the Cyclops, and Zeus with his thunderbolt, and various abductions of Helen. But the interpretation of some at least of the Levantine originals, for example a sheet of bronze figures at Olympia, must have been as obscure to the 8th-century Greeks as it is to us.

In the structure of early Greek life there are a few factors which are so obvious that they are sometimes overlooked. One is the adoption of writing. The alphabet, learned from the Phoenicians, begins to appear in the mid-8th century. Writing created or intensified the sense among the Greeks that the world could be controlled, first in morality and of human behavior, then in the whole field of history and politics, and finally in philosophy, in science, and in religion.

Religion

Another dominant factor in the late 8th century is religious. Images emerge that tell the same stories as those of the written literature from a slightly later date. Yet they are more solemn than Homer, and sometimes more terrible. Polytheism continually corrects

itself by proliferating, it is always alive at the edges, in its newer cults. There is some evidence that more or less professional prophets and holy men played an important role in Greek religion about this time.

The oracular shrines also existed, but their immense prestige was only beginning; still, it is remarkable how rich the offerings were both at Delphi and at Olympia at a relatively early date. The cult of Demeter existed at Eleusis, just northwest of Athens, as it existed probably at sites all over Greece. By the early 7th century Eleusis was a holy place and a shrine of pilgrimage.

It is worth wondering why the gods are Olympian. Homer already records that Mount Olympos was the home of the gods. Since we know now that most of the names of the gods are Mycenaean, we may suspect the choice of Mount Olympos for their home is 1,000 years earlier than 700 BCE. It is at least likely that whatever people first colonized Olympos with gods had at one time lived in the shadow of that mountain. On the other hand, the home of the gods may have been put on the borders of the known world, to the north, just as Homer located the entry to the Underworld just beyond the western borders.

Eighth-century Greek polytheism was an open system. There was a constant receptiveness to the gods on the borders of the Greek world, and an identification of foreign gods with existing names. Astarte influenced Aphrodite, Artemis is an Oriental Mistress of Animals, Aiolos the wind god was accommodated, and so on. But the process did not break the supple coherence of Greek mythology. Among the other results is that stories about the Mycenaeans, stories about distant people, and the religious mythology of the Greeks and of their neighbors became hardly distinguishable.

▶ *The religious rites held in the Telesterion at Eleusis were and remain secret. Centered on the events of Demeter's life, the Mysteries were celebrated annually.*

Archaic Religious Practice

The decision to send out colonists and where to send them, the right behavior in a national emergency, even legal and constitutional questions, were all sometimes determined by oracle. They were religious questions before they were political, and this occasional power of oracles over politics lasted into the 4th century BCE. Both at Delphi and at Olympia the dedications of ruling families and of nation states, some colonies of recent origin, were very rich. Some of the athletic contests, at least the horse racing and chariot racing, were the sports of kings. As the conception of the temple as a glorious house for the cult statue of a god gained ground in the 7th century, the dedications at great temples became another kind of rich man's or rich nation's competition.

Delphi

Delphi was a herdsmen's shrine on an old Mycenaean site. In the 8th century it grew up where a spring of water tumbled out of the lower rocks of Mount Parnassos, under tall cliffs. The sanctuary is on a steep slope, and the stadium for the Pythian games, one of the four great athletic festivals, balances further up on the mountainside. The whole site is a natural theater (the man-made theater was not built until the 4th century). The temple of Apollo was rebuilt more than once, but we know of no temple before the late 7th or the early 6th century. The ruins that stand today are substantially 4th century. The columns, which were rebuilt by French archaeologists in the mid–20th century, are simply piles of ancient column drums of different dates.

Delphi is the most dramatic sanctuary in Greece. Eagles and white-tailed Egyptian vultures ride in the air above it, the waterspring is still abundant, it is a place of pilgrimage. Euripides in the play *Ion* has a chorus of pilgrims arriving at Delphi, lost in wonder at the monuments.

Later in history, in the sunset of the place, Plutarch (c. 50–c. 120 CE) sets a leisurely dialogue at Delphi. The difference is great. In his day the priests are learned and cultured historians; they respect their shrine; intellectual curiosity and aesthetic pleasure play over the surfaces of stones; tourism and scholarship have begun. Delphi had played an important role in Greek history, and the remnants of many great historic monuments are still to be seen there. It was the richest and greatest of the oracles of Apollo, at least in mainland Greece. The Greeks had once believed that Delphi was literally the center of the world.

The monuments at Delphi are highly competitive. Both sides in the great wars of the 5th century BCE built memorials there to their victories. When the Athenian family of the Alkmaionidai was exiled from Athens, they maintained their position internationally by rebuilding the temple of Apollo at Delphi and entering horses in the Olympic games. One of the charges brought against Pausanias of Sparta at the time of his disgrace was that he made the victory dedication for the battle of Plataiai personal to himself by its inscription, which was then altered.

The base of that memorial still exists near the temple of Apollo. It was once a tall gilded bronze pillar of three entwined snakes. At the top the three heads looked outwards, with a gold tripod balancing on their three noses.

It was Nero who first looted Delphi, but Rome was filling up with Greek treasures before his time. In the first two centuries CE the last great buildings were being constructed at all the Greek international showplaces, but at the same time works of art were disappearing. At Delphi it is Herod of Athens, a rich patron of scholars, who built the marble facade of the stadium in the 2nd century CE, and the theater, typically of Greek story, was restored in the 2nd century BCE by a foreign king, and again under the Roman empire.

No great archaeological complex is the pure relic of any one moment in the past, least of all Delphi, which is vulnerable to

▲ *The round temple, or tholos, at Delphi, much restored and damaged by earthquakes, was built in the 4th century. It had a peristyle of 20 Doric columns.*

65

Delphi

The Delphic oracle had a small sanctuary on a steep slope under the cliffs of Parnassos, a little inland from the north coast of the gulf of Corinth. It grew up where spring water broke in two places out of the mountainside. The oracle gained rapidly in importance in the late archaic period. Greek cities sought its advice for their colonizing expeditions, and Delphi gained importance as a meeting-place with the establishment of the Pythian games about 590 BCE.

In Classical times the sanctuary was a place of tall monuments, each craning up like a sunflower to be seen. They were often damaged by earthquakes. From the southeast corner of the walled temenos or enclosure, the Sacred Way wound up past the treasuries of the Greek city-states and the monuments they erected to mark victories and great events, to the temple and the oracle itself, and on to the terrace above.

In the sanctuary, the theater is a late (4th-century) addition, and the restoration of the temple of Apollo is particularly inauthentic. Still, that is better than heavy-handedness. It is hard, but it is necessary, to relate the intricate contents of the Delphi museum to the bare stones out of doors. In this pure air, in this remote place, the masterpieces of many generations were crowded together.

The Oracle of Apollo

The great oracular shrines of the Greeks started very small. Delphi is essentially a mountain herdsmen's shrine. There are a number of others. The early records of the replies of the gods to the questions that were asked of them are inextricably entangled in folktales and embroidered stories. Oracular power was probably less dramatic than we used to think. But they were holy places, the essential symbol of the unity of the Greeks. International festivals grew up at oracular sanctuaries which already existed.

In their last stage, oracles embodied the conscious traditional wisdom of the Greeks, the final distillation of what it was thought the gods had to teach. The uninspiring but innocent precepts of the god at Delphi were copied and recopied far across Asia, where they have been found on stone tablets as far away as the borders of Russia and Afghanistan. The sanctuaries themselves were places of pilgrimage and centers of learning even under the Roman empire.

▼ *At the center of ancient Delphi was the temple of Apollo. It was surrounded by treasuries and monuments. The theater could seat about 6,500 people.*

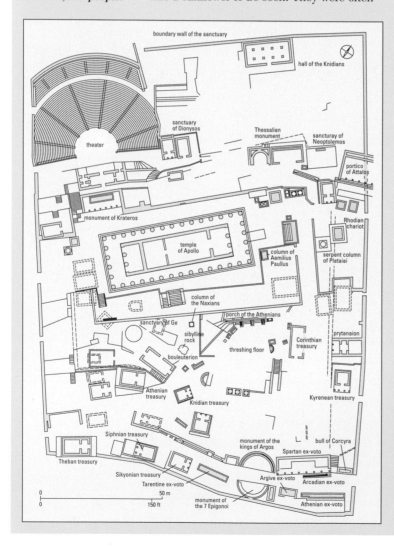

landslides, earthquakes, and falls of rock.
The monuments have often been rebuilt and
shifted from place to place. The most telling
evidence of rebuilding is the marks of
building clamps in the stones, which can be
dated. From the earliest Delphi we have a few
bronzes and some foundations, and the two
huge statues of Kleobis and Biton. There is a
naivety and heaviness about the pair that
speak of a more innocent age than anything to
be found much after 600 BCE.

The liveliest sculptures at Delphi belong to
a time of transitions. They are inventive with
no loss of dignity, and mobile with no loss of
strength. Their purpose is to decorate, not
only to impress. They compete for attention
but not for space. They are the frieze of the
treasury of the Siphnians.

The island of Siphnos played little part in
history, but it had gold mines and silver

mines, and the Siphnian treasury at Delphi
competes successfully with those of the
greatest Greek cities. There were 16 of these
buildings at Delphi, each of which was the
embodiment of city-state or national prestige,
built to shelter the small, rich dedications to
the god that Athens or some other great
power might offer. The temple would not hold
all the offerings, and the city-states liked to
keep their own treasures in one place.

The competition for prestige had its roots
in the honor and shame system of Homeric
heroes and of undeveloped peoples. The
wealth was not in the strict sense for use,
but in this context show was itself a use. It
provoked the kindness of the god, it engaged
the favor of the oracle, and it bonded national
self-respect; in addition, it asserted
internationally the standing of Athens,
Siphnos, or other dedicators.

▲ *The original
temple of Apollo
was detroyed by
earthquake in 373
BCE, but it was rebuilt
on the same plan.
The columns have
been partially
restored in
modern times.*

Olympia

▲ *Restored columns help give the visitor an idea of the layout and appearance of the structures around the sanctuary of Zeus at Olympia.*

The most characteristic expression of archaic Greek religion is Olympia. Associated with a jumble of legends, Olympia was a grove, an open-air sanctuary with a dozen or more altars dotted around among the trees, some sacred relics, great dedicated wealth, a fine water supply, and a huge extent of flat land suitable for an athletic festival. Sport had in Greek religion something of the same function as sculpture, which therefore often represents naked athletes; it was a display of strength and skill and animal quality in which the gods might delight. Of course it was essentially competitive and it retained from the heroic society in which it began the quality of its principal reward: an immortal and universal fame. There is a continual gesture in Homer to link this glorious status with breeding, ancestry, and inherited wealth.

Olympia was not a shrine of pilgrimage like Dodona or Delphi; it had little political or religious power. It was a meeting-place, and so, in virtue of their position, were Nemea and the Isthmus, the other international sporting centers. The landscape of Olympia is not typical of Greece, but we know that to ancient taste it was the most beautiful in the world. Its central monument was not built until the 5th century BCE, the huge and strangely shaped temple of Zeus.

Olympia lies in a bend of the Alpheios, a broad, powerful river coming down from the mountains of Arcadia. At Olympia the river is about to break out into the fertile coastal plain; at one time it must have divided the upper from the lower grazing grounds. From the ruins in winter you can see the snow on the Arcadian mountains, and from the nearest mountain you can see the sea.

Olympia

Olympia was a sanctuary, a sacred wood called Altis, in the unpoliticized countryside of western south Greece, on the banks of the river Alpheios. It was named for the Olympian gods, and the hill that overlooked it belonged to Kronos, father of Zeus, and perhaps to his mother.

By the 8th century, Olympia had become immensely rich and powerful, and the center of an international festival of athletic games. The sanctuary has been reconstructed from the mud of the Alpheios floods which buried it. The altar of Zeus was made of ashes, and it was dissolved; but his temple, built in the 5th century, has survived in colossal ruins.

There were cults of heroes, legendary human beings of divine ancestry, as well as of gods at Olympia; in the end the athletes themselves came to seem half-divine.

The Gods of Olympos

There are 12 great Greek gods, but not always or everywhere the same 12; some important and interesting gods never join the 12, while some of the 12 have multiple personalities. The most famous include Zeus, king of the gods; Aphrodite, goddess of love; and Poseidon, god of the sea.

Each city-state had its own patron or patrons, to be appeased and flattered, and a farmer would offer to Demeter for a good harvest, a sailor to Poseidon for safe passage.

There were also countless minor gods, and in the country Pan and the nymphs were important. In later times the "mysteries" and more personal philosophies, and foreign deities such as Kybele from Asia Minor, Isis, and the Greco-Egyptian Serapis gained in popularity.

▼ *The temple of Zeus, the largest Doric temple in Greece, was at the heart of the precinct. To the east was the stadium, which could hold about 40,000 spectators.*

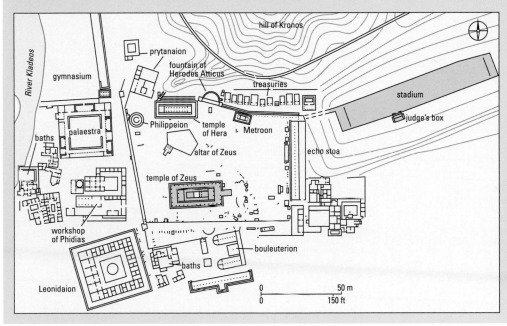

The altar of Zeus was made of the ashes of its own old fires. In the end it had become a huge construction with steps and a high core, but it was all swept away in the Middle Ages by the floods of the Alpheios. The whole site was covered under 10 feet (3 m) of mud; it was a long time before it was identified. The altar of Zeus has left no discernible trace; all that we can look for is where there was space for it. It must have been hard to find room in the 5th century for the temple of Zeus; a number of older monuments are close to it. Pieces of an Ionic building have been found built into its foundations.

▶ *Artemis, the sister of Apollo, is a huntress, and a goddess of initiation She was also Hekate, a death goddess, and had an interest in childbirth, although she was a virgin.*

The floods that inundated Olympia have preserved piecemeal the fragments of a few historic memorials. The river silt has confused traces of the dark age and the Mycenaeans. The fine early bronzes, the helmets dedicated after wars, and a golden bowl like half a pomegranate are the spoil of the floods. So are the pediment sculptures of the temple of Zeus. Apollo's blank expression—which has been overstressed by inappropriate cleaning of the marble surface—has a terrible power. This is not a cult statue with a benign smile, it is the god of mythology. In several of these statues one can make out the beginnings of portrayal of human character and emotion, and of an attractive naturalism. The harmony of the limbs is both stony and bodily, the frozen action is a ballet of violence. The solid and crisp strength of the marbles from the temple of Zeus marks the end of an epoch.

The workshop where Pheidias made the statue of Zeus still survives in ruins. A cup that Pheidias marked with his own name has been recovered from it; so have some of the molds for the draperies of the statue. Some of the finest of the small finds from Olympia are the terracottas, the colored architectural decorations mostly of the long row of city treasuries that stood on a terrace below the hill called Kronion, at the edge of the sanctuary. The color is not garish, indeed some of the best are black and tan, produced by Pheidias' workshop, but their boldness and simplicity as an architectural scheme are stunning.

It is appropriate to add a word here about the Hermes of Praxiteles. There is no doubt at all that this famous statue is a fake, a copy made in the Roman period. But the excavators knew that Pausanias recorded a Hermes of Praxiteles here, and when they found this one in 1877 they were naturally excited. It is a brilliant copy, but to idealize it is false. The arguments against its really being the work of Praxiteles are too detailed to be set out here, but they seem to me overwhelming. They depend on fine points of sculptural technique.

There were an enormous number of victory statues at Olympia, and later political statues, and most of the greatest artists of the best period worked there, yet of all those masterpieces almost nothing has survived but the inscribed bases of the monuments and one ear of a bronze bull. The four horses of the Cathedral of San Marco which came to Venice from the sack of Constantinople started their journey at Delphi or at Olympia, at Corinth perhaps, or at Chios, assuming they were Greek.

Contemplation of the loot of the ancient world, particularly when it is wrenched out of context, has a tendency to wither historical judgment. The evidence that tells us most about the archaic Greeks includes many fragments of their written literature, the cities in which they were beginning to live, their laws and institutions, and the always extending map of their activities.

Delphi was hidden among remote mountains and Olympia was a sacred city with no permanent population; indeed, the Eleians had no city at all until a late stage in their history, and when one was built they were reluctant to live in it, preferring an old-fashioned life in the countryside. Is that not because water, with all its benefits, was comparatively abundant all over Eleia? The temple of Zeus is in many ways a monument of social transition; it was the first act of self-assertion of the first Eleian democracy. How interesting that it was built at Olympia and not at Elis.

The Birth of City-States

The old laws had been known by heart, or they had been general principles like proverbs. With the coming of writing, the elaboration of legal institutions became a continual process. This happens more slowly than one might think. In Athens Solon's laws were written after 600 BCE, and the laws of the newly founded Greek city of Marseille (Massilia) were publicly inscribed very little earlier. The laws of Dreros may date from the 7th century, the laws of Chios from about 575 BCE. At the end of the 6th century at Aphrati in Crete the laws were codified by a high official, a scribe and remembrancer, apparently for the first time. Some 7th-century legal fragments do exist, but they are always fragments. No doubt the great Cretan cities inscribed their laws early, but many inscriptions must have perished.

The longest archaic law code we have is that of Gortyn, in southern central Crete. It comprises 600 lines carved into a series of stone tablets; its likely date is just after the mid-5th century. The laws themselves are earlier, and the oldest part probably dates from the 7th century. They indicate a clear division of classes: the free, those without political rights, the serf, and the slave. The law distinguishes between cases where a judge is bound to decide according to statute and according to witnesses, and all other cases, in which he decides freely.

Tyrants

An active lawgiver is implicit in the wording of the law of Gortyn. He revived in Greece in another form, particularly in the area of the Isthmus, a little before 650 BCE. As in Egypt and Lydia, at Corinth outsiders (Kypselos,

followed by his son Periander) took over and vigorously controlled the state; the same happened at Megara (Theagenes), Sikyon (Orthagoras, Kleisthenes), and Epidauros (where Periander seized control), and in the late 7th century Kylon nearly took control of Athens by force of arms. Early in the 6th century a public arbitrator was elected at Lesbos, who held office 10 years, and at the same time Solon of Athens as public arbitrator and lawgiver altered aristocratic government and reversed some of its social results. However, Peisistratos and his son subsequently made themselves tyrants, or unconstitutional rulers, of Athens (546–510 BCE). Other tyrants imposed themselves in the city-states of the east (Miletos, Ephesos, Samos, Naxos) and west (Akragas, Gela and Syracuse, Himera, Selinus, Rhegion).

This rash of local tyrannies may well have been partly due within Greece to the influence of Pheidon, a tyrannous king of Argos, probably in the mid-7th century. It indicates also some general social conditions. There was unrest everywhere, the aristocracy was sufficiently powerful and disunited everywhere except Argos to throw up outsiders who could take over the state. The new dynasties caused a conflict of loyalties, and usually ended badly. But they usually increased public wealth; they were lavish and showy patrons, and in this way expected to acquire worldly success and heroic prestige. Tyrannies arose first in trading cities with small territory. The same pressures, social or economic, which caused these entangled civil quarrels and tough regimes must have operated also on the colonial movement. The competition in trade

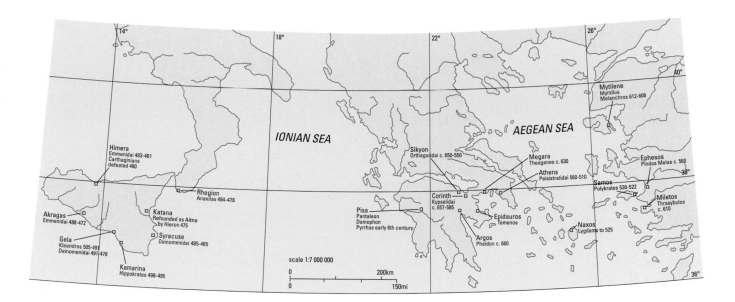

Map labels:
14° · 18° · 22° · 26° · 40° · 38° · 36°

IONIAN SEA

AEGEAN SEA

Mytilene
Myrsilus
Melanchros 612-608

Himera
Emmenidai 483-461
Carthaginians
defeated 480

Sikyon
Orthagoridai c. 650-550

Megara
Theagenes c. 630

Ephesos
Pindos Melas c. 560

Athens
Peisistratidai 560-510

Rhegion
Anaxilas 494-476

Corinth
Kypselidai
c. 657-585

Samos
Polykrates 530-522

Miletos
Thrasybulos
c. 610

Akragas
Emmenidai 488-472

Katana
Refounded as Aitna
by Hieron 475

Pisa
Pantaleon
Damophon
Pyrrhos early 6th century

Epidauros
Temenos

Naxos
Lygdams to 525

Gela
Kleandros 505-491
Deinomenidai 491-478

Syracuse
Deinomenidai 485-465

Argos
Pheidon c. 660

Kamarina
Hippokrates 498-495

scale 1:7 000 000
0 · 200km
0 · 150mi

▲ *This map shows the location of tyrannies between the 7th and 5th centuries BCE. Rule by violence and distribution of land to their own supporters were characteristic of Greek tyrannies.*

may well have been a disturbing factor; as a direct influence it fell first on the rich. It was they who fought civil wars, who founded colonies, who imposed tyrannies.

The European context

It is useful to see this troubled Greek renaissance in a European context, even though most of the influences, after 700 BCE, are from Greece and from the east on Europe, with almost none from Europe on Greece. The first European long iron swords and iron harness appear at that time. Wealth increased, so did population, and so therefore did fortification. From the 10th century to the 7th the strong places grew in strength and numbers. From the Greek expansion onward, there was even some influence of Greek building techniques. Were Europe's walled towns not city-states? Does the city-state not arise from similar reasons both in Greece and in the north? Whether this is so or not, in Greece the community of language, and the geographically determined stability of tribal territories, created an advantage.

As for direct eastern influences, Oriental metalwork reached Europe. Down to 500 BCE, the Scythian penetration of central and even of western Europe is remarkable, and hard to explain without a big migration. The mixture of influences, some of them directly Oriental with no Greek transmission, that produced the material culture of the early Etruscans sets some difficult problems. Before the 8th century, local styles and local skills were similar all over Europe. Greece recovered first, perhaps because it was closer to the east. The bronze bowls that the Greeks loved have their origins in Urartu, to the east of Lake Van in modern east Turkey. (Urartu was taken by the Medes in 585 BCE.) Those cauldrons have been discovered at Angers, Auxerre, Sainte Colombe, and Stockholm. But from about 600 BCE France, Spain, and Scandinavia were being supplied with imitations, made in Britain and Ireland.

Even the early La Tene style in bronzework in the early 5th century, the first version of one of the most idiosyncratic and brilliant of all European styles, is visibly close to Greek, as well as to Oriental models. From 700 to 500 BCE Europe was more Orientalized than Hellenized, but Greek influence continually increased. By about 800 the Mediterranean was politically, economically, and culturally dominant in Europe, and Greece within the Mediterranean. Much of the Greek penetration of Europe can be seen in terms of movement toward the sources of metal, in Spain, Brittany, Cornwall, and Sardinia.

The rise of Sparta

The archaic age was a period in which peoples conflicted. The tradition of literary historians strongly suggests, and the evidence of dialect does confirm, that there had been some redistribution of peoples in Greece, and the end of the process was still going on in historical times. When the Spartans took over Messenia in the 8th and 7th centuries, we have no knowledge of any refugees, but after the third Messenian war, which began at the earthquake of 464 BCE, the refugees settled at Naupaktos, on the north shore of the gulf of Corinth, unapproachable except by sea.

They retained their identity for 100 years, and in 369 BCE Messenia was restored. In the dark age there must have been many

unrecorded movements of peoples which were at least on a similar scale.

Spartan expansion in the Peloponnese was an arduous policy. The first conquest of Messenia took place between 735 and 715 BCE, but in the next generation, in 669 BCE, Sparta was defeated during a move against Argos, and about 660 Messenia rebelled. In the 6th century the Spartans reached the east coast of the Peloponnese, and the island of Kythera in the south.

By war and diplomacy, the Spartans established a dominant position against Argos and a protective alliance with Arcadia. In the second half of the 6th century Spartan armies were active abroad. They ended tyranny at Sikyon, and so gained an ally on the Corinthian gulf. They menaced Polykrates of Samos off Asia Minor, and expelled Lygdamis of Naxos. They attacked Hippias, son of Peisistratos, and drove him from Athens. By the end of the century, Sparta dominated the Peloponnese in a formal league of allies with set procedures

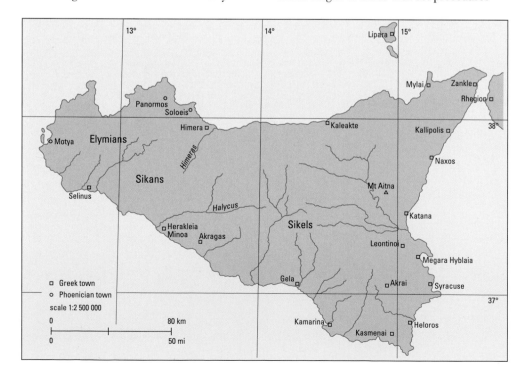

ΛΟΤΕΛΟΝΑΕΤΟΝΡΟΤ
ΕΙΜΕΝΤΟΛ:ΛΙΝΤΕ
ΡΑΛΕΝΟΔΡΛΛΟ
ΚΟΚΟΣΜΑΣΚΑΝΕΣ
ΔΟΝΙΣΟΡΓΑΝΟΣ
ΟΛΝΤΣΚΡΕΘΑΣΚΑΤ
Α:ΕΝΜΑΜΕΝΑΤ
ΑΜΕΣΟΝΤΟΜΕΓΣ

ΕΝΙΚΟΤΝΟΤΤΑ
ΑΣΙΝΑΤΡΣΤΡΑΓΕ
ΛΟΣΤΟΝΕΝΟΤΡΑΤ
ΡΑΙΝΝΕΝΟΝΝΤ
ΤΡΛΚΤΑΜΕΛΑΣΤ
ΑΣΚΑΝΝΑΝΤΑΣΚΑ
ΟΣΡΣΑΤΜΕΣΤ

and assemblies. Only Sparta could summon the Peloponnesian league, and on a majority vote of its members the whole league backed Sparta in arms.

Sparta had to pay a heavy price in military alertness, and in a cruel discipline. From early Spartan society we have an impression of vigorous gaiety. In the early 6th century Spartan trade abroad began to die out, and in Sparta itself the import of luxuries withered. By the late 6th century the hard disciplines of Spartan life were fixed. True Spartans were an elite; the farm work was done by serfs.

The Spartan system was complete and extreme concentration on producing strong, violent, disciplined, and ruthless young men, and more or less similar young women. The Spartans were ruled in battle and in matters of religion by two royal families. Sparta was a city without walls; it was considered that the heartland of the Spartans would never be assailed. Religious festivals were much concerned with group initiation; at one of them a boy was flogged unconscious. The Spartans prided themselves on brute strength, courage, and brevity of speech.

The Persian threat

Meanwhile in the east a storm cloud had been moving slowly westward out of central Asia for 1,000 years. Between 560 and 546 Kroisos of Lydia conquered the Greek cities of Asia Minor, all but Miletos. The Lydians were in some ways a Hellenized monarchy; they offered reparation to Greek gods, they consulted Delphi, and they dedicated very rich offerings. At the same time, however, revolution brought Cyrus to the throne of the Medes and Persians. The Lydians were conquered, Sardis fell, and with it the cities of the coast. The Persian empire was now immensely strong, and directly threatening

Greece. Before the end of the century the Persians had ravaged Samos, and conquered Egypt, Cyprus, and Kyrene. On the northern shores of the Mediterranean, through Thrace, the Persians extended their influence toward central Europe.

By the end of the archaic period then, the Assyrians had been replaced by a single, vast empire in western Asia. The Spartans had to some degree unified the Peloponnese. At the same time the increasingly competitive Greek colonies in the west had provoked serious countermeasures from the Phoenicians based at Carthage, and an even more frightening southward thrust from the Etruscans. Rome itself was beginning to be successful: the Romans expelled their last Etruscan king in 510 BCE.

Athens

In the 300 years between 800 and 500 BCE, the city in Europe that altered in the most startling way was Athens. It was slow to alter, and at the end of the period it was not a world power. The dominance of Athenian pottery in colonial and foreign markets had been established only in the course of the 6th century, and Athenian coinage began to be minted only at that time.

The small island of Aegina in the Saronic Gulf introduced coinage at least 50 years before the Athenians, from Lydia via the Greek cities in Asia. Aegina was the commercial rival and embittered enemy of Samos, at a time when Athens was still inward looking. It is possible that Aegina had blocked the early commercial expansion of the Athenians, even as early as the late 8th century; Herodotos tells us of "an ancient hatred." (Later this rivalry was to result in war and, in 459, the defeat of Aegina and its inclusion in the Delian

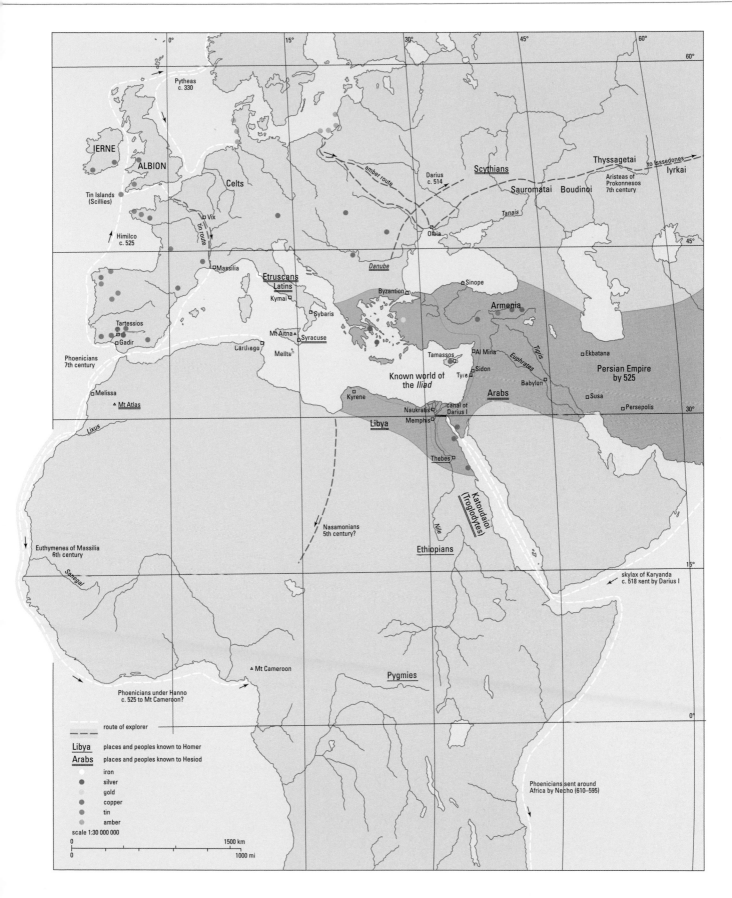

Pytheas
c. 330

IERNE

ALBION

Tin Islands
(Scillies)

Celts

amber route

Darius
c. 514

Scythians

Thyssagetai

to Issedones

Iyrkai

Aristeas of
Prokonnesos
7th century

Sauromatai Boudinoi

Tanais

Himilco
c. 525

Vix

tin route

Olbia

Massilia

Etruscans
Latins

Danube

Sinope

Byzantion

Kymai

Armenia

Sybaris

Mt Aitna

Syracuse

Phoenicians
7th century

Tartessios

Gadir

Carthago

Melite

Known world of
the *Iliad*

Tamassos

Al Mina

Sidon

Tyre

Babylon

Ekbatana

Euphrates

Tigris

Persian Empire
by 525

Susa

Persepolis

Arabs

Melissa

Mt Atlas

Kyrene

Lixus

Naukratis

Memphis

canal of
Darius I

Libya

Thebes

Nasamonians
5th century?

Katoudaioi
(Troglodytes)

Nile

Euthymenes of Massilia
6th century

Ethiopians

Senegal

skylax of Karyanda
c. 518 sent by Darius I

Mt Cameroon

Pygmies

Phoenicians under Hanno
c. 525 to Mt Cameroon?

route of explorer

Libya places and peoples known to Homer

Arabs places and peoples known to Hesiod

○ iron
● silver
● gold
● copper
● tin
● amber

scale 1:30 000 000

0 _____ 1500 km

0 _____ 1000 mi

Phoenicians sent around
Africa by Necho (610–595)

77

Sparta

Sparta was protected not by walls but by its remote location in the valley of the Eurotas among high mountains. But its arts and monuments in the archaic period were wonderfully fine.

The Spartans and the Persians were reluctant adversaries, but the military power of Sparta was necessary to the honor, prestige, and influence of the chief member of the Peloponnesian league. It was also inspired by the ambitious and high-handed Spartan attitude to race, and the dominant position of the Spartan elite over territories acquired through war. The Spartans were more stylish and brilliant than we used to think, but probably also more odious.

The city occupied a large area including several low hills. In its later history, walls marked the boundary, which was some 6 miles (10 km) long. At the eastern end of the acropolis was the sanctuary of Athene Chalkioikos, which from the 2nd or 1st centuries BCE overlooked the vast new theater. On the banks of the Eurotas, at the sanctuary of Artemis Orthia, Spartan boys were ritually flogged.

▼ Even in its heyday the city of Sparta had few grand public buildings. Its naturally protected position and the strength of its army, meant that it was not walled.

league dominated by Athens.) However, Athens was not without exports: Athenian olive jars have been found all over the Mediterranean world, but they likely were the product of the richest farms. In the 7th century, in the countryside even more than in Athens itself, the landholders were buried with great riches, government was by hereditary oligarchy, and the poor became poorer. In 620 BCE Athens adopted a new code of law, known as Draco's code, in which the only progressive rule was for state trial and punishment of murder, with the consequent abolition of family vendetta.

The reforms of Solon

Solon, whose reforms were introduced a generation later, was an aristocrat, a poet, and a traveled man with experience of Cyprus and Egypt. He rescued the Athenian poor from the penalties of debt. Outstanding debt was canceled, and enslavement for debt was abolished. Athenians in exile to avoid slavery, Athenians sold abroad, and those enslaved in Attica became free. Solon also forbade the export of corn or of any produce except the olive.

In law, Solon introduced the right of appeal. In politics, he removed the criterion of blood for holding authority in the state and substituted graduated criteria of wealth, removing the power of hereditary aristocracy. He graded the people into divisions based on wealth in measures of corn: "500-measure" men, riders, rankers (infantry), and laborers. It has been suggested that Solon used this measure to tie gentility to landholding, but it is likely that the wheat measure was a traditional unit of value at a time when money was still new and confusing.

The nine governors or chief officials of Athens were chosen from 40 elected

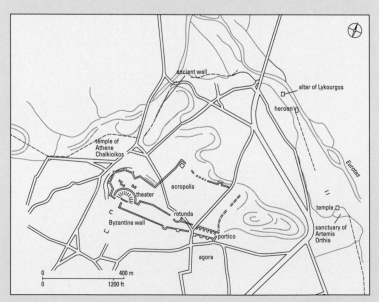

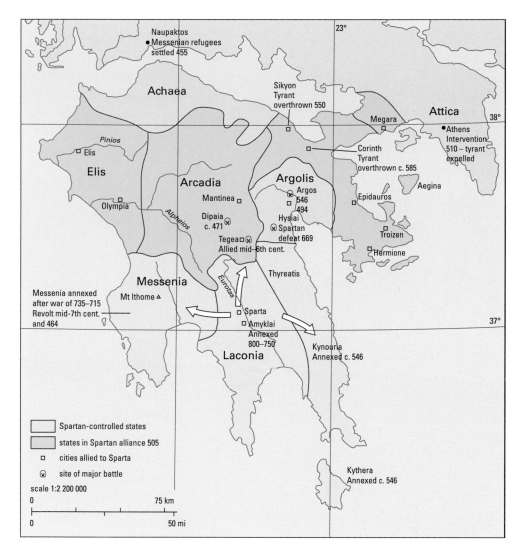

candidates who fulfilled the criterion of wealth. Governors joined the state council after their year of office. Below this was the general assembly of the people, with a smaller assembly invented by Solon between the two, of 400 elected members, who set the agenda for the general assembly.

It was only in the days of Solon that the Athenians captured nearby Salamis. Under Solon, whenever Salamis fell, the Athenians had taken an important step in national consciousness; scholars recognize in the beginnings of democratic justice an articulate social identity, the liberation of a powerful and confident spirit, a creative breath.

To concentrate attention on what was developing fastest in the Greek world and to ignore more conservative or less successful societies gives the false impression that history is a linear evolution. In Arcadia, for example, life was quiet, and the energetic young emigrated. A few cities grew from clusters of villages: Tegea, Heraia, and Mantinea. The Arcadian dialect was very old-fashioned, and some of the religious cults of the mountains were conservative or eccentric, or both. Even in Asia Minor there were small oligarchies of landowners, and the ritual curses of Teos look very ancient indeed compared to the laws of Solon.

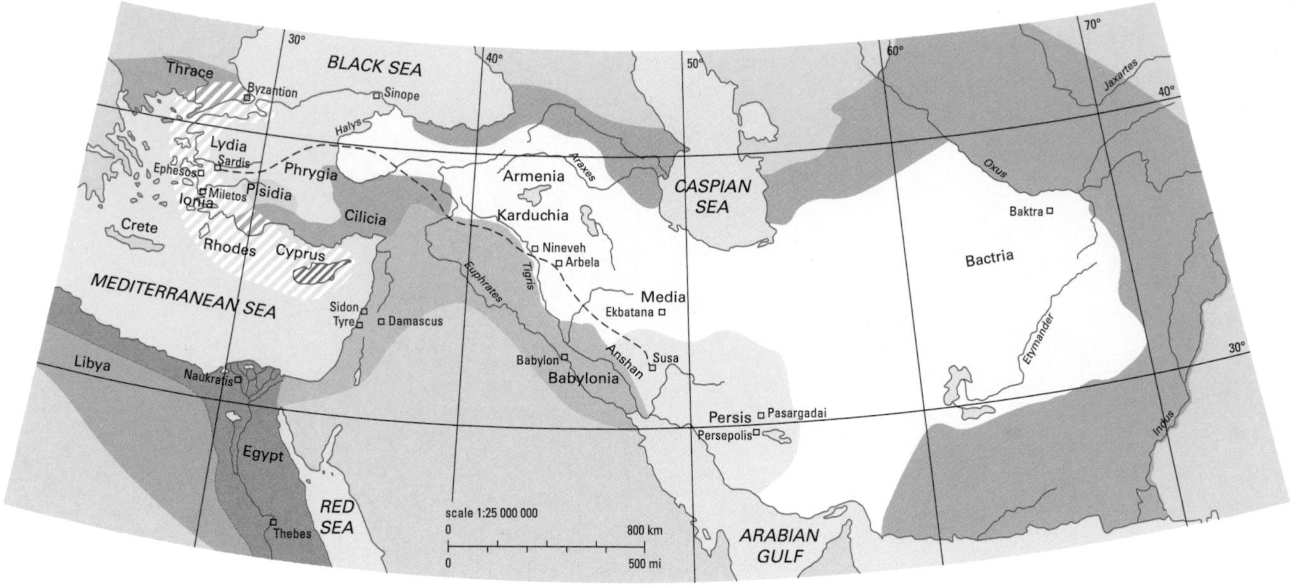
BLACK SEA
Thrace
Byzantion
Sinope
Halys
Lydia
Sardis
Ephesos
Phrygia
Miletos
Pisidia
Ionia
Crete
Rhodes
Cilicia
Cyprus
MEDITERRANEAN SEA
Sidon
Tyre
Damascus
Libya
Naukratis
Egypt
Thebes
RED SEA
Armenia
Araxes
Karduchia
Nineveh
Arbela
Tigris
Euphrates
Media
Ekbatana
Anshan
Susa
Babylon
Babylonia
Persis
Pasargadai
Persepolis
CASPIAN SEA
ARABIAN GULF
Oxus
Jaxartes
Baktra
Bactria
Etymander
Indus
30°
40°
50°
60°
70°
scale 1:25 000 000
0
800 km
0
500 mi
Persian homeland under Cyrus before 550
Kingdom of Medes – annexed 550
Kingdom of Lydians – annexed c.547
Kingdom of Babylonians – annexed c.539
Kingdom of Egyptians – annexed c.225
Final annexations of Darius and Xerxes
Persian royal road
zone of Ionian revolt 499-493

▲ This map shows the expansion of the Persian empire in the 6th century BCE under Cyrus.

It is interesting that Teos had grain hunger in common with Athens. That perhaps was why the first Athenian colonies of the late 7th century BCE looked toward the Black Sea. Wheaten bread was a luxury, and the poor seldom ate it; they lived on various cakes and breads and mashes of mixed grain: barley, millet and so on. It was Solon's law that the official diners who were entertained in the council house at Athens should have barley cakes on normal days and wheaten bread for festivals. Economic historians suggest that, certainly at a later stage in history, Athenian farmers could not compete with cheap wheat from abroad.

The great families

This was an age of great families, of which the Peisistratidai and Alkmaionidai were the greatest. But they were mostly doomed to get above themselves. One of the most famous cases is that of the Alkmaionidai at Athens. In 632 Megakles, a member of the family, was principal magistrate, and when Kylon, an Athenian nobleman, attempted to take Athens, Megakles had many of his supporters dragged from sanctuary and murder was committed in a holy place.

A generation later Kylon's supporters contrived to get all the Alkmaionidai banished as being under a curse. But Alkmaion, son of Megakles, commanded the Athenian army, and by 592 he had acquired wealth. He became a diplomatic agent of the Lydians at Delphi, and won the chariot race at Olympia. His son, another Megakles, married the daughter of the tyrant of Sikyon. There were several more expulsions of the family, but the later members of the same family include Kleisthenes, Perikles, and Alkibiades. The last time the curse was invoked was by the Spartans against Perikles, unsuccessfully as it turned out. It

► Sparta lies near the head of a long river-plain protected by the spectacular barrier of Mount Taygetos, which lies between Sparta and Messenia.

▲ The Acropolis is an outcrop of limestone that rises about 295 feet (90 m) above the modern city of Athens. It has been a citadel and sanctuary since ancient times.

was the Alkmaionidai in exile in the late 6th century who built the archaic temple of Apollo at Delphi, the first massive architectural use of marble in mainland Greece. It was the Peisistratidai in power in Athens who began the enormous early temple of Olympian Zeus.

There are some glimpses to be had of the decline of these great families through the development of technology. The availability of heavy armor and weapons for infantry, and the consequent evolution of mass formations of drilled soldiers, removed the personal basis of power from horsemen, and also from those noble individuals who had behaved in battle as their fathers had instructed them. The change in tactics became also a social change, and the new infantry became a new and powerful force in Greek politics.

However, the conditions of Solon's day were not quite altered at a stroke. Before the mid-century, Peisistratos had seized the acropolis and was governing Athens. He was Solon's relative, an aristocratic adventurer with international connections, a successful soldier who had taken the port of Megara, and a rich man. He installed Lygdamis as tyrant of Naxos, and there he exiled Athenian nobles. As tyrant of Athens he was vigorous and successful abroad, and a strong administrator at home. Roads and public buildings, the circulation of judges to country districts, and a property tax to subsidize the farmers, who by now were back in debt, constitute a policy not hard to understand. It was actively continued by his children. The great Athenian summer festival, the first glorious buildings on the acropolis, and the

patronage of artists are their memorial.
Simonides and Anakreon came to Athens,
Peisistratos collected the works of Homer.
He also brought miners from the north. Soon
after 500 BCE the deeper and icher veins of
Laurion silver and the finest marble from
Mount Pentelikon near Athens, used in the
Parthenon and other 5th-century buildings,
began to be exploited.

When the tyranny fell, it fell to aristocratic
opposition and Spartan intervention.
Peisistratos's son Hippias had taken over the
state. The assassination of the new tyrant's
brother Hipparchos in 514 was carried out
by Harmodios and Aristogeiton, two young

members of the Gephyraei family, and a year
later the Alkmaionidai invaded Attica from
Boeotia. The invasion was a tragic failure.

Kleisthenes unifies Attica

Kleisthenes of the Alkmaionidai was a friend
of Delphi, and Delphi brought the Spartans,
who under Kleomenes overthrew the last
tyrant of Athens. After a period of quarreling
between great families, Kleisthenes carried
through a complete social reorganization late
in the 6th century. The old four clans were
allowed to retain some religious functions,
but 10 new "tribes" were instituted for all
political purposes; each tribe was named for

▼ *By the 7th century
BCE Attica was a
unified political
entity. During the 6th
century Salamis and
Oropos came under
its control.*

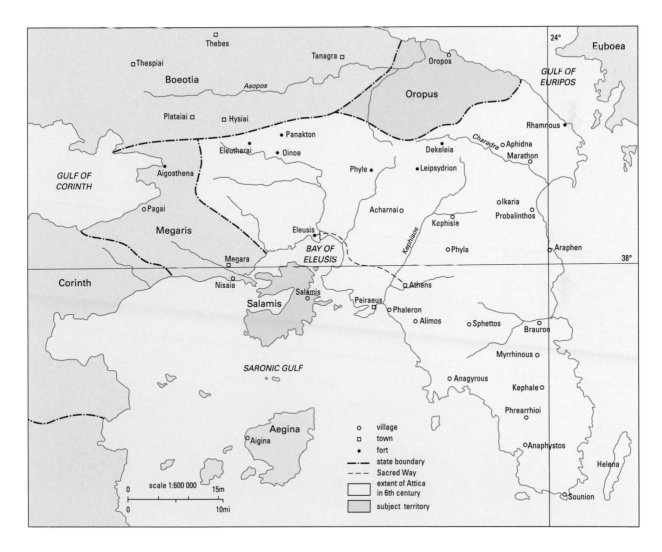

a hero as its patron and "ancestor." Apart from one at Salamis and one at Eleusis, these were all mythological heroes buried in Athens; clearly some attempt was involved to substitute state cults for the heroic ancestors of clans or families venerated in the countryside. At the same time the towns of the countryside were registered, and each of the three regions of Attica—the coast, the interior, and the mountains—was subdivided into ten; each of the tribes had one division in each of the three regions. There were difficulties and anomalies, but in principle, the new military and political organization did its work. It confused any possibility of territorially based baronial conflict; it also sharpened class conflict by setting aside territorial loyalty.

In certain places the boundaries of the new divisions deliberately cut across ancient association. We are not to imagine a new order's influence in daily life, but in elections. The opposition claimed, surely rightly, that Kleisthenes enrolled new citizens who had no ancient claim to that title. The reforms were not passed without a further struggle, a failed Spartan intervention, an appeal to the curse on the Alkmaionidai, and another Athenian nobleman occupying the acropolis and withdrawing into exile. But by the very end of the 6th century, the system was working.

The ancient council of the Areopagus, consisting by now entirely of former state officers, since its last hereditary members had died out, was still a supreme judge and constitutional guardian. A new elected board of ten tribal military commanders had important potential power. The newly registered country towns were given uniform local government. The 10 tribes sent 50 members each to the council of 500.

It is evident that Kleisthenes unified the state. It is also evident that the Athenian state around 500 BCE must have taken some unifying. It was Kleisthenes who instituted ostracism, the system of voting any one troublesome citizen in a year into exile for 10 years. The minimum of total votes (cast in the form of ostraka, potsherds inscribed with the name of a citizen) had to be 6,000, and once it was voted that someone should go, he had to leave within 10 days.

The unification of Attica was on a scale smaller than that of the Peloponnesian League and much smaller than that of the Persian empire. But the changes in Attica were more intricate and ambitious. Its development from this time was headlong. That is partly for economic reasons, partly by the chances of war, partly through the contributions of foreigners, but it is also because the Athenians invented the social basis of democracy. That is the reason people remain so interested in them today. If another reason exists, then it must be their startling literature, though the humanity and rationality that we recognize there belong at least as intimately to their architecture and their democratic experiments as they do to their writings.

In Athens literature flowered late, and so did architecture. By 500 BCE other Greek centers already had a distinguished record for both. That is particularly true of the eastern Greeks. Even the small colony of Poseidonia in western Italy, which we know as Paestum, could have rivaled Athens in archaic architecture. In the 5th century the rich powers of the Greek west did continue to rival Athens, in some ways successfully, but in the east already at the end of the 6th the Persians had cut off the life of the Greek Levant. Most of what Greece learned from

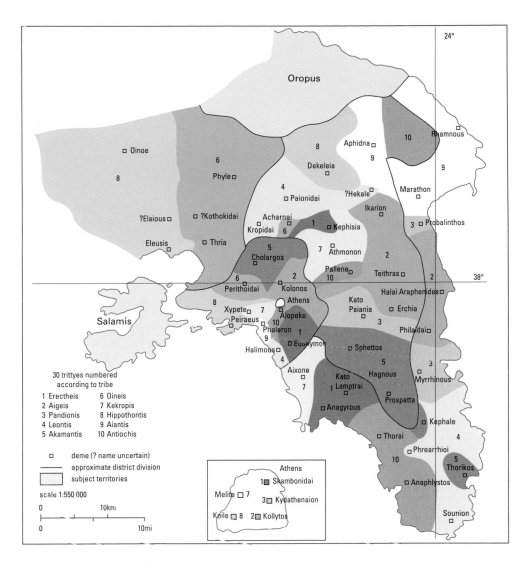

Oropus

24°

□ Oinoe

Phyle □ 6

8

Rhamnous □ 10

Aphidna □ 8

9

Dekeleia □

Marathon 9

?Hekale □ 4

Paionidai □

?Elaious □ ?Kothokidai □

Acharnai □ Ikarion □

Kropidai □ 1 Kephisia □

Probalinthos □ 3

Eleusis □ Thria □ 6

Athmonon 5

Cholargos □ 7

Pallene 2 Teithras □ 2

Perithoidai □ 6 Kolonos □ 10 38°

Athens ○ Halai Araphenides □

Xypete □ 8 7 Kato Erchia □

Peiraeus □ Alopeke Paiania

Phaleron □ 10 3 Philaidai □

Halimous □ 9 1 Euonymon □ Sphettos □

Salamis Aixone □ 4 Hagnous 5

Kato 7 Myrrhinous □ 3

Lamptrai 1

Anagyrous □ Prospatta

Kephale □

Thorai □ 4

Phrearrhioi □ 10 Thorikos 5

Anaphlystos □

Sounion □

30 trittyes numbered
according to tribe

1 Erectheis   6 Oineis
2 Aigeis   7 Kekropis
3 Pandionis   8 Hippothontis
4 Leontis   9 Aiantis
5 Akamantis   10 Antiochis

□   deme (? name uncertain)
___ approximate district division
▨   subject territories

scale 1:550 000

0   10km

0   10mi

Athens

Melite □ 7   1□ Skambonidai
              3□ Kydathenaion
Koile □ 8   2□ Kollytos

◀ **Kleisthenes united
different sections
(trittyes) of Attica
into 10 new tribes.
Men were registered
in their local demes
(country districts or
villages) at the age
of 18. A man's tribe
and deme were
hereditary; he kept
them even if he
moved residence.**

the east was learned by soon after 500 BCE.
Much was learned in the last generations,
and from refugees like Pythagoras of Samos.
In an earlier generation Thales of Miletos
had proposed a united east Greek state; his
pupil Anaximander drew a map of the world.
The Orientalizing period in Greek art ended
with the growth of the Persian empire, but
Athens more than anywhere inherited the
fertility of the eastern Greeks.

Akragas, a Greek colony

Of all the Greek colonies none has a more
brilliant history than Akragas in southern
Sicily (Agrigentum to the Romans, modern

Agrigento). The site is a vast natural
amphitheater locking in a large area of
fertile and protected ground.

The most spectacular remains of Akragas
are the series of temples that stand in line
along the southern edge of the ancient city,
above the plain and silhouetted against the
sky or the sea. It was a fortified city,
deliberately chosen for its position.

Akragas was founded in 581 BCE by a
combined party from Rhodes and Gela, a
rich colony some miles to the southeast. The
new foundation was a strong colonizing act;
the dominant cultural influence was
Rhodian, and the policy was that of Gela,

Akragas

Ancient Akragas was a rich and powerful Greek colony on the south coast of Sicily. Its backbone was a long ridge of mountain curving forward at each end to join hands in a low ridge enclosing a vast hollow of land, naturally defended. Akragas was founded about 582 BCE from the existing colony of Gela. After a number or tyrannies and a huge agricultural and commercial development in the late 6th century, Akragas became rich enough to challenge and defeat the Carthaginians in 480 BCE. Its magnificent ruins are a monument to the triumphant century that followed, when Akragas was one of the largest of Greek cities, with a wealth based on the grain trade. The Carthaginians destroyed it in 406 BCE. It was revived later and became a prosperous Roman town, but the mid-5th century could never be brought back.

▶ *Akragas was one of the largest of Greek cities, with a wealth based on the grain trade. The Carthaginians destroyed it in 406 BCE.*

1   temple of Zeus
2   agora
3   temple of Concord
4   temple of Hera
5   ancient road grid
6   rock sanctuary of Demeter
7   temple of Demeter
8   walls
9   acropolis
10 necropolis

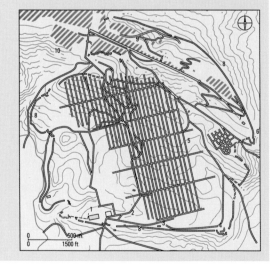

▶ *The temple of Concord is one of several well preserved temples at Akragas. It was turned into a church in the 6th century CE.*

grounds. The best of the olive crop was sold peacefully to the Phoenicians at Carthage. The Akragantines were despotically ruled, and at the beginning of the 5th century one of their more successful rulers, the tyrant Theron, married his daughter to the powerful ruler of Syracuse. This was a case of dynastic alliance with an imperial aim.

The city of Himera in northern Sicily had traditionally been on good terms with Carthage; Theron of Akragas took over Himera in 483, and the exiled ruler called in the Carthaginians. It was Syracuse rather than Akragas which three years later won the battle of Himera. Himera was never rich again, and before the end of the century Carthage had wiped out Himera, Selinus to the west of Akragas, and finally Akragas itself in 406. There were several restorations of Akragas, even a short Indian summer in the late 4th century BCE, but in the 3rd it became a Carthaginian fortress.

The conflicts of Greeks and Carthaginians in Sicily were over trading concessions, and above all over precious metals. Akragas needed peace. It was immensely rich by agriculture and by horse breeding, as well as by trade. But it was the battle of Himera which created the architectural grandeur one can see today.

The captives became slaves, and there were those who owned 500 slaves. They built public buildings, aqueducts, even an artificial lake inside the city. The temple of Here and the temple of Concord crowned the southern aspect. The most amazing ruins lie to the south of the modern city: the remnants of the figures of giants who once stood high up under the entablature of a huge temple of Olympian Zeus. It was begun before Himera, probably in the late 6th century BCE, and was unfinished when the city fell in 406.

which controlled much of the trade of southern Sicily.

In the 6th century Greek influence penetrated the innermost native settlements of central Sicily. The Greeks were traders, and native cities controlled the upper grazing

▶ *Sokrates (469–399 BCE) was an Athenian philosopher whose life, ideas, trial, and death were to have a profound effect on the evolution of European thought.*

5th century. But a love poem by Archilochos has raised his reputation now to what it was in antiquity, second only to Homer's. In this gentle but vivid description of persuading a girl to sleep with him, he speaks directly and at the same time in many changes of tone, using all the resources of poetry.

Early lyric poets

In the second half of the 7th century, choral lyric poetry was already mature and complex in the work of Alkman, and before the end of it Alkaios and Sappho, the fine craftsmen of individual song, were growing up on Lesbos. Alkman lived and composed in Sparta, but in a happier society than Sparta would know in later generations. He seems to have been born in Sardis, but he was surely a Greek and not a Lydian. For the simple joy in life which is so attractive a feature of archaic Greece, Alkman has a special place among poets. The gods are very lightly sketched; familiar peasant activities such as milking are simply transferred to a world of gods, where the milking pails are made of gold and the milk comes from lionesses.

Alkman's most famous poem, and the longest fragment we have of his work, was written for an initiation festival of young girls, a ritual of dancing and singing with strong agricultural overtones. Its liveliness and charm are remarkable enough, but its joking allusiveness also suggests an intimacy of atmosphere, as if this were a small, local scale of celebration.

The songs of Sappho, and to a lesser extent of Alkaios, express personal emotion in precise circumstances. With a delicate confidence that belong to aristocratic life in all ages, Sappho sings her heart out. She tells us the details of her love life, which recall in some measure the passionate crushes of a

schoolgirl. Archilochos tells us as much, but without hints and without the full-blooded description of passionate emotions. He does convey passion, and more sharply, in fewer words, but Sappho is more nostalgic, more lingering.

Mytilene, the chief city of Lesbos, lurched in the lifetime of Sappho and Alkaios from tyranny to tyranny. By 606 Alkaios was fighting under Pittakos against Athenian colonists. His great hatred was the next tyrant, Myrsilos, and he went into exile after an unsuccessful attempt to get rid of him. Alkaios at some point went to Egypt and Sappho to Sicily. Alkaios knew Thrace, and he had dealings with the Lydians. Sappho's family once had land on the mainland of Asia Minor; the brother of Alkaios fought as a mercenary for the king of Babylon.

Sappho's wedding songs and the political songs of Alkaios were among the substantial attainments of Greek literature in its early flowering. Both poets use a variety of four-line stanza forms, with similar rhythms but very different effects. It is clear that the Lesbian stanza forms belong to a special and very ancient musical tradition that grew up in that particular dialect; it has been suggested that the same tradition underlies even the hexameter, the epic rhythm. That remains doubtful. We can at least say that a profuse tradition of song rhythm was in flower, and that its use by Sappho and Alkaios was a special development. Their social position to some degree determined their handling of it.

Similar four-line stanzas were in use 100 years later in Athens; many political verses of the last aristocrats as well as of the democrats were composed in them. So were invocations to the gods, and since Alkaios also wrote hymns in these stanzas, it is quite possible that hymns were their origin. It may

easily be that the 7th-century aristocracy were the first to adapt the stanza forms of traditional singing to political and to very personal uses, and that they were also the first to construct long songs of linked stanzas.

The highly developed rhythmic sense of the early poets seems to owe more than a little to Asia Minor. The limit of a stanza form is one human breath. The variety of forms, which by the 5th century were beginning to mingle, owe everything to the comparative isolation of so many islands, and the confluence of so many traditions in Asia Minor. We must not overestimate the contributions of the few poets we happen to know today.

Prose and developments in poetry

The problem is not so much that poetry is early, as that prose is late. Poetry was still disputing the ground of history with prose in the late 6th century, because verse was the traditional device to make memorable. Early written prose used many verse devices that were devices of memory. Written prose had to be invented, and the process was slow.

The written or inscribed verse epitaph or epigram cannot have existed in Greece until the 8th century BCE. We have five before 600, and only one before 730; all but one are written in hexameter verse. The hexameter was the natural verse to use in the beginning because it was the established verse of epic and of impromptu lamentation. Elegiac verse is a more elaborate eastern version. A lament would be remembered and live in the mouths of later generations.

From a superficial point of view at least, all these poets wrote comparatively simply. The technical forms of Greek choral poetry became complex probably under the influence of writing, when it became possible to immortalize difficult and subtle rhythms, and long, wandering sentences, by writing them down. The movement was international; Stesichoros of Himera, Ibykos of Rhegion, and Anakreon of Teos in the 6th century are unlike each other, but their styles are not regional as the Lesbian style was. The style in favor at Samos seems to have been love poetry. We are dealing with poets of some social grandeur, probably in the case of Stesichoros and certainly in that of Pindar. He had family connections in several cities; but by the late 500s it seemed natural to learn his art in Athens.

It imay seem surprising that Greek poetry should be more complicated the more public it is, and simpler the more private it is. Stesichoros and Ibykos composed for public rituals; they celebrated the sacred mythology of all the Greeks. Stesichoros went so far in originality as to invent new episodes, some of which became very popular.

The style of these poets is clear and their language striking; it is quite intelligible in spite of its ornament. Even the grandeur and boldness of their themes, which are reflected in the visual arts of the same period, have a long history; they are to be found in the Homeric hymns, and sometimes in later fragments of epic poetry. Only the rhythms are different, and a few aspects of diction and style that depend on the new rhythms: long, flowing sentences sharply ornamented, and richness confused, climax postponed, more than they would be in straight narrative.

In the poetry of Pindar the same boldness and clarity prevail, but his style is more rhapsodic, and the patterns he weaves are riskier and even more splendid, more complicated.

The public grandeur of Pindar and the private brilliance of Sappho are both

aristocratic. The contribution of democracy was to come. The poetry of reason was to come. But the objective power of the dramatic poetry of Aischylos arises from the form, from the social situation, from the convention of the stage. Aischylos is not as progressive as used to be thought; the dramatization of tragic conflict is bound to make him hit hard.

The idea of that conflict, of a rebellion which must fail, of a fall or a curse which must be feared and pitied, was built into the structure of Greek mythological thought long before Homer. To understand the origins of tragedy, it is necessary to presuppose both polytheism and history.

The impact on Athenian consciousness of the city's success against Persian invasions and Spartan dominance was so overwhelming that it can hardly be exaggerated. The Athenians took on confidence, deepened their daring, grasped their destiny in their hands. In some sense, by hindsight, we know the confidence was false, and the fate of Athens itself was tragic. But the supreme confidence of the Athenians is justified both by what they inherited from the world, and by what they offered it.

▲ *This fresco from the 1st century CE depicts the poet Sappho holding a stylus. She lived most of her life on Lesbos and is renowned for her lyrical verse.*

Athenian Society in the Fifth Century

◀ The Parthenon on the Acropolis in Athens is one of the most famous ancient sites in the world.

▼ A fragment from the marble frieze that ran around the central block of the temple of Athene (later known as the Parthenon) in Athens.

We may fail to understand the Greeks of earlier centuries because our information is defective; in the 5th most of our failures come from staring too long at familiar information. There are still some gaps in the evidence, though clear patterns can be traced. In the Ionian cities of the Greeks in Asia, after they regained their freedom from the Persians in the 5th century, there were very few public buildings newly or splendidly constructed. Usually it had been one of the functions of aristocrats to display their wealth by such buildings. A lavish public display added to their honor, and therefore also to their power. But these were the days of the Athenian alliance of sea-states, including the cities of

west Asia Minor, and the islands from Lesbos to Rhodes and most of the Cyclades, who paid a heavy financial tribute to the Athenians. Is that the explanation? Are we to think of poor and democratic city populations that favored Athens, and old oligarchs who retired to their farms and ignored the cities?

In Athens itself the 5th century saw a dramatic change in popular morality. Isokrates, who was born in 436 BCE, says that in his youth the possession of wealth at Athens was a secure and socially impressive quality in a man. He refers to a time when the old values of public honor and public shame prevailed. But the action of the state depersonalized the public expenditure of the

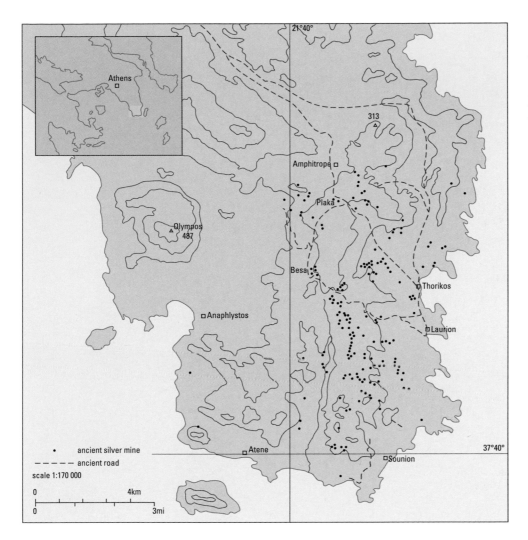

◀ *The silver mines at Laurion belonged to the Athenian state. The mining was done by slaves, who worked in wretched conditions.*

rich. It was systematized as public duty; it became an entire system, a sort of super tax, alongside the general tax system. Those who contributed bore a burden, but with little credit. It was the dramatist, not the rich man paying for the production, who was applauded. In the 4th century it was common for Athenians to hide their wealth in order to avoid these public impositions. From the 7th century, public display had attracted the ancestors of these rich men; they had built public buildings, commanded their own warships, and sacrificed generously, the meat being shared out. In the 4th century they still anxiously insisted in the law courts on their generosity to the state, but in later history

generosity was exercised only for the sake of policy by foreign princes, by Pergamon, Macedon, Egypt, Rome, and the wealthiest individuals in the Roman empire. The Athenian-born historian Xenophon in the 4th century BCE could no longer understand the ethos of a Sicilian tyrant like Hieron.

Rise of the lower classes

At the same time as this collapse of honorable ambitions in the upper class, the lower class at Athens became for the first time money-minded. In the archaic period the Athenian economy had been essentially a household matter, an elaboration of subsistence economy, with constant exchange

▶ *The 5th-century Erechtheion looks directly down from the acropolis northwest toward the sacred road to Eleusis. Its south porch is held up by stone women, or caryatids.*

▼ *The plan shows the ancient city of Athens from Archaic to Roman times. In modern times it has been restored to its appearance at the end of the 5th century BCE, when Perikles promoted extensive rebuilding.*

Athens

Athens has wonderful temples and state buildings, but rather dingy private houses. The acropolis, which was always the central fortress and principal sanctuary, was enclosed by the 13th century BCE by a massive Mycenaean wall. Around 800 BCE Athens comprised a few villages in the shadow of the acropolis. Even at the time of the Persian wars it was hardly a city. The acropolis had its fine architecture, and the Peisistratidai had begun construction of the temple of Olympian Zeus to the southeast,

but the agora to the north was little more than one row of buildings, including Kleisthenes' new council chamber.

After the Persian sack of Athens in 480 BCE and the Athenian victory at Plataiai came the great period of rebuilding, first under Kimon and then under Perikles. The acropolis maintained its general appearance into Roman times, and today again presents its magnificent Periklean aspect.

The Parthenon on the acropolis was designed to honor Athens's city goddess, Athena, but also to celebrate Athens's role as leader of Greece against the Persians. Its sculpture, inspired by Perikles and designed by Pheidias, glorifies both the gods and the heroic character of the Athenians.

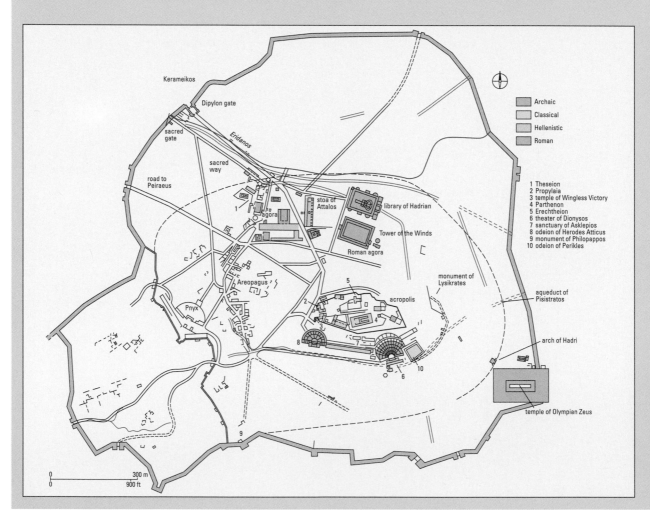

Olynthos

The great city of Olynthos, which dominated the region in the 5th and 4th centuries, stood on the Chalkidic peninsula a little way inland from the sea, commanding the great gulf between modern Saloniki and Mount Olympos. It was at the gate of ancient Macedonia. The Persians took it in 479 BCE, and from that time onward it looked east to the cities of Chalkidike and to the Macedonians, becoming around 432 BCE the capital of the Chalkidian confederacy. Its alliances with Athens in the 5th century and Sparta in the 4th were for temporary expediency. But in 349 Olynthos bravely combined with Athens against Philip of Macedon, and the next year the Macedonians destroyed Olynthos, with little opposition from the Athenians.

About 100 houses of ancient Olynthos have been more or less excavated, and a whole district of the ancient city surveyed in great detail. The district seems to have been developed as a unity, with continuous rubble foundations for each block of houses. No two houses were exactly alike, so individuals must have taken over, but the general patterns are very similar, and follow rather closely the same ideas that are to be found in Xenophon and in Aristotle.

The houses of Olynthos are the best evidence that survives in mainland Greece for developed Late Classical living conditions. The southern court, sheltered in winter, and the northern portico, giving a wall of shade in summer to the principal rooms, represent a traditional formula for comfort. The walls were mudbrick, the bathrooms adequate. The chief rooms or courtyards were floored with magnificent pebble mosaics.

▼ *This artist's reconstruction shows one of the 100 or so houses excavated at Olynthos, all of which follow the same basic pattern.*

Olynthos

Athens

between equals, and with certain communal festivals. But under Perikles in the mid-5th century, the peasants were cut off by war conditions from the earth. The extent to which they lived inside Athens by public doles and payments may have been exaggerated, but that system did exist and there was also military pay. More importantly, many became small tradesmen. Both their economy and the morality that went with it became money-oriented.

Trade

How far was commercial exchange publicly organized? The corn trade at Athens was publicly regulated, as two-thirds of the city's grain needs had to be met from overseas. The great colonnades built for it in the Peiraeus were one of the monuments of the main harbor. At Olbia, which was one of the centers supplying corn from the Black Sea, and a prosperous city in the 5th century, there were big private houses with storage areas that suggest they must have belonged to merchants. These houses stand closely behind the great public agora, the public business area, and the agora of Olbia is remarkable for the vast size of its public colonnades. Olbia was an organized, public, commercial enterprise, and it was successful. On the same scale the king of kings, ruler of the Persian empire, traded through his provincial governors or special officials. But at Athens, and probably everywhere else in mainland Greece during the 5th century, trade was more ramshackle.

The system of the corn trade was inherently instable; conditions were competitive, and did not remain the same for long. It was corn starvation and the loss of the fleet that doomed the Athenians at the end of the century. At the other end of the

Mediterranean, competition for silver and for bronze, sharpened by the hunger for coined money, had disastrous consequences. Even the horse trade inside Greece itself could have experienced severe difficulties, although we do not know that it did so. In Athens some of the horses that the cavalry used, at least in the 4th century and later, came from three different areas of Thessaly, from Macedonia, and from Corinth and Sikyon. Among these, the use of Thessalian horses certainly goes back to the 6th century.

The supply of corn, the breeding of horses, the silver of the coinage, and the sacrifices of the gods must have seemed as secure as anything in nature unless there was a crisis. Humankind was defined as "those who eat the corn of Demeter." Since those who worshiped the Greek gods shared the meat of their sacrifices, the worship constituted Greekness. It is interesting that the Eleusinian definition is wider; can this be the origin of the universalism that can be detected, later, in the Eleusinian mysteries? But Athenian society in the 5th century was utterly exclusive, for instance, of slaves and of women; wives and daughters of citizens had no more political or legal rights than did slaves. Every Greek city had to do something about the status of foreigners, as their numbers grew, just as it had to do something about bastards and half-breeds. In the 5th century Athens coped with those problems. Slavery was another matter.

Slavery

Chattel slavery, the buying and selling of human beings like a dog or a piece of furniture, is supposed to have entered the Greek world through Chios, but the people of Chios claimed that the slaves they bought and sold were non-Greek. Neither war nor piracy

nor even slave raiding could have maintained effectively the systematic slave states of the 5th century without organized trading and organized markets, so the importance of Chios may have been great. In Athens, slaves' nationalities were mixed. Aristotle observes that, in any area where slaves were numerous, a racial mixture among them was a useful deterrent against slave revolution. The greatest concentration of slaves was at Laurion in the silver mines, where there were 20,000 to 30,000, nearly the equivalent of the free population of Athens, half that of a really large city of this period like Miletos.

The conditions at Laurion were proverbially nasty, although this was not the only nasty work slaves did. The Athenians had prisoners of war working as slaves at the stone quarries of the Peiraeus foreshore before their own expeditions of the late 5th century reached Sicily, before many Athenians of the last, doomed expedition had died in the quarries of Syracuse. At Laurion the system was one of numerous short-term state leases, quickly exploited. That is probably why the area, as it was left at the end of the Classical times, was such a honeycomb of tiny pits and shafts, holes and galleries, and why what smelting and refining installations have been found have been on so small a scale

Rich and poor

An inscription of ownership from the Laurion mines claims "the ground, the installations, and the andrapoda" (the human cattle). Yet a mile or so away, in what is now the same idyllic countryside near Sounion in southern Attica, inland from the fringe of seaside bungalows, there are irises and orchids and anemones and the ruins of farm after farm; their honey was famous, it was mentioned in

◄ *Doric columns are the simplest of the three styles found in Greece. The Parthenon in Athens is probobaly the most famous ancient Doric building.*

poems. This is one of the best-preserved ancient agricultural landscapes in Greece. It was a proverb in the 4th century BCE that one lifetime might compass the appalling contrast between life on a farm and work in the mines. It was a steeper difference than any modern division of wealth and poverty. At Athens, a poor city population accumulated in the second half of the 5th century, but there it was not permanently marked by any contrast of accent or religion. However, the distinction of slave and free was absolute, and few slaves were freed, while war and piracy reduced many to slavery. The difference between wealth and poverty at Athens in the 5th century was a continuum; few propertied families of the time can be traced more than three generations, and there were no wealthy town houses. Country houses were fortified stone farms, rectangular yards with a corner tower, like the farm buildings of the Scottish border.

There are not many regions of Greece thoroughly enough explored to offer a comparison, but the pattern of contrast between town and country is known to be variable: at the colony of Istros (Histria) on the west coast of the Black Sea mudbrick houses clustered outside the city walls; were they native houses? At rich Olynthos in Chalkidike graceful villas grew up outside the city on the extended lines of the same symmetrical grid of roads that existed inside the city; whose houses were they? Were they built on the landholdings, which would be good land close to the city, of the founding families? The egalitarianism of early colonial land division not only ossified into an aristocracy of founding families, but was swiftly disturbed in other ways, even by the laws of inheritance and the equal rights of kinsmen in successive generations.

At Megara Hyblaia in Sicily, which was destroyed in 483 BCE, rich and poor were buried in common graveyards until about 550 BCE. From that date the rich separated and isolated their tombs in family groups. But even in the early graveyards, three-quarters of the dead died poor. What offerings there were in the graves came in reused oil or wine jars. Of 250 burials, 42 percent had no offering at all; 13 percent were bodies simply dumped in the earth. There is a certain poetic justice about the wars that so badly afflicted 5th-century Greece; in wartime the slaves escaped more easily, and slave owners were enslaved more easily. Nikias, the defeated Athenian general of the Sicilian expedition of 415–413, owned some 1,000 slaves in the Laurion silver mines, and hired them out to Sosias the Thracian, the number of slaves to be kept at 1,000 by Sosias. It is very likely Sosias was once a slave himself.

Modern analysis of ancient societies has revealed several points of paradox. The Greeks in the 5th century had no state policy on a number of questions we think important.

In a sense there was no state, no deliberate, longstanding, self-knowing, self-organizing entity that knew what it was doing and accepted consequences. We are told that the Persian economy could function well only while its wealth was prevented from circulating. It has been said that the Spartan social system was based on war, and yet it threatened to collapse when war broke out. The Athenians prided themselves on the arts of peace, and yet their economy threatened to fall apart under peacetime conditions. The poor were threatened, and not eased, by the increasing reliance on slave labor, which once it was available inevitably penetrated every enterprise. An extreme solution was calmly suggested in a minor work of Xenophon: that the state itself should acquire slaves, just as an individual might do so, in the hope of profiting for ever by their labor; he thought the right proportion might be three slaves to every Athenian citizen.

Religion

In view of these contrasts and paradoxes, something more must be said about Greek religion in the 5th century. The system of the gods was apparently unalterable, although every element in it was variable. The names of individual gods cover more than one function, and the roles of the gods vary even when their names stay the same. What Zeus does at Elis is partly done by Athene at Athens. In a calendar of festivals inscribed on a rock face in Attica, all the celebrations are sacred to Hermes. But what was expected and demanded of the gods, taken together, was the same: rain, bread, wine, physical wealth, healing, oracular wisdom, peace.

The contradictions in the nature of individual gods troubled no one but philosophers; the individual aquired his religious wisdom from tradition and elected from it automatically.

That is why Athenians were open to such bold conceptions as those of Aristophanes or of Plato's *Symposion*. Theirs were brilliantly inventive and unashamed minds; to whom no

▼ *The theater (or odeion) of Herodes Atticus, of imperial Roman date, was one of the last great public buildings to be built at Athens in ancient times.*

Bassai

The temple of Apollo the Helper stands near a water spring, very high up in the Arcadian mountains. It belonged to the people of Phigaleia, a powerful ancient hilltown not far away across country. It is said to commemorate the turning away of a plague, and the architect is supposed to have been one of the architects of the Parthenon. It is an extremely peculiar monument with a unique ground-plan, a side door for its main entrance, and its north–south orientation. There is something mysterious about this great temple among high mountains, and the weirdness of its atmosphere at night or in winter still recalls some nuances of ancient religion.

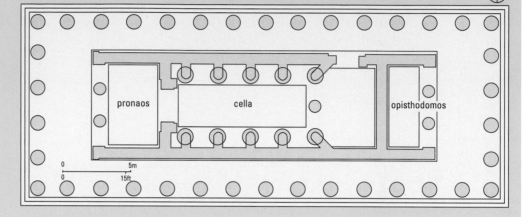

▶ *The temple of Apollo the Helper is unusual because it has Doric, Ionic, and Corinthian columns. The Corinthian column is one of the earliest known.*

pronaos

cella

opisthodomos

0 5m
0 15ft

god was all-important and who knew of no creed. In their adaptations of existing forms they showed an astonishing power. The craftsmen of the Parthenon frieze must have learned to carve horses from an art preoccupied with heroes and the dead. After the work was complete, a few tombstones appeared, surely by the craftsmen of the Parthenon, which readapted its figures. The tombstone of Sosinos, a smith from Crete who lived and worked in Athens, and the tomb of the cobbler, Xanthippos, who seems to have been a slave, model their portraits on the seated gods of the Parthenon. The crop-headed slavegirl Minno sits spinning on her tombstone like a goddess.

But there is no doubt that Athenian religion had its dark side, which was taken seriously by the citizens. There were ceremonies of exorcism, and many primitive rituals. Sophokles was more respected in his own century as the servant of a holy snake than he was for his dramatic poetry. Nikias, who delayed military action at Syracuse because of an eclipse of the moon, was not unique in his superstitious anxiety. Before the battle of Salamis in 480 BCE, when the Greek fleet decisively defeated the Persians, the Athenians performed human sacrifice, and apparently combined their disgusting ritual with a wild barbarity in the execution. There was talk afterward of miracles, a magic apparition from Eleusis, and the omen of a dove, of an owl, of a snake, even of a dog. The Athenians believed that a dead hero rose from the ground to fight on their behalf at Marathon, scene of an earlier famous victory over the invading Persians in 490 BCE. Here and there in the countryside Dionysos was ivy or he was the fig tree.

Annual processions with transvestite dancers placated this or that god, commemorated this or that initiation. In the ritual of child initiation at Brauron, a little human blood had to flow.

It is against this dark and disoriented aspect of the century that the intellectual pride and confidence of the Athenians are to be measured. The 7th century BCE had lesser problems, but the spirited and attractive poetry of Archilochos is equally to be measured against them. The new element in the 5th-century darkness is disorientation, a condition which is something like nervous fatigue, which entails loss of meaning, something close to the *anomie* described by sociologists. The ancient ritual forms of Greek religion, the public and collective rituals which were integral to a whole society and way of life, had lost their force to some degree at the end of the 6th century. They had lost their "natural" context, and many crucial functions had by now been taken over by the state. The Athenians no longer understood the precise significance of the rituals they were performing (hence the mock rationalism of the sophistic generation of the tragic poet Euripides) and widespread anxiety was the result as well as the cause. It was accompanied at a later stage in Athenian history by an otherwise unaccountable increase in the popularity of wild and exotic cults, and in private religious and magical indulgence.

▼ *The Hephaisteion (left foreground) was the first great building of the reconstruction in Athens following the Persian wars. It is the most complete example of a Doric hexastyle temple.*

The Persian and Peloponnesian Wars

The entanglement of the Greeks with the Persian empire was inevitable, and the Greek cities of Asia Minor were almost all eaten at once. Thrace was at first safer in spite of its neighboring barbarians, and the Black Sea colonies in spit of the Scythians. Since the fall of Kroisos, king of Lydia, to Cyrus in 546 BCE, most of the Greek cities in Asia and all the Lydians had been ruled from Sardis, Phrygia and the Greek cities there from Daskylion, by Persian governors, although each city had a ruler of its own. He was independent as long as he paid his taxes and produced his regiment. As a class, these men were not loyal to Persia; they were self-interested local barons.

The Persians invade Thrace

In 512 BCE Cyrus' successor Darius invaded Thrace, then crossed the Danube to adventure north against the Scythians. On the tribes of the region he had little effect, and the three Greek cities of Byzantion, Perinthos, and Chalkedon rebelled behind him. Darius retired into Persia, but he left an army in Europe that in the end conquered the coastal states from the mouth of the Black Sea to the Axios west of Chalkidike; Macedonia acknowledged Persian supremacy. Yet these were not secure conquests; the Scythians retaliated by raiding into Thrace and driving out a Greek ruler the Persians had appointed.

Aristagoras and the Ionian revolt

An oligarchy of great families, thrown out of Naxos by the population, appealed to Aristagoras of Miletos. He was inspired to suggest to Darius a plan to subdue not only Naxos but the rest of Euboea as well. In 499 BCE an expedition of 200 ships against Naxos achieved nothing in four months, and Aristagoras was suddenly in disgrace. His reaction was devastating. He organized a series of rebellions, the tyrants were expelled from every Greek city he could reach. Aristagoras himself resigned the tyranny of Miletos, silver coinage was issued by the new democracies on a single standard, an appeal to Sparta failed but appeals to Athens, and to Eretria in Euboea, brought a fleet of 20 warships and a flotilla of five. The Persian empire was slow to act. Aristagoras had burned Sardis, the chief city of Lydia, before the Persians defeated him near Ephesos. The tide turned, and he fled to Myrkinos.

Aristagoras died, and his erstwhile allies in Athens, in a sharp reversal of their anti-Persian policy, elected Hipparchos as chief magistrate. Darius sent troops to put down the rebellion. Miletos fell after a sea battle in which the Greek fleet was little more than half the size of the Persian. The Lesbians and the Samians deserted, and only Chios fought effectively. The surviving men of Miletos were removed to the mouth of the Tigris, and all the women and children enslaved. The nearby sanctuary of Apollo was burned down. Far away in Athens, the news of what happened at Miletos was heard with an outburst of grief and anger.

The Persians advance

The Persians had already subdued Cyprus and now they did the same in Caria, in southwest Asia Minor. In the north Darius' son-in-law Mardonios moved in 492 BCE to restore Persian supremacy in Thrace and Macedonia, and to destroy Eretria and Athens. He lost much of his fleet in a storm off Mount Athos, so Athens and Eretria escaped. In 490 the Persians entered Europe for the third time. This time they sailed straight across the Aegean, conquering island after island as they went. The city of Naxos was burned down, but Delos, the sacred island of Apollo, was spared. The Persians were not ideologists or political or religious maniacs. When the local rulers of Greek Asia showed themselves reliable, the Persians governed through democratic local systems, so long as taxes were paid, and so long as the tribute of ships and men was still forthcoming. The action against Athens was in one sense a baronial civil war, with Hippias son of Peisistratos on one side and Miltiades son of Kimon on the other.

The battle of Marathon

The invaders burned Eretria after a campaign of seven days, and sold its people as slaves. The Persians then landed at Marathon, perhaps on the advice of Hippias, since this was where his father had landed to capture Athens 50 years earlier, on a wide marshy plain remote from the city.

Athens had already appealed for help to the Spartans, but it was full moon, a holy time in Sparta, and no help came. Some 9,000 Athenians, with no allies except about 1,000 men from Plataiai, faced a big Persian army alone. The Persians expected to overwhelm them with arrows and then cut them to pieces with cavalry. Against all probability, the Athenians won. They charged on foot, cut the Persian center away from its flanks, and turned in against the central division. The result was a massacre for the Persians; the Athenians lost only 192 men. The mass of the Persian fleet of 600 ships sailed on around Sounion to Athens. The same Athenian army met them again, and they withdrew.

Memorials at Marathon and Delphi can hardly express the Athenian triumph. There were poems, a painting, legends, and written histories. Those who fought were known as

▼ *The extent of the Persian empire under Darius in 486 BCE. The Persians traded with people as far away as India in the east and Phoenicia in the west.*

Aegina

The island of Aegina was wealthy and independent until Athens grew strong enough to overwhelm it in the 5th century BCE. In the 7th century and the 6th it was a great sea power. It has a number of fascinating archaeological areas and has produced at least one great treasure of gold, dating from the Bronze Age, or so it seems, and buried in an old tomb just outside the sanctuary of Apollo, at the island's modern capital. Aegina's silver coins were the common coinage throughout much of Greece and circulated widely in the Mediterranean; Aeginetan late archaic sculpture was of international significance. The island lies about halfway between Athens and the Peloponnese. It is mountainous and partly forested.

The most important surviving temple is the sanctuary of Aphaia, a local goddess, which stands on a low hill above the sea. This temple was built in the early 5th century, but the sanctuary had earlier buildings and the cult dates at least from the 7th century BCE. The sculptures of the later building point to an identification of Aphaia with Athene.

▼ *The plan of the temple of Aphaia indicates which sections of the structure date from the 7th, 6th, and 5th centuries BCE.*

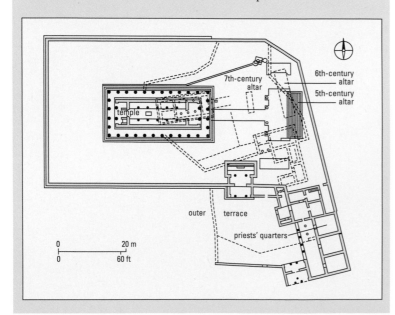

the "men of Marathon" for the rest of their lives. The Athenians undertook the strong older Parthenon, which was still unfinished 10 years later, when the Persians came back. In foreign affairs the Athenians were occupied with the continuing struggle of their city against Aegina. It is instructive that in, an action in 487 BCE, the Athenians still had only 50 ships and dared not attack Aegina without borrowing another 20 from Corinth.

At home, Athenian politics developed toward direct democracy. The board of state officers was now appointed by lot, and authority in war was given to a board of ten elected generals, one from each tribe. In 487 Hipparchos the chief magistrate was exiled, and in 486 Megakles, a nephew of Kleisthenes, followed him. Miltiades, the hero of Marathon, died a disgraced adventurer. One at a time, the menace of individual members of these great families was being nullified. In the same years Themistokles was active. He first held office before Marathon and also fought there; his family was rich and noble, though he may himself have been a half-member of it; in the end he too died in exile, having been ostracized, as governor of a Greek city in the Persian empire.

It was Themistokles who fortified the Peiraeus. In 483 and 482, when the mines of Laurion first produced silver in quantity from a deep level, he built up a fleet of 200 ships. When the Persians struck again, in 480 BCE, Athens was for the first time in its history strong enough to win a victory greater than Marathon.

The invasion of Xerxes

Darius died in 486 and was succeeded by his son Xerxes. Two years later, Xerxes moved carefully and in massive force. He had a canal cut on the inland side of Athos,

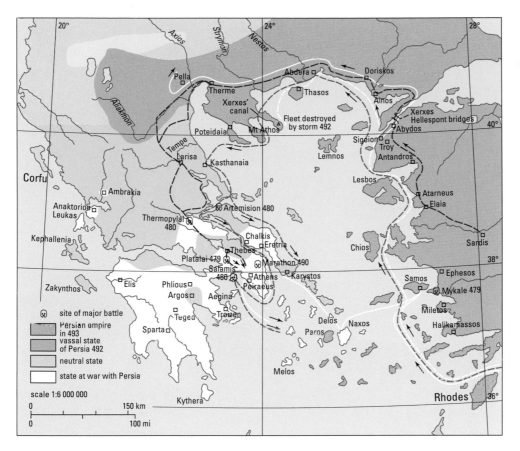

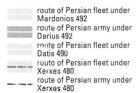

route of Persian fleet under Mardonios 492

route of Persian army under Darius 492

route of Persian fleet under Datis 490

route of Persian fleet under Xerxes 480

route of Persian army under Xerxes 480

to avoid a repetition of the 492 destruction of the Persian fleet, and ordered a bridge to be built over the Strymon; his army gathered; in 481 he came down to Sardis, and spent the winter there.

The numbers of the enormous host Xerxes led were recorded by the historian Herodotos, contemporary to the events, but only as a young boy at the time. The army included Ethiopians, Persians, Indians, central Asians, and Thracians. We are told of more than 1.5 million infantry and 80,000 cavalry; the real number of the whole land force was more likely fewer than 200,000, among whom elite troops numbered 10,000,

and the Persian fleet comprised perhaps fewer than 1,000 ships.

The Spartans held a congress at Corinth, attended by 31 states. Thessaly, most of Boeotia, and the smaller groups of the north stayed at home; they stood in the immediate path of Persia, and did not expect the south to protect them. Argos stayed at home because of an old hatred of Sparta. So, for various reasons, did Crete, Corfu and Syracuse. Only Athens and Aegina seem to have been reconciled. But an army of 10,000 Greeks occupied the vale of Tempe, between Thessaly and Macedonia, and a fleet gathered; both were under Spartan command.

The army at Tempe retreated, because it was learned that Tempe was only one of several passes, and it was felt that the Thessalians were insecure allies to have behind one's back.

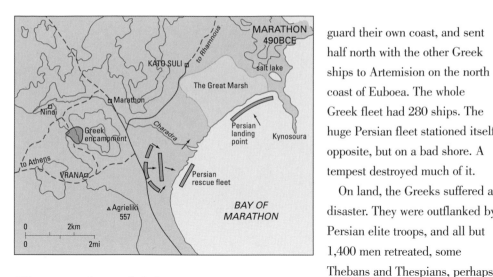

▶ *In 490 BCE 9,000 Athenians faced the might of the Persian army at Marathon. Against all the odds the Athenians won for the loss of 192 men.*

Thermopylai and Athens

Seven thousand men under King Leonidas of Sparta took up a new position opposite the north end of Euboea, at the top of a rocky pass above Thermopylai, the Hot Gates. The landscape has altered utterly; the Spercheios River has silted its estuary, and a coastal plain now carries the main road from north to south Greece where the ancient terrain was impassable. The army of 7,000 would have fallen back further to the Isthmus itself, but the Athenian fleet was now a crucial factor, and Athens must be defended at least symbolically. The Athenians prudently evacuated their civilian population to the Peloponnese, retained half their fleet to

guard their own coast, and sent half north with the other Greek ships to Artemision on the north coast of Euboea. The whole Greek fleet had 280 ships. The huge Persian fleet stationed itself opposite, but on a bad shore. A tempest destroyed much of it.

On land, the Greeks suffered a disaster. They were outflanked by Persian elite troops, and all but 1,400 men retreated, some Thebans and Thespians, perhaps because their own country was so close, and 300 Spartans. Leonidas and his few men held the western end of the pass against the main body of the Persian army. After a ferocious defense, the last Spartans died surrounded.

The Persian army and the remnants of the fleet hunted the Athenians home. The Greek army mustered at the Isthmus, all but the last Athenians abandoned Athens. It took two weeks for the acropolis to fall. The sanctuaries, except those of Demeter, were left in ruins as a monument of what had been done to the Greeks.

Persia's retreat

But it was at Athens that the Persians were checked. Themistokles provoked a ferocious battle at sea, between Salamis and the mainland. It was a complete victory for the Greeks. Xerxes, with an army of 60,000 men, retired into Asia, and set up headquarters in Sardis. The Persian army then reassembled in Thessaly to besiege fortified cities. Meanwhile, the Greeks were building monuments, settling accounts, and distributing loot. They had won a victory at

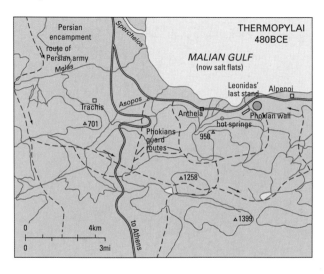

▶ *In 480 BCE a small Greek force led by Leonidas fought to the last man to prevent the advance of the Persian army through the pass of Thermopylai.*

sea and a moral victory on land; the retreat of those vast Persian hordes for the second time in ten years confirmed that it was worthwhile to continue to resist.

The Persians sent the king of Macedonia, their subject, with an offer to Athens of free and equal alliance. Athens stayed loyal to Sparta, but as the Persians advanced, the Spartans at first excused themselves before, fearing what would happen if Athens were to surrender her fleet, they gathered the greatest army ever to emerge from southern into central Greece: 5,000 Spartans, 5,000 tribal soldiers subject to Sparta, and 20,000 serfs, joining an allied army of 8,000 Athenians and the other regional contingents. They met the Persians below Plataiai, on the road to Athens and the Peloponnese. The Persian expeditionary force was cut to pieces, and its Theban allies taken to Corinth and executed.

The Persian empire had passed its high tide and war moved back to the eastern Greek cities and the islands. At sea Athens was supreme, and it thus expanded its influence in the east. The Spartan general Pausanias, who had commanded the Greek army at Plataiai, liberated most of Cyprus and the city of Byzantion, but he behaved like a tyrannical warlord and was recalled to Sparta. The day of his like, and of the likes of Themistokles, was over.

The Delian league

Already in the early 470s Athens had based on Delos a new alliance or league of cities (the Delian league) with a common treasury filled by taxation and a common military policy dominated by Athens.

Step by step, Athens itself became a fortified city, and a great military power. Kimon, son of Miltiades, completed the liberation of the Greeks from Persia with a victory at the Eurymedon estuary in southern Asia Minor in about 468 BCE. When any city seceded from the Delian league, a severe sanction was automatically applied. Karystos in south Euboea was brought into the league by force, the loyalty of Naxos was forcibly renewed, and when Thasos rebelled, it was defeated at sea, its fleet confiscated, and its city walls pulled down.

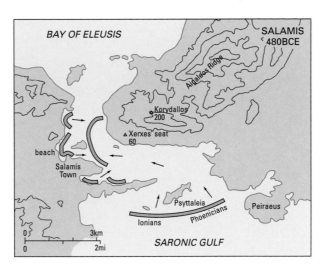

◀ *In 480 BCE a Greek fleet defeated the far larger Persian fleet at the battle of Salamis, sinking about 300 Persian ships and scattering the remainder.*

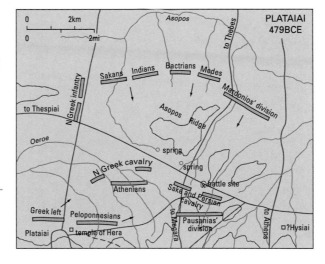

◀ *During the indecisive battle of Plataiai in 479 BCE, the Persian commander Mardonius was killed and the army was forced to withdraw.*

▬▬ Greek forces
▬▬ Persian forces
——— main road (passable by cart)
– – – track
▬▬ modern road
VRANA modern name
Athens ancient name

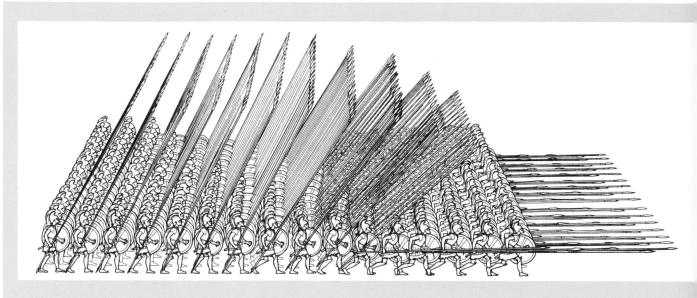

Soldiers and Fortifications

▲ This artist's impression shows a part of what was called the phalanx, a large mob of drilled men at arms used rather like a battering ram. The first five rows of spear points projected beyond the front rank.

There is nothing specially interesting or instructive about the techniques of gut-spilling and throat-slitting in the Greek world. Most wars were unjust, most generals were incompetent, as in more recent history. Weapons were designed as much to inspire terror as to hurt. The capital L for Laconia on the shields of Spartan armies, the nodding crests, the tinkling bells around the shields of one country, the fine-looking but almost useless cavalry of another, were among other things a kind of ballet. Still, it is as well for any student of ancient Greece to come to terms with what arms and armor were like, since they were part of everyone's experience of life. The fineness of the design and workmanship of the best bronze armor was meant to express and to generate confidence. At the same time, the edges of the best bronze swords of 5th-century Athens were tipped with steel. In the Classical period the principal weapon of infantry in formation was the long spear, a radically different object from the short throwing spear, together with arrows, slings, and swords.

Greek fortresses go back to the Bronze Age and the Mycenaeans; the acropolis of Athens which the Persians took in the 5th century still had Mycenaean defense walls. In the 5th century not only were fortresses and castles walled, but whole cities, and in the case of the long walls of Athens and of the city of Akragas in Sicily, miles and miles of ground. The walls of Rome show Greek influence. The whole Peloponnese was defended by a wall across the Isthmus. The 5th and the 4th centuries saw constant technological progress in the weapons and defenses of war. This progress produced a succession of building styles and devices, and of course of methods of attack. Indeed, it was continuous in spite of setbacks until the invention of the aeroplane made walled towns obsolete. Key developments included the use of catapults mounted in towers of a long defensive wall which, if arranged well, could provide a great density of firing power against attackers; complex forms of mechanical crossbow; and mobile battering rams enclosed in a protective shell.

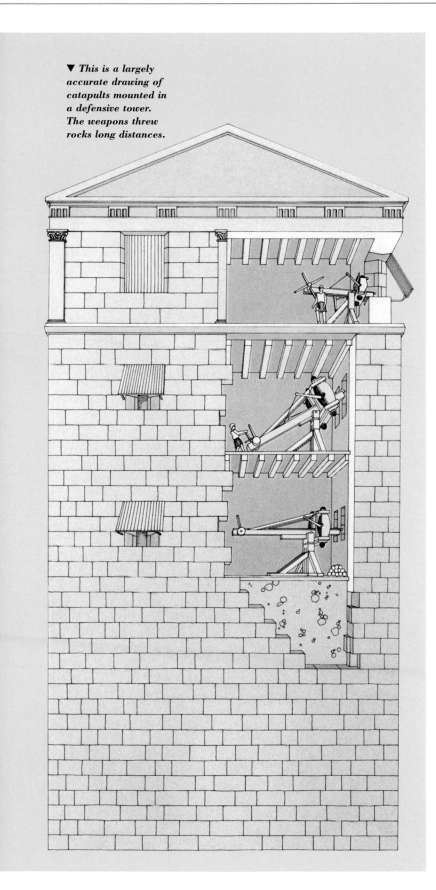

▼ *This is a largely accurate drawing of catapults mounted in a defensive tower. The weapons threw rocks long distances.*

Seeds of the Peloponnesian war

The next 10 years were the hinge of the century. Athens was ascendant, and between 463 and 454 it came close to supremacy. But it was a supremacy that no one city could sustain, and the Athenians could no more finally dominate the eastern Mediterranean than the Spartans could: the Spartans were eventually to the Athenians what the Greeks were to the Persians.

In 464 BCE Sparta was bleeding; the Messenians had rebelled, and Sparta had summoned its allies to besiege Ithome, the ancestral stronghold of Messenia. Among others, Kimon of Athens went to help with 4,000 men, but he was insultingly sent home. In 461 Kimon was ostracized. Athens allied itself with Argos, in a diplomatic move against Sparta. Meanwhile, unsteadily—but irreversibly—Athenian democracy increased. In 459 Megara, in a quarrel with Corinth, left the Peloponnesian league and accepted the alliance of Athens. A fierce war followed against Corinth. At the same time Egypt rebelled against the Persians, and the Athenians were called in to support the rebellion. That war dragged on (456–454), and it ended badly, with the Persians back in control and Phoenician ships defeating an Athenian fleet. But meanwhile Aegina had finally fallen, and in 456 paid its tribute to the Delian league.

In 457 Athenians fought against a Spartan army at Tanagra. The Spartans and their allies defeated the Athenians and their allies. The battle was a measure of how far things had gone. State confrontation had once been unusual; now it was league against league. In 454 BCE, Athens removed the treasury of the Delian league from the holy island to the city of Athens. By 449 the Athenians ruled as far north as Thermopylai and in the late 450s

Delos

Delos is the central island of the Cyclades, and the central shrine of Apollo in the Aegean. The island was sacred to the god from before the time of Homer, and there is at least some remote possibility of a continuity of religious cult since Mycenaean times. Apollo and Artemis were born on Delos.

In the 7th and the early 6th centuries Delos was controlled by its large neighbor, Naxos, but from that time onward the Athenians were more and more dominant, with a short break at the end of the great war with Sparta. But in 314 Delos became independent, and remained so until 166 BCE. Its importance grew as a center of banking and of commerce, and in 166 the Romans made it a free port subject to Athens. It declined in the disturbances of the mid-1st century BCE as Roman central power increased.

▶ *Notable buildings in Delos included a number of temples, a processional way lined with statues of lions, a theater, two agoras, the stadium and the gymnasium.*

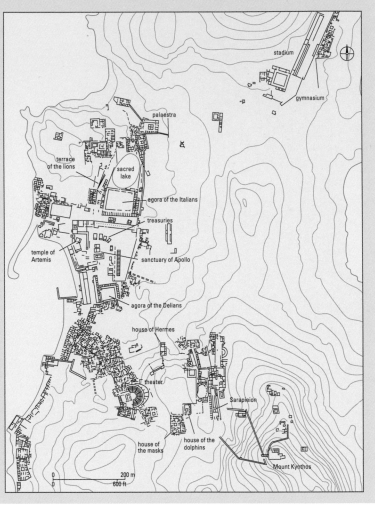

and early 440s the Athenians adventured further in the Corinthian gulf.

A peace of five years was patched up between Athens and Sparta, and a longer peace of 30 years between Argos and Sparta, from 451 BCE. Athenian action against Persia continued until Perikles, forced to choose between war in the east and war at home, chose war at home, and about 449 BCE he negotiated peace with Artaxerxes, the successor to Xerxes. With the pressure of the Persian war being lifted, the more ambitious acquisitions of the Delian league soon began to disintegrate. In 447 Boeotia was lost, then Phokis and Lokris. Megara and Euboea rebelled with Spartan help. Athens made concessions and obtained a treaty of 30 years with the Peloponnese in 446 BCE, just as Argos had done five years before.

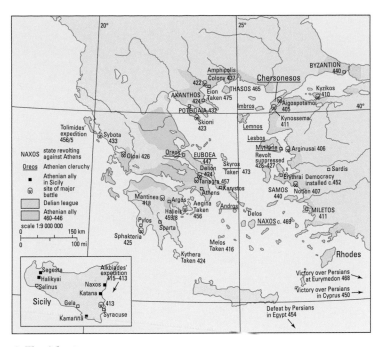

▲ The Athenian empire between 460 and 446 BCE, detailing the battles, rebellions, and alliances of the period.

▼ Athenian and Spartan alliances in 431 BCE at the beginning of the Peloponnesian war. It would last for 27 years, ending in the destruction of Ahens.

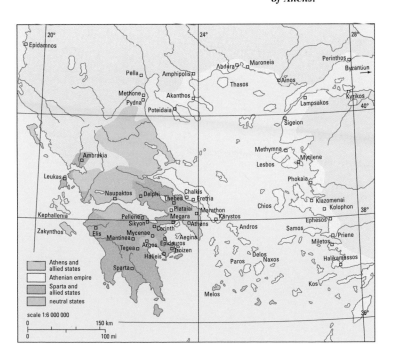

Inside the Delian league, Athenian policy was in some ways toughening. Athenian coinage was compulsory. Athens was now well fortified, glorified with works of art, and within limits directly democratic. The Thracians and the Macedonians still barred the land route north into Europe. But by sea, eastward and westward, the Athenians were active, and although Egypt, the Persians, and the Phoenicians still guarded Africa, Athens did trade with North African cities.

Perikles himself sailed to the Black Sea to install a garrison in the rebellious city of Samos. But the oligarchs of Samos handed over the garrison to the Persian governor of Sardis. The conflict ended with a blockade by 200 ships for nine months, a huge fine, and the destruction of the walls of Samos.

The Peloponnesian war

In the west of Greece the same competitive policy produced worse results. A dispute arose between Corfu (Kerkyra) and Corinth. After a naval victory over Corinth in 435 BCE, Corfu appealed to Athens for protection. Then Perikles proposed a decree to exclude Megara, now for 15 years back in the Peloponnesian league, from every port and market that the Athenians controlled. The highhanded imperialism of Athens had brought it close to war. The Spartans were angry, probably frightened, certainly envious, and at least as arrogant as the Athenians.

Apart from one year of truce between 421 and 420, the war was to last 27 years, from 431 to 404 BCE. It ended in the destruction of Athens and the fragmentation of Greece. Still, during the course of the war the influence of the Greeks, and particularly the Athenians, in Macedonia and Thrace, in Asia, and in Sicily and Italy, even among the

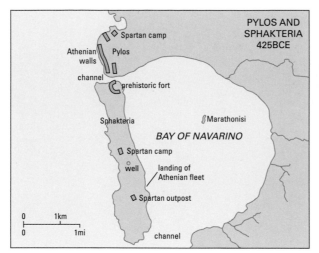

▶ *A brilliant coup enabled Athens to seize Pylos in 425 BCE after capturing crack Spartan troops, previously believed invincible.*

Celtic peoples, even as far south as the Sudan, was still increasing.

In 431 a commando of Thebans attacked Plataiai, which was friendly to Athen. The Spartans invaded Athenian territory, and most of the population—probably something like 300,000—crowded into the city. The Athenians colonized Aegina, secured some western alliances, set up reserves of money and of ships. The Spartan invasion became an annual fixture, counterbalanced by offensives of the Athenian fleet. The people of Poteidaia on the edge of Macedonia, before they surrendered to Athens, had eaten human flesh. Under siege, the Athenians began to die of plague, and Perikles himself

died in 429 BCE. Predictably enough, in 428 an island seceded from the league; it was Lesbos, and the Athenian reaction was devastating; the sovereign people's assembly at first proposed a general massacre but instead pulled down the walls and confiscated the fleet and the whole of the land; colonists were appointed, who employed the Lesbians as tenant farmers. Just as predictably, at this time the outlying hill-town of Plataiai fell to the Spartans, but Corfu, after prolonged and ghastly convulsions, preserved a democracy.

War continued with increasing violence in subordinate cities throughout the 420s. In 425 the Athenians captured some Spartan soldiers in a daring campaign on the southwest coast of Messenia, in Pylos bay. Elsewhere the Athenians were not so successful; they failed in Boeotia, and lost Amphipolis. The area of the war was too great to be dominated. Both sides were exhausted, both were losing, neither was winning. After a failed attempt at truce in 423 BCE, a treaty of 50 years' peace was agreed in 421 BCE. Corinth, Megara, and Boeotia rejected its conditions, and stayed outside the peace. When Athens and Sparta entered into positive alliance, the Peloponnesian league began to break up.

Corinth, Mantinea and Elis allied themselves with Argos. In 419 Athens allied itself also with Argos, and with Elis and Mantinea, for 100 years. This new alliance then moved together to attack Epidauros: Sparta

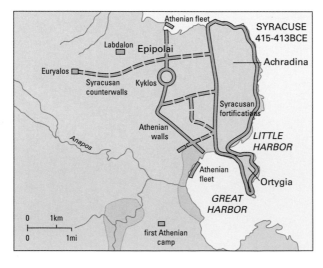

▶ *Athen's most ambitious venture was the attack on Syracuse. The long seige from 415 to 413 BCE was mismanaged and ended in defeat.*

supported Epidauros and the war was on again (it was formally renewed in 414). Its first great battle was at Mantinea in 418 BCE; the Spartans won, and the Athenians temporarily lost all their new-found allies at a stroke. The politics of direct democracy had not had a good effect on the Athenians; the dangers were expressed in an unprovoked attack on the neutral island of Melos in the south Cyclades, the massacre of all Melians of military age, and the enslavement of the survivors.

Sicily and Athens's surrender

Athens was bent on self-destruction. In 416 BCE, the sovereign people entered into the convoluted quarrels of Sicily. Sparta sent a force under Gylippos to lead the defense of Syracuse against Athens.

The war in Sicily was a disaster that no one had imagined. It ended, after a long mismanagement, in 413 BCE, with the massacre of most of the retreating Athenians when the siege of Syracuse had failed.

Athens was sinking. About 20,000 slaves deserted to Dekeleia, a Spartan outpost in Attica north of Athens, and the mines at Laurion were shut down since they were insecure. Coinage was in gold, borrowed from temple dedications, and in copper thinly plated with silver. Thracian soldiers were brought to Athens, and sent home again for lack of pay. Athenian allies seceded. Persian provincial governors increased their activity and took some part in the war on the Spartan side. A movement toward oligarchy in Athens began to be discernible, and in 411 BCE a council of 400 men took over Athens, and governed it tyrannically for three months, but Sparta was too slow or too vengeful to come to terms, and democracy was restored. Even at this stage, a victory at sea came near to

Miletos

Miletos was perhaps the greatest of the Greek archaic cities of Asia. Its extent was vast, its antiquity venerable, its wealth and influence very great. Monuments survive there from every period of its history, to which the key is its position at the mouth of the river Maiandros.

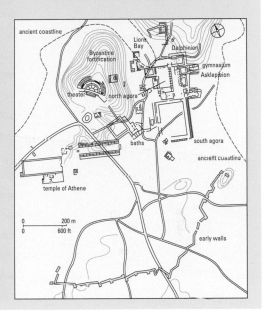

▶ *Extensive remains of the classical city from the 5th century BCE to Roman times include the biggest and grandest theater in Asia; it held 15,000 people.*

restoring the balance: in 410 it was the Spartans who asked for peace, and Athens who refused. The war was now being fought mostly at sea and in the east. Finally, the Athenians lost a naval battle. Their fleet was surprised in the Hellespont in 405 BCE, and 160 ships were destroyed. Athens lived on for some months under blockade by land and by sea, but was starved into surrender. The Athenians were made to pull down their own walls to the music of flutes, they forfeited almost every ship of the fleet, and all foreign possessions. Nominally, Sparta was supreme at the end of the century, as it was at the beginning, but there was no real supremacy.

The Classical Revolution

Aischylos fought at Marathon, therefore his grandson was a mature man at the fall of Athens. In historical terms, the 5th century seems to be one part of a single, long process, a swift decline, a steady succession of consequences. In other ways it was a moment of unusual balance. The intellectual serenity and restless curiosity of the best philosophers, poets, and historians of those few generations were certainly inherited from an age of greater innocence, but in Athens, where so many streams met, they flourished peculiarly. Polygnotos of Thasos was brought to Athens by Kimon; both the indirect evidence of his influence and the opinion of ancient critics suggest that he was the greatest painter the Greeks ever knew; it is still just possible to trace the development of the art of painting under his hand. Pheidias was a supreme sculptor; his work was at Ephesos and Olympia as well as his native Athens, but his influence was most alive in Athens; he was the designer of the sculptures of the Parthenon.

There is no monopoly of art, even of developed arts; Polykleitos, the greatest and the most influential sculptor in the generation after Pheidias, was born and trained at Argos, and he was not the only important sculptor in the Peloponnese. But we are forced to judge by what we can see; sculpture had achieved an international style. The small 5th-century boy in a strange and coarse-grained island marble effectively contrasted with the smoothness of its Polykleitian shape, now in the Ashmolean Museum at Oxford, must from its technique be by a pupil of Polykleitos and a near contemporary, but it could have been made anywhere in the Greek world. Yet it is

Athens where we should concentrate inquiries, if only because, except for Sicily, the more interesting the developments are in other parts of the Greek world, the more on the whole they appear to resemble Athens, while it is only in Athens that we have all the elements together that attract us here and there in other places.

The self-conscious claim Thucydides puts into the mouth of Perikles cannot be quite disregarded, though it must be treated warily. "That the city is in general the school of Greece, and that the men here have each one of them disposed his person to the greatest diversity of actions, and yet with gracefulness and the happiest versatility," is a claim only to power and success, "For we have opened to ourselves by our own courage all seas and lands." The more interesting claim is "For we study good taste, and yet with frugality; and philosophy, and yet without effeminacy." The claim is justified and fascinating. It was at Athens, in the mid-century, that restraint, with complete mastery of means, and some austerity of conception, became a keynote of Greek design. The revolution in the arts was to break away from the robust fullness of the archaic style; and the moving simplicity that followed, the brief, delicate balance before the reaction, is what we call Classical. It was engulfed at once in extravagant and baroque styles, it never held the whole field even in its own day, but it marked an important and a recurring ideal.

At Athens the tough and shaggy Herakles, beating up Egyptians, murdering a whole sky full of birds, wrestling down a lion, and in one local story breaking a boy's skull by mistake with a flick of his finger, gives place

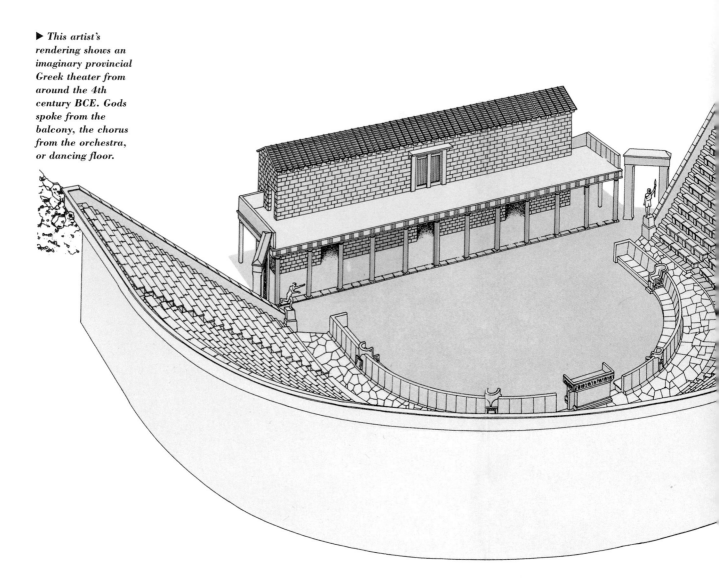

▶ *This artist's rendering shows an imaginary provincial Greek theater from around the 4th century BCE. Gods spoke from the balcony, the chorus from the orchestra, or dancing floor.*

to Theseus, a boyish hero in his youth who becomes a civilized king. Sometimes the adventures of the two heroes were drawn together. This is not only a change of heroes but a change of styles. It may be that in vase painting too much was sacrificed to it. The decorative power of Exekias and the riotous expressiveness of so many Dionysiac painters would no longer be possible. The concentration of attention, the unity of theme, as if art had to be seen through a telescope, put a new strain on the meaning of its subject matter. Solemnity, sentimentality, and dramatic emotion were the new temptations.

It is curious that the invention of perspective drawing by the Greeks was bound up with the theater, with the art of scene painting. The first wall painting in a private house was commissioned by Alkibiades from a theatrical designer. Just as the stage concentrates attention powerfully on who is to blame, or on what one is to do, so the new conditions of visual art which the Athenian theater to some degree generated threw a dramatic light on the traditional silhouetted figures. The new conventions had an earlier prehistory. The best and nearly the only example we have of archaic or early

Classical painting on a flat surface is the tomb of the Diver, the painted slabs of a stone sarcophagus from Poseidonia, the Roman Paestum, on the west coast of Italy. The diving boy was freshly painted when the tomb was closed, on the underside of the slab that covered it. This is one of few representations of diving that survive from the ancient world, and it poses a number of questions. Since the rope-marks on the paint show it was freshly painted, the subject was probably commissioned. Was the tomb for a boy who liked to dive? Is the stone diving-board realistic? None higher than a foot or so has ever been found and no writer refers to one. How does the diver climb up to it? Is the boy diving from a statue pedestal? He is not drawn from life, since the angle of his feet and his raised head are not true; this is a special scene, not an old subject. Paestum was near enough to Cumae, the mysterious caves and the river of Lethe; can this be a boy diving into the water of death, to return somehow to life? Or is it some unknown myth, perhaps about a statue by a swimming place which came to life, as one does in a minor Greek poem 250 years later? The isolation of the boy in mid-air, the fine formal ornaments at the corners, the two bare trees, the bare stone and bare water create an extraordinary singleness of impression. The banqueting scene around the four inner, walls of the sarcophagus compares very well with similar scenes by great masters of vase painting, by Douris and even Euphronios.

The tomb at Paestum was painted quite early in the 5th century, and a tradition of fresco painting on plaster must already have been widely rooted. Paestum was a colony of Sybaris, a little over 100 years old. Sybaris itself has perished with such a reputation for luxury and so little trace that it would be foolish to dogmatize over the style of this unique painted tomb, beyond saying that in its own day it was certainly not unique. We do know that the big change in painting came with Polygnotos, not one of whose works has survived. But the description of his compositions, and the evidence of a visual and intellectual earthquake in the work of his contemporaries, make it profitable to pursue an inquiry. The abandoning of the baseline in drawing, the implication of mighty events in a few details, the setting of things in space, an ease of movement, and a restfulness characterize him as a new kind of narrative painter.

Professor Martin Robertson has written with intuition and scrupulous scholarship about this stage of Greek painting. "On many other vases ... a figure lays hand to chin, or rests elbow on knee, face on hand. Such gestures are loved at this time, their brooding character according with the taste for stillness and the indirect expression of the action. So in contemporary tragedy there is little or no action on the stage. Set speeches magnificently describing events there are; but the actual drama, played out in words between a few characters and a chorus, culminating often in a violent deed offstage, perhaps revealed in a tableau of the slayer and the slain, is surely akin in spirit to the art we have seen some reason to call Polygnotan." The greatest example of it must

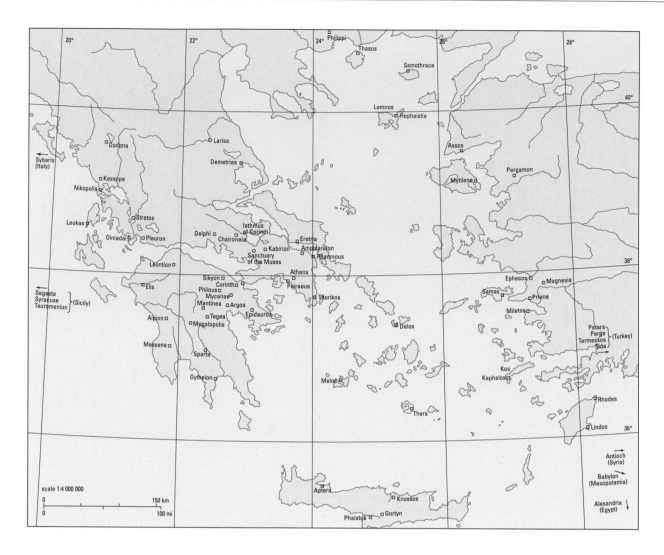

▲ *The map shows the sites of the best-known theaters of the Greek world. Many were built when the Classical moment of the Athenian theater was over.*

▶ *Two very different theaters. The theater of Dionysos Eleutherios, Athens (top), sat 15,000 people; on the coast, the Amphiareion (bottom) held an audience of just 3,000.*

have been the big wall painting of Odysseus and the Underworld at Delphi, in which tallness created a sense of distance. The whole painting was a composition of groups, some very strange, but the central group, below the wood, showed Agamemnon standing with his stick among the greatest heroes, all beardless except the king.

The economy of means, the frugality of Classical art after the first break away from traditional grandeur and vitality, clearly represent a confident and a sophisticated movement. The draperies fall more simply, the inexpressive faces fix themselves as if they were posing for eternity. While sculpture inches forward into a solemn realism,

drawing takes on a sculptural quality. This is a more self-conscious art. There had been nothing like it in the history of the world. It was in the 5th century that the Greeks took off finally from their predecessors and contemporaries. Technical books began to be written by artists: Polykleitos on sculpture, Parrhasios on painting, Iktinos on the Parthenon, Agatharchos on wall painting, Sophokles on the tragic chorus.

The reaction to this movement is most apparent in literature, where it struck first. Herodotos, as late as the early 420s, was still an archaic writer. He balanced his anecdotes, composed his sentences as well as his chapters and whole books, with an intuitive formal sense. Thucydides started to write soon after 431 BCE and continued for some 30 years, but his clarity of composition, his conscious restraint, and his monumental effects, place him as purely Classical. This is a mannered style, and Classicism is nothing if not mannered, but the result is clarity of materials and ease of comprehension. These close contemporaries belong not only to different generations of writing style but to different worlds, to Halikarnassos overwhelmed by the Persians and to Athens in its heyday, to the old Ionian community and the 5th-century Delian league.

Thucydides already lived in the time of the sophists. Their effect on prose style was on the whole retrograde; they regularized into ornamental rhetoric the old-fashioned devices of public speech which had existed before they could be recorded. Speech became an impressive performance which could be taught. This new rhetoric was west Greek, but it was not the only sophistry. They specialized also in the art of argument, often of a perverse kind, and sometimes in philosophical positions of radical originality but with little regard for common sense or morality. None of this was new, but in the sophistic movement they got out of hand. But in so far as their effect on style, which is after all a kind of good manners, a social gesture, was to make it more conscious, they did well. We owe to them to some degree the prose style of Thucydides.

The reaction into extravagance and wildness can be measured in the late plays of Euripides, their powerful and complicated impressionism, the structural brilliance and confusion, the exotic coloring. The greatest is surely the *Bacchai*, though underlying that there is almost certainly a lost masterpiece by Aischylos. But in dramatic poetry, the

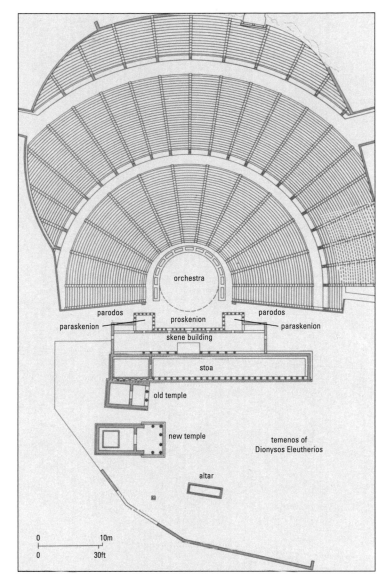

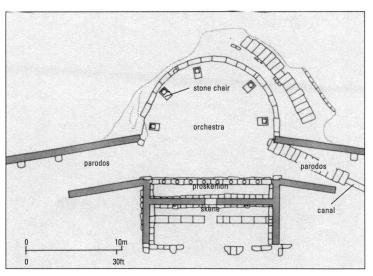

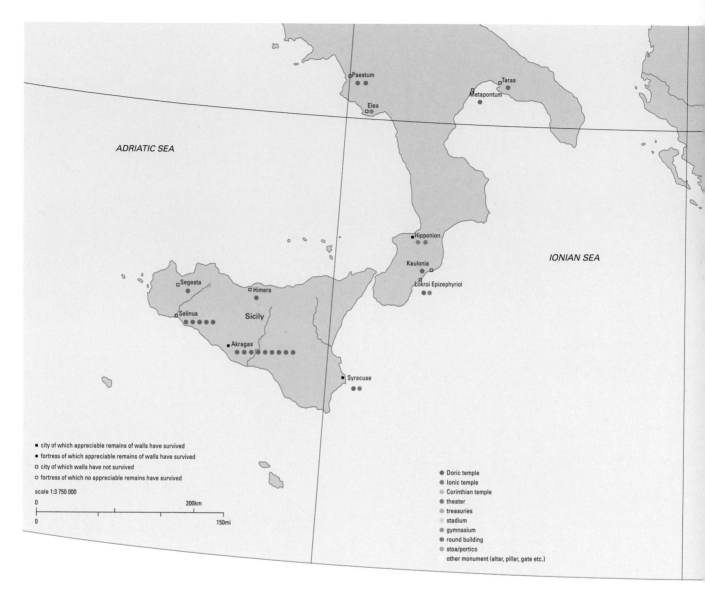

ADRIATIC SEA

IONIAN SEA

Paestum

Taras

Metapontum

Elea

Hipponion

Kaulonia

Segesta

Himera

Lokroi Epizephyrioi

Selinus

Sicily

Akragas

Syracuse

■ city of which appreciable remains of walls have survived
● fortress of which appreciable remains of walls have survived
□ city of which walls have not survived
○ fortress of which no appreciable remains have survived

scale 1:3 750 000

0   200km

0   150mi

● Doric temple
● Ionic temple
○ Corinthian temple
● theater
● treasuries
○ stadium
● gymnasium
● round building
○ stoa/portico
○ other monument (altar, pillar, gate etc.)

Classical moment is usually said to be Sophokles. The deadly concentration of arguments, the simplicity of conceptions, and economy of structure are strongest in Sophokles. His material is wild, even appalling, but not extravagant.

Dramatic poetry is wholly Athenian, while the sophists and philosophers, except for Sokrates, who satirized the others, were foreigners. They were mostly Ionians, Protagoras from Abdera, Prodikos from Keos, and so on. Their greatest influence at Athens was probably in the late 430s. The first plays of Aristophanes were produced in the 420s

and later Plato set his *Symposion*, the golden age of Athenian conversation, in 416 BCE.

There is no need to take too seriously the kind of accusation that is always made against intellectuals and foreigners after a crisis in the state. It was no more the sophistic influence that brought down Athens politically than it was Voltaire who caused the French revolution. When things go well, no one blames the intellectuals for exactly the same kind of conversation that on other occasions brings down Olympian wrath. Protagoras was prosecuted at Athens, nor was his case unique; the most famous victim was

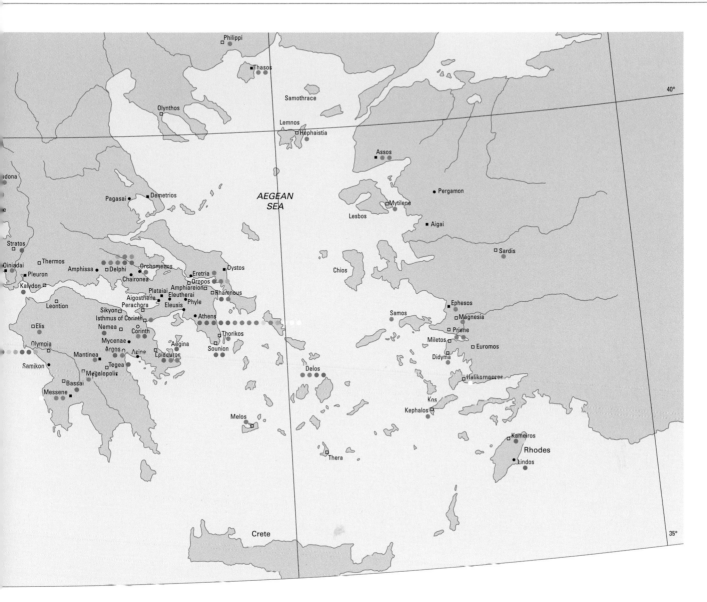

Philippi

Thasos

Samothrace

Olynthos

Lemnos

Hephaistia

Assos

AEGEAN
SEA

Pergamon

Pagasai   Demetrios

Mytilene

Lesbos

Aigai

Stratos

Sardis

Thermos
Oiniadai   Orchomenos   Dystos
Pleuron   Amphissa Delphi   Eretria
Chaironea   Oropos
Kalydon   Amphiareion   Rhamnous
Plataiai Eleutherai
Aigosthena   Phyle
Leontion   Sikyona Perachora Eleusis
Isthmus of Corinth   Athens
Elis   Nemea   Thorikos
Mycenae   Corinth
Olympia   Aegina
Mantinea Argos   Asine Epidauros   Sounion
Samikon   Tegea
Megalopolis
Bassai
Messene

Chios

Ephesos

Magnesia
Samos   Priene
Miletos   Euromos
Didyma
Halikarnassos

Delos

Knos
Kephalos

Melos

Kameiros
Rhodes
Thera   Lindos

Crete

40°

35°

Sokrates. He was condemned because of the dangerous behavior of his pupils, but that was after a coup d'etat, at the end of a lost war, when the Athenians were angry and confused. Whether one approves of the sophists or not, and Sokrates did not, Plato makes them seem rather innocently bad.

It is doubtful whether they genuinely affected belief or disbelief in the gods. The behavior of the Athenians at the end of the century shows hysterical anxiety, but public religion continued without faltering, and private cults increased rather than falling. In every sanctuary where worship was continuous, so far as I know, small offerings of the late 5th century are even more numerous than those of the early century. The sophisticated arguments of Euripides by no means suggest atheism, and the Athenian women at Delphi in his *Ion*, who cry out at a statue of "Athene, my own goddess," are likely realistic. For poetry of real religious awe, and of many levels, the *Bacchai* has few rivals even in Greek.

The most interesting index to what was going on inside Athens in the 5th century is the career of Aristophanes. The differences between his styles are very great. The first

▲ *The key sites of the Classical Greek world include cities, fortresses, buildings, and monuments.*

▶ *In this illustration a teacher shows his pupils how to play the lyre and to set Greek poems to sing to the music.*

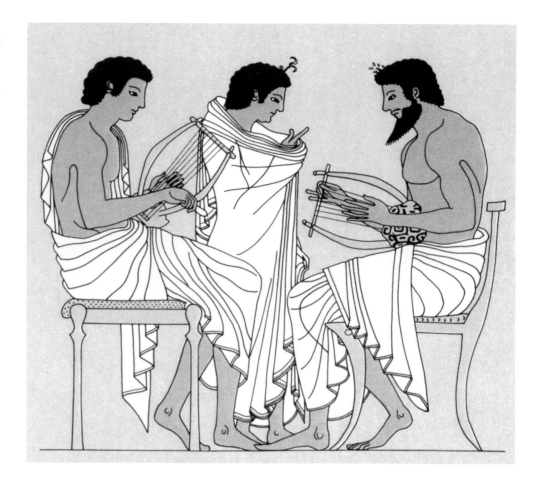

▶ *The lyre was made of a tortoiseshell sounding box with a frame made of cane and gut strings plucked with a plectrum.*

plays are spirited, lyrical, and terribly hard-hitting. After 424 the political edge is slightly blunted: in the *Clouds* he mocks Sokrates, in the *Wasps* a mad old man obsessed with the law-courts, and in the *Peace* in 421, in which year peace was a topical subject, he is as lyrical and as vehement as he was in 425, in favor of the farmers, but now with less fury. By 414, to judge by the *Birds*, the theater has become more spectacular, more musical, and more Utopian: there are still some sharp remarks, but the plot is amusing, the atmosphere that of a happy never-never land.

The *Frogs* (405) has another brilliantly invented animal chorus, the same rhythmic mastery and lyricism, enough jokes, and for the first time some penetrating literary criticisms. One would expect the play to be plunged in gloom, since Athens faced defeat, but not at all. It adapts a device of Eupolis, in which the towns of Attica send down to the Underworld to bring back a statesman from the dead to save Athens. There are hints of this in Aristophanes, but in his version no one saves anything; what is wanted is only a good tragic poet, Sophokles and Euripides having joined Aischylos among the dead. The chorus of the Eleusinians in the Underworld could hardly be more otherworldly.

The last plays of the Athenian theatrical poets before the fall of the city are Sophokles' *Oedipus at Kolonos*, Aristophanes' *Frogs*, and Euripides' *Bacchai*. On this evidence, whatever else was in disarray, wit was not, religion was not, and poetry was not. It is possible to argue that Aristophanes' *Lysistrata* of 411 BCE, a knockabout comedy

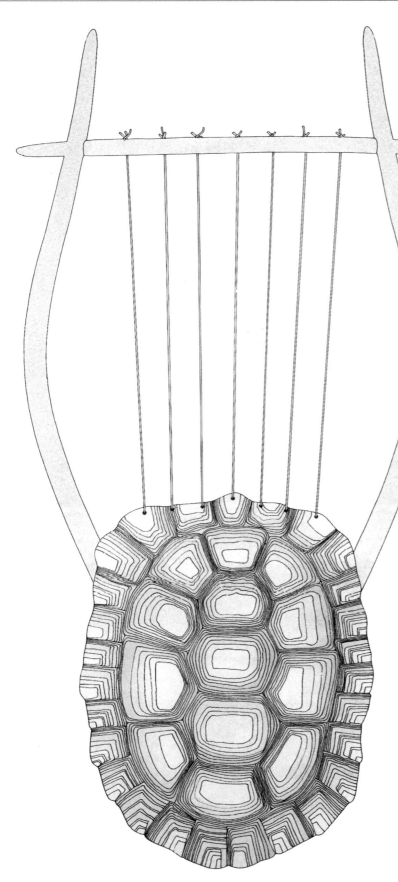

in which the women of Greece refuse sex to
their lovers until the men agree to peace,
shows a healthier political tone.

The public buildings of Athens in the
last years of the Peloponnesian
war are smaller in scale than the
Parthenon, but in delicacy of
detail and subtlety of composition
they show no falling off. The
Erechtheion was begun in 421 BCE
and after some interruption its
friezes were carved in 408 and
407. It owes its complicated plan
to a whole group or involved knot
of elements of ritual: a sacred
snake, the twin temple of
Poseidon-Erechtheus and
Athene, a solemn balcony, and a
deep hole in the rock, to name
not quite all of them. To make
matters worse, in the course of
building a prehistoric tomb was
discovered which was identified as the
resting place of a legendary king, and
allowance had to be made for it. The
Erechtheion itself is a triumph, different
from every aspect and yet transforming
perfectly from view to view. It is a slender,
catlike Ionic masterpiece, both beautiful and
brilliantly clever. After the Erechtheion, no
Greek temple would again be rebuilt that was
not less beautiful than one it replaced.

One can tell something also from the
funeral vases called white-ground *lekythoi*
that were decorated for their purpose, and
used almost nowhere but in Athens and in
Athenian colonies in the second half of the
5th century. Hypnos and Thanatos, the twin
brethren Sleep and Death, who carried away
the body of Sarpedon in the *Iliad* carried
away the bodies of many Athenian soldiers.
Sleep is young and beautiful, but Death is

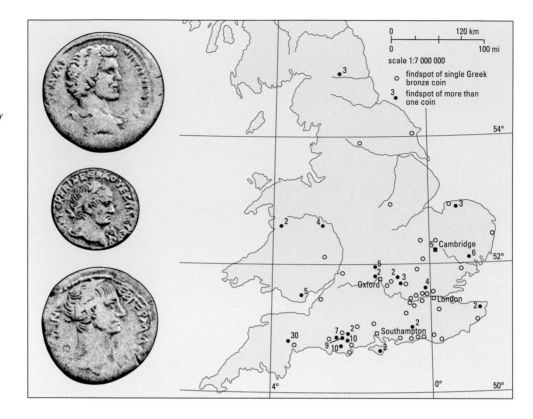

▶ *Greek coins have been found at a number of sites in Britain. Coins of Antoninus Pius, Trajan, and Vaspian (illustrated) probably reached Britain in the 2nd century CE.*

0   120 km

0   100 mi

scale 1:7 000 000

○ findspot of single Greek bronze coin

●3 findspot of more than one coin

▶ *This black-figure amphora from the 4th century BCE portrays two atheletes taking part in a boxing match.*

not, and nor is the ferryman Charon, who appears on many of these vases. In the Charon vases only the ferryman and the stern of his boat appear; Hermes guides the dead. Some of the later scenes have a curious ambiguity, as do the carved tombstones of the same years. Grief is expressed, there are scenes of departure, last looks, gestures of mourning, but it is not obvious who has died; the sorrow is ambiguous and universal.

And what had happened to the gods? Their representations had become more and more human. Athene leaning on her spear in mourning at a stone memorial was evidently not drawn from life, but completely convincing as life. The male gods had the bodies of athletes, Aphrodite was sexually attractive, and even Pans and satyrs were elegant nudes, and a great deal less wild than they had been. What had altered? The answer seems to be that in some areas, or among some people, not much had altered

except art, and even that less than we think. At the court of Polykrates on Samos, Zeus and Hera were mischievously erotic figures, and the *Iliad* confirms that such a conception of gods was not a new or impossibly shocking idea even in the archaic period. The Zeus of Pheidias had great dignity. The wild Oriental Zagreus (the Cretan god with whom Dionysos was identified) prancing on a bull on a bronze disk from a Cretan cave from centuries earlier was a being in another idiom which had never been Greek at all. The simpler dedications remained conservative through the 5th century. Zeus Ktesios was still the name for the household snake, Apollo Aguieus was still a stone post, and Hermes still received wreaths on his perpetual erection. Religious poetry was almost too clever and versatile to be taken seriously, but that proves little: it both was and was not serious, like the conversation at Plato's *Symposion* in 416 BCE.

New Patterns in Literature and Religion

In the 4th century BCE archaism had already entered into literature, and into visual art. The great high tide of nostalgia was to come 100 years later. Epic poetry was already in the past in the 5th century; by then Athenian children had to learn strange words in order to understand Homer. Homer was still a sort of god, but his poetry seemed remotely ancient. Already by the end of the 4th century BCE the three great Classical tragedians—Aischylos, Sophokles, and Euripides—had been recognized; their works were preserved by the state of Athens. The reemergence of Athenian fleets and Athenian alliances after 400 BCE, the rebuilding of the city walls ,and the recovery of wealth were not able to bring back the 5th century.

Even Thucydides in the late 5th century archaizes as a stylist, but Athens believed old-fashioned language had a greater dignity and poetry than everyday speech. The interest to us of 4th-century archaism is not that innovation then ceased, but that a process began which was to continue a very long time. Critics were more severe in their devotion to the past than poets or sculptors or architects: Aristotle thought Sophokles the greatest tragedian, Plato went back to Pindar for nourishment; the 4th-century elegiac poets are underestimated to this day, and so is the best of 4th-century sculpture.

Theokritos and pastoral poetry

At the same time we have the strong impression of a more level Athens. The severely beautiful blushed a little deeper into prettiness until it was all but overblown. Representations of the Gorgon's head had once been terrible, then grotesque, then by

the early 5th century partly funny, and now she could be a beautiful woman. The Cyclops had been an antigod, then a terrible monster, then a pantomime creature, and now in the early part of the 3rd century he was pathetic and hopelessly in love with a sea nymph.

Theokritos, a Sicilian Greek, learned the conventions of pastoral poetry from Philetas of Kos, and lived at the Macedonian Greek court of Ptolemy in Alexandria. He wrote in Doric dialect meant to be a peasant speech. But Theokritos exaggerates, likely deliberately; his dialect was never really spoken. It is partly a joke, partly a device like stage dress or pastoral scenery.

Theokritos and other dialect poets of the 3rd century mark a development in Greek consciousness of the world: a logical extension of the curiosity of Herodotos, combined with social curiosity, and a nostalgia for simplicity, poverty, and security, for beliefs no longer shared, emotions no longer felt by intellectuals.

Public ritual

Something had altered by the 3rd century BCE in the emotions and the beliefs even of quite simple people. Theokritos wrote a poem about a royal festival of Adonis at Alexandria. The worship of Adonis was well known in 5th-century Athens, though its origins were Babylonian; Adonis was wounded Thammuz, a dying god of vegetation. We first hear of his worship by Greeks in a fragment of Sappho. In Athens his festival was in April, but at Alexandria in September; there were deeper differences. Theokritos' characters are Syracusan women, who make an excited excursion to see a

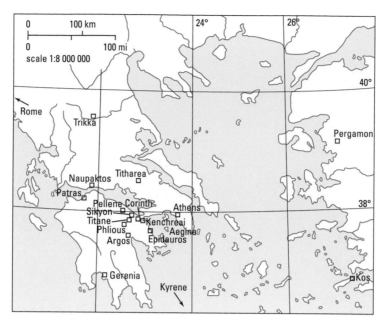

a central bower is a couch of ebony and gold. Here figures of Adonis and Aphrodite lie with a fine display of food in front of them.

The same process was at work on a lesser scale even among the state rituals of Athens. The lavishness of celebration increased, and the crowd increased and diversified. The ritual duties of the young men doing military service increased in their ceremonial quality. Not unnaturally, the young men in their fine new cloaks appealed more to the city than the mysterious and ominous private processions that also appeared in the streets. It is easy to see how the increase of cults will have infuriated the intellectuals and the conservatives equally. It is also easy to see how on the edges of society, an increasing area in Athens, it might find converts.

spectacular tableau of Aphrodite and Adonis feasting together on a couch, in a bower of green branches. They are from poorer, remote districts; they despise native Egyptians and their own slave girls, they are terrified of horses, they have a proverbial humor. The festival has an exotic charm but its character is secular, a popular show put on by Ptolemy for the crowd. Even the sequence of events in the festival is strange. In the poem, the festival begins with the union of Adonis and Aphrodite, goes on to death and lamentation the next day, and then closes—not with the god's resurrection, as in earlier accounts. In Athens the festival of Adonis was private and confined to women.

In Ptolemaic Egypt at least, home of a new Greco-Egyptian culture, a public celebration of romantic love and death, taking place in the royal palace with an expensive display of devotion, had replaced the private ritual of a dying god who mysteriously came to life. The keynote of the palace festival is its richness. The place is hung with new and magnificent tapestries of Adonis dying in his silver chair, with Aphrodite lamenting. The centerpiece in

The cult of Asklepios

The biggest increase in religious cult from the late 5th century was that of a respectable minor god whose benefits were not invisible: Asklepios, god of healing. In many sanctuaries he took over from an existing god or hero, and he never controlled all healing shrines. The cult of Asklepios reached Athens in 420 BCE from the Peloponnese, probably by way of Aegina. But the great parent sanctuary of Epidauros was recognized in the name of the new festival of the god at Athens, the Epidauria. It was usual for any new sanctuary of Asklepios to

Kos

The island of Kos is in the southern Sporades. It belonged to the southeastern union of Lindos, Knidos and Halikarnassos. At the end of the 6th century the Persians took it; in the 5th century it was an ally of Athens and saw the birth of Hippokrates. Destroyed in the Peloponnesian war, it was refounded in 366 BCE. In the Hellenistic period, it bred the inventor of pastoral poetry, Philetas, and Theokritos set one of his most remarkable poems in its countryside. Its monuments and sanctuaries are still appearing.

The famous sanctuary of Asklepios, where Greek medicine began, is close to the city of Kos. It was once the sanctuary of Apollo; some time after the death of Hippokrates, in the mid-4th century, building of the temple of Asklepios and its surroundings were undertaken. It contains several 3rd-century features. The Askelpian festivals probably took place on the third terrace; the remains of Roman temple stand on the second.

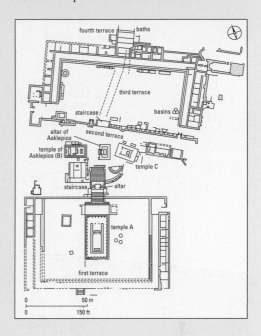

▶ The Asklepion is built on three levels. The middle level houses the temple of Asklepios, built in the 4th century. Festivals were probably held on the third terrace.

Ephesos

Ephesos was another of the teeming, mixed Greek cities of the Asian coast. It rivaled Miletos and later Alexandria in importance and size. The ancient local mother goddess was identified with Artemis, and by the Romans with Diana; the Ephesian Artemis was covered in egg-like breasts or breastlike eggs. Her great sanctuary, one of the seven wonders of the world, incorporated 117 columns, each over 60 feet (18 m) tall. Ephesos was the great city of Roman Asia, and nearly all the remains uncovered are of Roman date. It declined like its predecessors and successors when its river estuary silted up, but it was still important in the Middle Ages: indeed, more magnificent than ever.

▶ *The street known as Arkadiane runs from the harbor to the theater, a distance of about 550 yards (500 m). The theater was built in the early 3rd century and survives in its Roman form.*

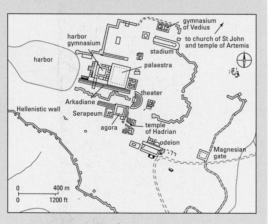

be formally set up by the arrival of a sacred snake of the god, brought from the mother temple. That is what happened in Athens, and the poet Sophokles entertained the snake until the new hospital was built. It is hardly too daring to call it a hospital. At Epidauros we have a series of inscriptions of the miracles of Asklepios. It is evident they involve surgery and a serious knowledge of some branches of medicine.

By about 400 BCE for Asklepios at Epidauros there was an international festival with athletics, horse races, music, and poetry. His new sanctuaries appeared at Kos (where Hippokrates in the 5th century laid the foundations of medical science), Pergamon and Kyrene by the 4th century, and at Rome in 293 BCE. Asklepios acquired sanctuaries at Sikyon, Corinth, Kenchreai, Phlious, Argos, Patras, and Pellene in the northern Peloponnese, at Tithorea and Naupaktos in Phokis, and proportionately many more further south. The increase was as much due to a special kind of religion as to the organization of medical science. It was a cult for individuals, and the rich paid for it. There are no state treasuries at Epidauros, but its buildings are lavish and decorative.

Oracles and places of healing are often the same, and in the 4th century the Greek oracles were already replying to individual questions, even on a small scale. Such questions probably took the form "Herakleidas asks whether to expect a child by his present wife," or "Nikokrateia asks to what god she ought to sacrifice to be rid of her illness." That is partly because each disease was believed to have its own god; Apollo for example was thought to cause and cure enteritis, because the symptoms resembled the droppings of swallows, his sacred birds. Asklepios was ambitious in curing all diseases; in a 4th-century apparition of the god his handmaid was called Panakeia, "All-Healing." The sick would go far to find such a god; we read in inscriptions of a man who had metal in his body for years until Asklepios cured him. Asklepios was also unlike the older gods in having no severe, terrible aspect. There is a legend about his being destroyed by the gods for raising a man from the dead. With the coming of Asklepios, divinity was tamed in an important respect.

Private philosophy

The 4th century saw the vast increase of small merchants and shaky commercial enterprises. The hazards of fortune had become extreme; one could rise and fall more easily in the city, and the city itself could rise or fall more easily. It was no longer possible for the Greeks perfectly to comfort themselves with the ancient gods, their proverbial morality, and their 5th-century concern for the state. There was a noticeable increase in religions and philosophies of withdrawal, of individual salvation and peace of mind. The gentle and austere Epicurus was born in Samos in 341 BCE and died in Athens in 270; he was by no means extreme among his contemporaries. He studied in Athens in 323, and lived at first in Kolophon in Lesbos and in Lampsakos in the Troad, at the east end of the Hellespont: his closest friends to the end of his life were from Lampsakos and Mytilene on Lesbos, places outside the great power struggles of the Macedonians; his community of disciples included slaves and women.

These movements entailed a new selection of mythology. In the 3rd century a new area of local mythology began to be exploited in Asia Minor. Some of the stories that became popular were those which eventually appeared in Latin in the *Metamorphoses* of Ovid. The gods were as slippery as fishes and unpredictable. These were tales "to keep a drowsy emperor awake." The intention, at least in the retelling, was no longer very serious. For serious analysis of experience, for criticism of life, the Greeks turned in the 4th century to philosophers. Serious philosophy and serious poetry were closer together than they are now, but from the time of Plato onward, there was a slightly literary feel about engagement in ancient mythology.

Epidauros

The city of Epidauros lies by the sea, on the Saronic gulf, but some miles inland a sanctuary of Asklepios grew up which had an international prestige that was at its height in the 4th century BCE. The theater there was thought the most beautiful in the world. It was simple and Classical. Games were held there, almost on a level with the greatest international festivals. Its architecture and sculpture were extremely rich, with a certain slight heaviness that marks the end of the Classical high summer. Of the late 5th-century temple of Asklepios itself and of the elaborate tholos, or rotunda, built in the 4th century, only the foundations and some fragments remain, some of them built into churches.

The ancient roads that connected the sanctuary of Asklepios with the coastal city can still be traced, and some distance away stray blocks of finely carved decorated marble from the shrine of the god can still be spotted built into the walls of churches. The sanctuary, or hieron, was a place of healing, innocent of history.

▼ *At the heart of Epidauros were the temple of Asklepios and the smaller temple of Themis. There was also a hospital, baths, and an abaton, where patients slept.*

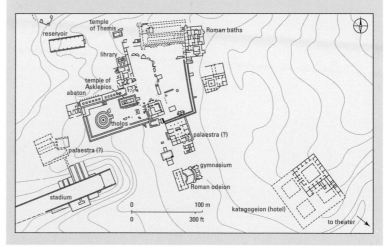

The Rise of Macedon

At the end of the war with Athens the Spartans entered a position of dominance which lasted more or less for one whole generation, from 404 to 371 BCE. It was challenged in 400 by war with Persia, now ruled by King Artaxerxes. The war was inevitable in face of Persian threats to Greek cities, but it was not energetically carried on. When Konon of Athens contrived to command a Persian fleet, he took Rhodes from the Spartans in 395. A year before, Agesilaos king of Sparta had crossed into Asia. He did well in Phrygia, but Konon annihilated his naval force in 394 BCE.

In mainland Greece the Spartans had also provoked fierce resentment. In July of 394 a confederation of their enemies faced them in an indecisive battle near Corinth. In August, the Boeotians and Athenians defeated Agesilaos at Koroneia. Sparta was blockaded inside the Peloponnese, at least by sea. Konon, with Persian connivance and Persian money, restored the long Athenian walls and the walls of Peiraeus, and Athens recovered the islands of Lemnos, Imbros, Skyros, Delos, and Chios. For now the sun shone for Athens; in six years it had control of the entrance to the Black Sea.

Another central feature of the power struggle was the availability in vast numbers of mercenary troops. In a small action near Corinth in 390 BCE, under an Athenian named Iphikrates, they cut to pieces a force of 600 Spartans, and in 388 BCE, in an ambush in the mountains of north Greece, they obliterated a Spartan expeditionary army.

These events foretold the future. Persia was not invincible, nor was Sparta; sooner or later wilder Greeks and those on the edge of the

world would have a say. Meanwhile in 386 BCE a general peace was agreed by all sides.

In 382 the Spartans occupied the fortified area of the city of Thebes. They were less successful in the far norther, where they only put down the growing Chalkidic league of cities based on Oiynthos in 379 BCE. The following winter the situation at Thebes was reversed. In 378 BCE Athens allied itself with Thebes against Sparta, and undertook the leadership of a new Athenian league. But the key to the next few years was not Athens, but the revival of Thebes as a military force.

Year by year, the Spartans lost and the Thebans won, always on Boeotian territory. The Athenians utterly defeated the Spartan fleet, which threatened their grain supply. The war smoldered on, but Athens was overstretched in terms of its diplomatic and military network—and its money. In 371 a peace was concluded between the Athenian and Spartan forces; Thebes, which refused to dissolve the league of newly liberated Boeotian cities, was left out of the treaty.

By this time, between Thebes and Macedonians, Thessaly was controlled by Jason of Pherai. When the Spartans were defeated by Thebes at Leuktra in 371, Jason of Pherai rushed with cavalry to support the Thebans. The Spartans withdrew. On his way home, Jason smashed the Spartan fort that controlled Thermopylai. However, the following year, in 370, he was assassinated. His death heralded a period of increasing Theban power.

Meanwhile southern Greece suffered great civil disorder; the wealthy had control and the less wealthy and the poor were by now prepared to beat them to death, as they did at

▶ *This head belongs to a small portrait statue of Philip II found in a royal tomb. Philip was a brilliant soldier and diplomat, who united Greece under his personal authority.*

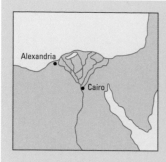

Alexandria

Alexander was buried in the city he founded in Egypt in 332/1 BCE, the first of 13 or more of the same name up and down the world. The masterstroke was to join the island of Pharos to the mainland by a long mole, creating two harbors. Under the Ptolemies Alexandria was for a time the commercial and cultural center of the world. It saw the world's first great library, the first poetry of a new kind and the first great literary scholars. The Romans dealt harshly with it, and the Arabs in the end destroyed it.

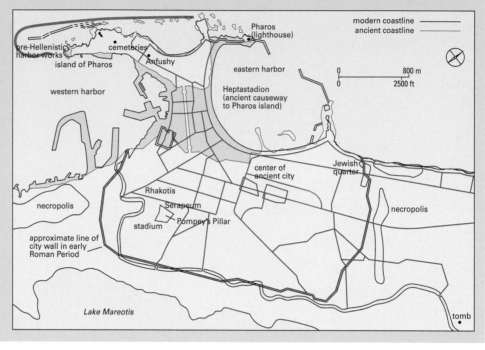

▶ *The Pharos lighthouse at the harbor entrance to the city of Alexandria was one of the seven wonders of the ancient world*

Argos. The Peloponnese was seething with discontent. An Arcadian appeal to Athens against Sparta failed, but an appeal to Thebes prospered; Epaminondas invaded the south. Sparta was in decay, with few pure Spartans left to resist an attack on their homeland. Sparta was saved only by its few allies, and by promising freedom to 6,000 of its serfs. Epaminondas refounded Messene in the southwestern Peloponnese to be used as a fortified base against Sparta. But Athens hated Thebes worse than it hated Sparta; it now took the Spartan side by formal alliance in 369 BCE.

Epaminondas invaded Sparta several times as alliances and realliances buckled under the weight of the conflict between Thebes and Sparta. Epaminondas died in 362. His legacy was not only the moral defeat of Sparta, but the survival of two cities designed to check any expansion of the Spartans: Megalopolis, formed from the populations of Arcadian mountain towns, and Messene, the capital of a new Messenia. But Theban military energy scarcely survived Epaminondas.

Philip of Macedon

Macedon now overshadowed the Molossians and the other tribes of Epirus. In 359 BCE Philip of Macedon, as regent of a kingdom under pressure from Paionians and Illyrians, came to power and organized his army.

Philip was 24 years old. He had 10,000 well-disciplined men at arms and 600 cavalry; in a murderous battle with Illyrian tribesmen, we are told that he left 7,000 dead. Once Macedonia was under control, Philip pushed eastward at once into Thrace. There he first ran counter to Athenian interest. He took Amphipolis and its gold mines in 357, and built his own fort to defend it. Other conquests followed, but by now the Paionians were reduced to vassals, the Illyrians crushed yet again, and the Thracians bought off. In 356 Philip assumed the title of king, and in the same year his son Alexander was born to his wife Olympias, the daughter of Neoptolemos the Molossian.

In the east at this time, Mausolos of Caria attempted like Philip to establish an imperial power, and inevitably clashed with Athens. He was a tributary prince of the Persian empire, and his authority was enormous in reality but undefined in theory. The Greek coastal cities had fallen one by one into his sphere of influence. He moved down from his old capital of Mylasa to Halikarnassos on the

sea. In 357 Chios, Kos, and Rhodes revolted against Athens; they were ripe to fall into the protective hands of Mausolos. In the resulting campaigns, the possibility began to loom of a full-scale war with Persia. Peace was agreed in 354, but the Athenian empire never recovered. The islands achieved their independence, oligarchies took them over, and Carian garrisons ruled them. Rhodes appealed against the new tyranny to Athens, without success. Meanwhile in 353 Mausolos died and Caria sank back into lethargy.

In the mid-350s a quarrel over the control of Delphi between Phokis and the council of neighboring states brought war to central Greece. Thebes provoked the conflict, but it spread until it involved Sparta and Athens, then Thessaly, and finally Philip of Macedon. The opportunity was heaven-sent. Philip took Methone, the last Athenian ally in his way, and moved south. He was checked by Phokians in Thessaly, but in 352 he defeated them. Unable to pass Thermopylai, he

▼ *Between the 6th and 2nd centuries BCE Celtic invasions spread over much of Europe. Celtic tribal organization surivived the Roman conquests of Gaul and Britain.*

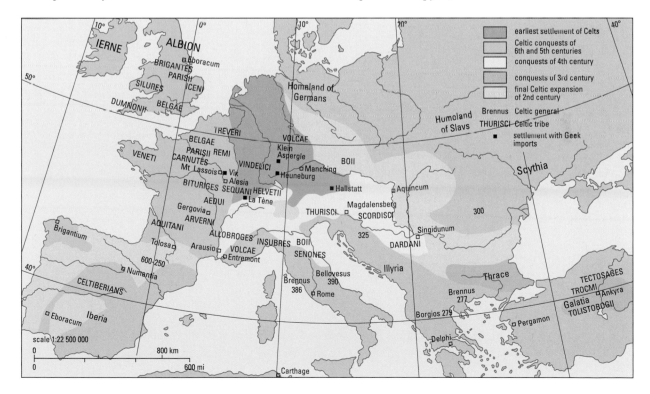

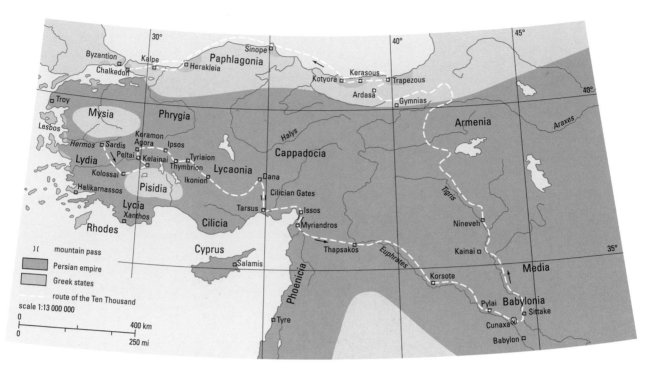

30° | 40° | 45°

Byzantion
Kalpe
Sinope
Paphlagonia
Chalkedon
Herakleia
Kerasous
Kotyora
Trapezous
Ardasa
Gymnias

Troy
Mysia
Phrygia
Armenia
Araxes
Lesbos
Hermos
Keramon
Agora
Halys
Sardis
Ipsos
Cappadocia
Lydia
Peltai
Kelainai
Tyriaion
Thymbrion
Tigris
Kolossai
Lycaonia
Nineveh
Halikarnassos
Pisidia
Ikonion
Dana
Cilician Gates
Lycia
Tarsus
Xanthos
Issos
Cilicia
Myriandros
Kainai
Rhodes
Cyprus
Thapsakos
Euphrates
Media
Salamis
Korsote
Phoenicia
Pylai
Babylonia
Tyre
Sittake
Cunaxa
Babylon

)(mountain pass

Persian empire

Greek states

route of the Ten Thousand

scale 1:13 000 000

0 — 400 km
0 — 250 mi

▲ *This map shows the extent of Persian and Greek lands in 401 BCE, and the route taken by Cyrus and his 10,000 Greek mercenaries when he made a bid for the throne against his brother Artaxerxes II. Cyrus was killed at the battle of Cunaxa and his men had to make their way home.*

attacked Thrace; only his illness saved Thracian Chersonese and the Hellespont.

In Athens, the personal vendettas of politicians in the crisis are all but incredible, albeit equally lucid. They lend an inevitability to events, like the long speeches of Athenian tragedy. The greatest of the orators, Demosthenes, affirmed that "If Philip dies you will soon raise up a second Philip."

Philip did not die; in 349 he invaded Chalkidike. In 346, by a treaty sworn at Athens, the Athenians abandoned any claim to Amphipolis, but to the east they kept most of the Chersonese. Meanwhile Philip conquered fortresses elsewhere in Thrace. Once peace was secure, and Phokis isolated from its provisions, Philip came south again. At the games at Delphi in 346 he was president, and gained membership of the Delphic council. He was now governor of all Thessaly. Kersobleptes of Thrace was his vassal; Messenia, Megalopolis, Elis, and Argos—those who feared Sparta in the Peloponnese—were his allies. In about 342 BCE he expelled Arybbas the Molossian

from Epirus and installed his wife's brother, Alexander. From Epirus, Philip was close to the Corinthian gulf and the western trade routes; little by little he extended the mountainous kingdom further south.

Athens reacted too late. The whole of Thrace, Macedonia, Thessaly, and Epirus constitute a formidable block of territory, and Philip had extended its boundaries; he had founded Philippopolis (now Plovdiv) on the Hebros, and held the western coast of Greece as far south as the Acheron. In 340 the Athenians seduced Byzantion and nearby Perinthos and also reestablished an independent Euboea. Philip attacked Perinthos, then Byzantion, but without immediate success. He spent the winter in northeast Thrace, at war with the Scythians on the Danube estuary, and in the following year returned to Greek affairs. Once again the excuse was a quarrel in the Delphic council, this time with the neighboring city of Amphissa. In 338 Philip swept down into central Greece, held Thermopylai, fortified a city in Phokis, and took Amphissa and

Naupaktos on the gulf of Corinth. Thebes and Athens, with other less powerful allies, opposed him; in August of that year the allied armies were utterly and finally defeated at Chaironeia in north Boeotia. Philip could now dictate his terms to the Greeks. He did so, but they were lenient, and in 337 BCE he announced a full-scale war of all Greece against Persia. That same year, on the morning of the incestuous marriage he had arranged between his daughter and her uncle, he was murdered.

Alexander the Great

Alexander the Great was then 18 or 19 years old, living in disgrace with his disgraced Molossian mother. His tutor had been the philosopher and scientist, Aristotle; Alexander was bold, imaginative, and violent. At once, in 335 BCE, after a year in which he confirmed his succession to his father's dominant role in Greece, he went to war in the Thracian mountains and on the Danube. As a commander, he possessed speed, tactical skill, and courage. In southern Greece the cities were restless; at a rumor of Alexander's death, Thebes rebelled. Within two weeks Alexander had crushed the city, killing 6,000 and enslaving the survivors.

Alexander invaded the Persian empire in 334. He crossed over into Asia in the north, performed religious duties at Troy, and at

▼ *The second Athenian league was set up in 377 to resist Sparta. In the mid 350s Thebes provoked a war that spread to all the central states and the league fell away.*

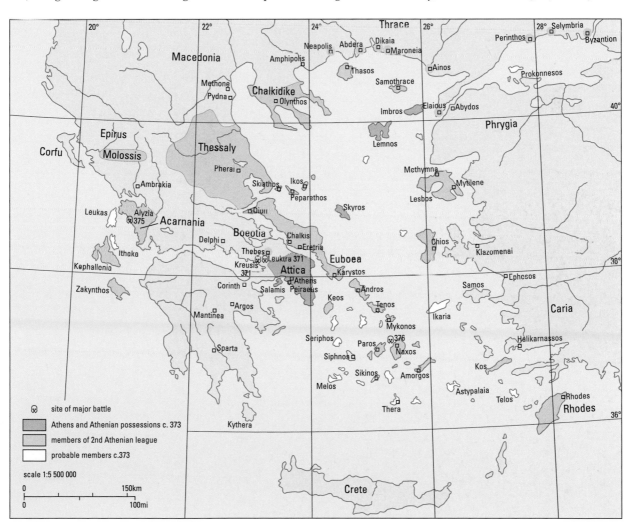

site of major battle

Athens and Athenian possessions c. 373

members of 2nd Athenian league

probable members c.373

scale 1:5 500 000

Salamis

Cyprus had been Greek for a very
long time. The legendary founder of
Salamis was Teukros, son of the king
of the island Salamis, near Athens. In
reality Salamis was the successor of
the Mycenaean city Enkomi.

In the 6th century Salamis controlled all
Cyprus. It was still at that time using a
syllabic script. In the 5th and 4th centuries
Salamis fought a long series of struggles
against Phoenician and Persian invaders but
in the Hellenistic world it flourished.

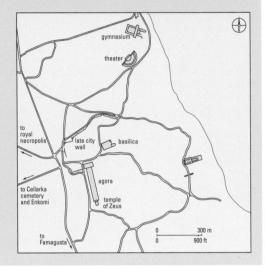

▶ *The great buildings
of Salamis include
the gymnasium with
its colonnaded
palaestra, the agora,
which was one of the
largest known, and
the 50-row theater.*

every fortified harbor in the Levant. The story
of the next two years is monotonously
triumphant. In October 333 BCE Alexander
encountered the king of kings, Darius III,
when the Persians caught up with the rear of
Alexander's rapid advance. The Greeks
defeated the Persians in a narrow coastal
plain at Issos; Darius fled. If the recorded
number of Persian dead is true, more soldiers
died at Issos than were again lost in one day
until the first day of the battle of the Somme,
110,000. There were 4,000 Macedonian
wounded, but we are told only of 302 dead.

Alexander moved next against Syria,
Phoenicia, and Tyre, which fell to him after
eight months of resistance in 332 BCE. After
Tyre, Gaza fell, and after Gaza, Egypt. After
Issos he had founded a city named after
himself, now called Alexandretta; at the
mouth of the Nile he founded Alexandria. At
Memphis on the Nile Alexander celebrated
Greek games, sacrificed to Egyptian gods,
and was proclaimed as king of Egypt. He
visited the oracle of Amun, whom the Greeks
called Zeus Ammon, in the Libyan desert,
where his soldiers thought later that he must
have asked whether he would rule the world.
The oracle may also have confirmed his
suspicion that Zeus was his true father.

Now Alexander plunged into Asia with
400,000 infantry and 7,000 cavalry, crossed
the Euphrates in 331 BCE and then the
Tigris, and at Gaugamela fought a second
battle with Darius. The battle was long and
complicated, but Alexander won, Darius fled,
Babylon surrendered, and Alexander took
Susa, the ancient capital of Elam and palace
of the old Persian kings. Effectively, the
Persian empire had all but fallen.

Alexander and his army pressed into the
Persian heartland toward Persepolis, as
conquerors and as explorers. At the Persian

once smashed a huge Persian army on the
river Granikos not far inland. In Asia Minor
he retained the Persian title of satrap for the
Macedonian governor he appointed, forbade
plunder, and left tributes and taxes at their
old level. Alexander refounded Troy and
liberated Sardis, the royal city of the Lydians.
Everywhere he made plain his intention to
govern. At Ephesos he restored democracy
but forbade reprisals, and this was the
beginning of a series of liberations and
restorations of the old Greek cities.

Miletos fell in spite of overwhelming
Persian strength at sea. Alexander's reaction
was to disband his own fleet, and to occupy

Gates in 330 BCE, he found a precipitous track that led behind a narrow, heavily defended pass, and utterly destroyed the powerful force that masked Persepolis.

The treasure of Persepolis can hardly be exaggerated; it was carefully carried away; some time later Alexander and his troops ran riot in the palace, and most of it was burned. Darius did not surrender. Alexander followed him back north to Ekbatana, capital of Media, then on by what is now Tehran and further east. But Darius was made hostage on the road by his kinsman the satrap of Bactria. By riding day and night Alexander overtook him at last; he found him wounded to death by his own courtiers. Some of them

continued in resistance and in flight, but one by one they were hunted down.

Many died. The Greeks who had enlisted only to fight Persia were sent home with treasures. New levies came out, but slowly. Alexander adopted some Persian customs, respected his new subjects, married a Persian noblewoman, Roxane (in 327 BCE), and set his ambition on all central Asia and all India. It was as if he and his diminishing army might consume themselves on an endless journey. During his conquest of the Punjab, Alexander was badly wounded at the assault of Multan, which he led personally. The troops never failed to respond to him, except that in India they refused to advance

▼ *In 359 BCE Philip of Macedon came to power, organized his army, and began to expand his empire. In 337 he announced a full-scale war of all Greece against Persia but was murdered not long afterward.*

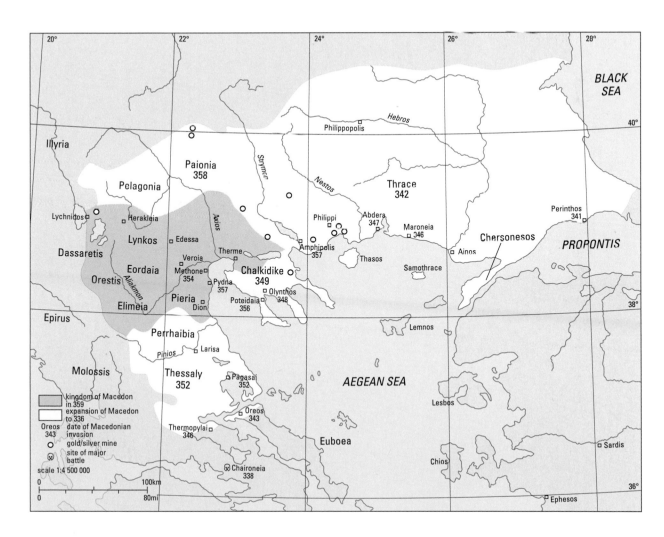

through desert country from the Indus basin to the Ganges; on the way home by way of the Indus delta and Gedrosia very many died in a desert.

At the end of 330 BCE Alexander had been on the northern edges of Afghanistan, the mountains and the Oxus (Amu-Darya) plains were his by 327, he had crossed the Indus in 326, and now returned to Babylon, where in 323 BCE he died, it seems of exhaustion, fever, and drink. He was 32 years old. It is a mark of his ruthlessness that no native people rebelled for a generation, and a mark of his simplicity and foresight, and of the objective situation of Asia as he left it, that history never quite covered over the achievement. From Gibraltar to what is now western China, there was intellectually one Greek world that lasted for centuries.

The over-extension of power

Imposed with difficulty, the political unity of Greece was by no means so secure. An alliance of cities was in open rebellion by 323 BCE, but the next year a victory at Krannon in central Thessaly restored Macedonian supremacy. Demosthenes committed suicide; democracy at Athens was restricted to the middle and upper classes, and a Macedonian garrison was installed.

In these few years Greece itself had exhausted much of its political power. At Athens, amid continuing quarrels, the schools of the great philosophers preserved the city's position as capital of the intellectual world. But the expansion of its own world had dwarfed it. In the east in the next century a flood of Parthian nomads would cut off the easternmost Macedonian provinces; but the isolated Macedonians would survive as kings for generations. The new Indian kingdom of Chandragupta would

bite at the southern frontiers in the east. In the west Alexander the Molossian, brother-in-law to the great Alexander, had already died fighting a campaign in southern Italy; Pyrrhos of Epirus would be the first Greek to fight against Rome. No mainland Greek city had the resources to compete. Any of the great Macedonian generals who now disputed the world, supplied from the treasury of Persia, could hire mercenaries on a scale no single city could match.

The disputing generals produced chaos on a world scale. The two natural commanders were Perdikkas in Asia, guardian of Alexander's posthumous child; and Antipater in Europe, the last surviving general of Philip. The other generals were local lords: Ptolemy in Egypt, Antigonos in Phrygia, Seleukos in Babylon, and Lysimachos in Thrace. Perdikkas was crushed first, killed in 321 BCE by his own men, and Antipater died in 319 BCE. His son Kassandros murdered Alexander's mother, brother, and heir: Kassandros himself died in 298 BCE Meanwhile Antigonos and his son Demetrios were active in Greece; their power was at its height from 307 to 303 BCE but the next year Antigonos died in battle against Seleukos. Demetrios survived until 285 BCE, when he was forced to surrender to Seleukos, and drank himself to death in two years.

The only direct successor of Alexander to die in bed was Ptolemy. He had married one of Antipater's daughters, and their son, Ptolemy the Thunderbolt, killed Seleukos in 280 BCE. But Ptolemy the Thunderbolt never ruled Egypt; his father left Egypt to a bastard son, the Ptolemy who was the patron of the last Greek poets. Ptolemy the Thunderbolt died in the raid of the Celts into Greece under Brennus in 279 BCE.

◀ *The wrestling ground at Salamis in Cyprus was the central courtyard of a vast gymnasium built in Hellenistic times but extended under the Romans. The columns and capitals were taken from a number of buildings destroyed in earthquakes in the 4th century CE.*

The Alexandrian Expansion

In a very few generations, the power structure of the world had altered irreversibly. When the dust had settled after Alexander's career, the Greeks had become inevitably conscious of remote peoples and traditions. Nomads in central Asia and on the borders of China, and peoples of the north and west, came into increasing contact with the Mediterranean centers. In the 2nd century BCE we know that an Alexandrian merchant ship of was wrecked off Anglesey as it rounded the coast of Wales. In Alexandria scientists had already begun to compute the magnitude of the earth.

But the economic consequences of the conquest of Persia were disastrous. Money had not existed for long, but it allowed any rich individual, such as one of Alexander's generals or the ruler of a barbarous territory, to buy himself a huge mercenary army. Mercenaries existed after Alexander's campaigns in vast numbers.

The supply of money had increased hugely because, by the generosity of Alexander, the hoarded treasure of the Persian empire, which in the past had not circulated, was simply given away, and flooded the Greek world. The resulting inflation was very sharp. In another important development at the same time, the great national sanctuaries of the gods, which had always lent from their treasuries to the state in time of emergency, now began to function as merchant banks to the public. There were even land investment banks. The results in terms of inflation and social disturbance were far-reaching. Class war amounting sometimes to civil war smoldered all over Greece. Piracy began again, and as time went on became a worse plague than it had ever been.

At the height of these upheavals, at the height of the increase of knowledge, when the overland silk route with China was open and Alexandrian ships were sailing as far as Britain and Southeast Asia, the Delphic oracle was asked who was the happiest man in the world. It named an obscure farmer on a smallholding not very far inland in the Peloponnese, who seldom left his own farm and had never seen the sea. There is something of the sense of this reply in Epicurean philosophy, and even in Stoicism: it had become clear that to be sane and happy in the new age one must limit one's desires and one's fears.

Nevertheless, on a wider scale the process was inevitable. The future belonged to rich farmers and rich merchants organized in the richest and most powerful community. Such a community would have to expand or perish; it would become a great empire.

That the new empire was to be Roman, not Greek, is immaterial; the civilized world except for China and perhaps India was imprinted with Hellenic life. The Ptolemies in Egypt and the great Greek dynasties in Asia brought to their kingdoms the Greek language and many Greek ways of doing things. Athens became a place of cultural pilgrimage, and its literature became the accepted model of purity and power of language in Latin as well as in Greek.

Alexandrian scholarship

One of the important means by which this happened was the growth of scholarly literature, the commentaries on the classics by the Alexandrian scholars. In the 3rd century at Alexandria the Ptolemies created

Pergamon

For little more than 150 years, from 282 to 133 BCE, under the Attalid dynasty, Pergamon in Asia Minor was a wealthy and formidable imperial power, with a reputation for scholarship. It gave its name to parchment, which was invented there as an alternative writing material when the Egyptians stopped exporting papyrus under the Ptolemies. Its library was second only to Alexandria's, with a reputed 20,000 volumes. Pergamon bred a new and spectacular school of baroque sculpture; it defeated the Celts and saw them settled in Galatia, held off the Macedonians, and kept the Romans friendly; it nourished the beginnings of the art of gardening. The sanctuary of Asklepios, a private foundation in 400 BCE, became under Hadrian a "wonder of the world." The theater, which could seat 10,000 spectators, had the steepest seating of any ancient theater.

The sculptures of the Great Altar of Pergamon have been removed to a museum in Berlin, Germany. Spectacular in its finish and fascinating in its detail, the altar was the grandest monument of the 2nd century BCE. The sculptures are on a vast scale, heavy and muscular and glittering.

▶ *Pergamon was built on terraces on steep moutainsides in a harmonious design of contrasting fine architecture and open spaces.*

▶ *The 2nd-century imperial temple of Trajan was built on the acropolis at Pergamon. It could be seen from every part of the city.*

impression were essential elements, the adaptations are almost impossible to chart. Already in the 2nd century BCE a Roman architect was employed by the city of Athens for the new baroque temple of Zeus. There was no longer a Greek world, only a world.

In that world victory belonged to colossal forces. Independent cities and lesser powers were doomed. In the 3rd century BCE the new kingdoms altered their frontiers on an imperial scale. Thrace was swallowed up, and the new kingdom of Pergamon in Asia Minor came into existence. Pergamon was rich, powerful, and influential. The art of gardening, of the pleasure garden, developed at Pergamon. The 2nd-century baroque ornamental sculptures of the altar of Zeus at Pergamon, with their huge, convoluted forms, add a new dimension and an almost new direction to the history of Greek art.

Commanders and mercenaries

The deadening process that slowly unfolded took place under the long pressure of forces

newly let loose. Mercenary soldiers, for example, did not become a regular resource available to all great powers until the 3rd century. At first the disloyalties of commanders who shifted their forces from king to king seriously disturbed what balance existed in the world, but eventually they were squeezed out of existence. The role of the Greek armies of the new kings in the 3rd century was colonial, and in Egypt, Asia Minor, and Mesopotamia, they held land in the new territories and their cities were cantonments outside the native cities.

Of course there were also special corps of professional soldiers. Their recruitment continued into the Roman army. There was also an important distinction among the land-holding reserve army; they were by no means all citizens, for citizen rights were owned only by official cities. By this time, every city in Greece depended heavily on the generosity of monarchs. The buildings of the kings of Pergamon at Athens, and the innumerable decrees of gratitude of the Athenian state, illustrate this dramatically.

Changes of taste

Middle-class taste was often cloying and hideous, sometimes appealing. Vases began to be made, at Centuripe in Sicily and in Alexandria, smothered in ornamental colors and shaped too elaborately.

Masterpieces often tell us less about social history. But the last masterpieces of Greek vase painting belong to the late 4th century; the last master is probably the Lipari Painter, whose works are found only on his own remote island and nearby. The magenta vases from Centuripe, and some sepulchral monuments in the Cairo museum, are much warmer, more fantastical, and less fine.

Not that nothing fine existed in the world. This was the age of illustrated manuscripts. We know of medical and surgical texts carefully illustrated, and even of entire epic poems illustrated with a cartoon version of

Ay Khanoum

Ay Khanoum is an isolated Greek city, perhaps once named Alexandria, on the borders of Russia and Afghanistan, not many miles from China. Its Hellenistic palace, once a great grove of columns, seems to stand on the site of a Persian palace. At Ay Khanoum the Kokcha, which flows from the lapis lazuli mines and the high pass into India, runs down to the Oxus. This is the only purely Greek city ever excavated in Afghanistan. It was discovered by chance, by the king of Afghanistan on a shooting expedition. It is a well-defended city, with a gymnasium, a temple, and inscriptions in Greek. Alexander

▶ *The huge palace dominates Ay Khanoum. It was defended by stout walls and its position on the Oxus river. The temple seems to have blended Hellenic and local religious beliefs.*

himself never came quite so far northeast, but this city is his signature.

the action. The drawing was very popular. It traveled where the language of verse was no longer understood, and when an early Buddhist sculptor in Gandhara, in what is now Pakistan, carved a scene showing the wooden horse at the fall of Troy; he used it as a miracle of the Buddha. A silver cup from Tibet has a scene on it which began life as an illustration to Euripides.

Elsewhere in the east the Greeks adapted to native life. We know of a Greek making an offering to the Buddha. Someone translated the Buddhist rules of life of the Indian king Asoka into philosophic Greek. The goddess of Baktra (Balkh), capital of Bactria, was Anahita, the great water goddess of the Oxus: she was worshiped in a confused cult as Artemis. The Greek sense of identity was

persistent, even when their institutions and almost their language were lost.

What survived was due to the scholarly revivals of antiquarians, or to the patronage of the new rich. The most beautiful of all surviving ancient books is one that contains a collection of botanical drawings made for Flavia Anicia, the daughter of a Roman emperor. The illustrations of the book, part of the *De Materia Medica* of Dioskorides, seem to be taken directly from life. They, or botanical drawings like them, were copied and recopied in the Middle Ages, more and more formally, less and less recognizably. But the codex of Dioskorides is the last point of a long and rich tradition. In it we have access to the best work of the Greeks under centuries of non-Greek patronage.

▲ *Columns from Ay Khanoum being restored as part of a project to build a Greco-Bactrian Museum to document the achievements of Alexander the Great.*

The Roman Conquest

Rome in the 3rd century BCE was a powerful city near the western Italian coast, and it had already conquered more civilized places. The 4th-century Gaulish invasion, which in Asia Minor ended with the Celtic settlement of Galatia in the 3rd century, had swept through Italy. After the sack of Rome (390 BCE) the Romans had challenged the Etruscans to the north, destroying Veii (396 BCE).

Militarily, Roman power had rested from the 5th century on a league of the cities of Latium to the south. But the Romans outgrew their league, and one by one, the Romans swallowed up their rivals. The Romans were now in Etruria to the north and in Campania beyond Latium to the south. Roman colonies established in the 4th century stood their ground in the 3rd. By 218 BCE there were Roman colonial cities on the Italian coast, at river crossings, in approaches to mountain passes, and where roads crossed. Between 343 and 263 BCE some 60,000 new Roman

Corinth

Corinth was one of the grandest and wealthiest cities of mainland Greece. With ports on both sides of the Isthmus, it was a great merchant city and an early colonial power. Its fortress was an almost impregnable rock, its land rich, its visual art, which absorbed many Oriental images, was magnificent. The Romans destroyed (146 BCE) and refounded (44 BCE) Corinth, which became capital of Achaea.

▶ *A 525-foot- (160-m) long stoa encloses the southern side of the agora. The theater held 15,000 people. The 1st-century odeon held 3,000.*

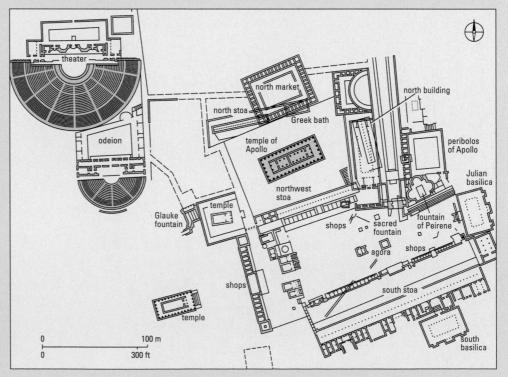

◄ *The temple of Apollo at Corinth is one of the oldest in Greece. The temple dates from the mid-6th century BCE. The surviving limestone Doric columns are all that is left of a rectangle of six at the front and back and 15 along the sides.*

landholdings were established, covering something like 50,200 square miles (130,000 sq km). The results of this advance were to last longer than Alexander's sweep.

Expansion produced war, and victorious war in turn produced further expansion. By the end of the 3rd century BCE they had annexed Sardinia, Corsica, and Sicily, and the vast riches of the Po valley. All Italy now belonged to Rome by irreversible alliance or by conquest. Since they now dominated the Greek cities of southern Italy, the Romans took over the Greeks' long quarrel with Carthage. The ensuing war, at sea, in Sicily and in North Africa, drew them into the center of the huge Carthaginian sphere of influence. In the first Carthaginian (Punic) war of 264–241 BCE, they fought the biggest naval battles the Mediterranean had seen.

Another invasion of Gauls brought an army of 70,000 men halfway down Italy; in 225 BCE it was annihilated at Telamon. In 237 BCE the Carthaginian Hamilcar Barca, a general of the first war, had set out to colonize Spain. The son-in-law who succeeded him advanced his frontiers to the Ebro, more than halfway across Spain. In 221 BCE the enormous power base passed to Hannibal, the son of Hamilcar, who for the rest of that century fought the Romans (second Carthaginian war, 218–201 BCE). The course of the war was dramatic, but by

▶ *After Alexander's death, his generals Ptolemy, Seleukos, and Antigonos divided the empire. This map shows the successor kingdoms in 303 BCE.*

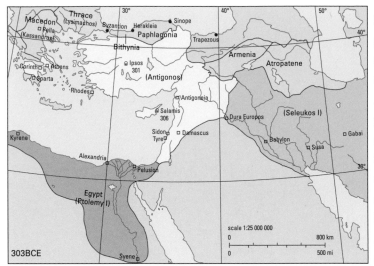

▶ *This map shows how much the Seleucid empire had expanded by 240 BCE.*

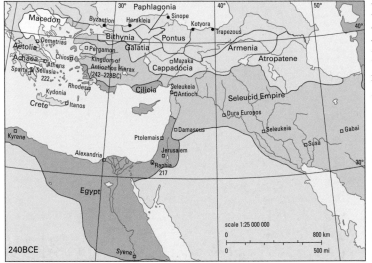

▶ *In 190 the Romans defeated the Seleucids for the first time and the empire continued to lose territory. This map shows its extent in 188 BCE. Parthia, once a Seleucid province, is now an expanding empire.*

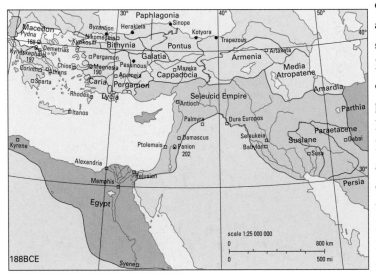

205 the Roman general Scipio had taken Spain and successfully invaded Africa. Carthaginian power was destroyed, and Rome was now as formidable, as wealthy, and nearly as far-ranging as any of the kingdoms of Alexander's successors.

First Macedonian war

In the course of their first Carthaginian war, the Romans had already landed on the eastern coast of the Adriatic. To close the Adriatic to Carthage they had established Brundisium (Brindisi), a fortified colony on a natural harbor, and in doing so provoked attacks on Adriatic shipping by the Illyrians. The Romans established a protectorate on the Illyrian coast. In 220 BCE a local adventurer, Demetrios of Pharos, began to trouble Rome. When Rome drove him out, Demetrios appealed to the nearest great power

in Greece, the
Macedonian court of
King Philip V. The
king, resenting
Roman expansion,
made an alliance with
Hannibal, then (in
215 BCE) at the
height of his success.
The Romans
controlled the sea,
and landed men in
Greece to make what
trouble they could. In
205 BCE, toward the
end of the second
Carthaginian war,
Philip made peace
with Rome.

Before the Roman
incursion, however,
the Macedonians
were already in
trouble in Greece. By
228 BCE the
Achaean league of
cities, the most
important power in
the Peloponnese, had
expelled the
Macedonians from the
huge fortress of
Corinth, from Sikyon,
Argos, Arcadia,
Megara, and Aegina.
However, the league
was a threat to Sparta,
and in the 220s the
Spartans had come
close to annihilating
it: the league in

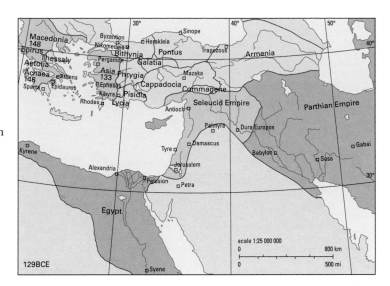

◀ *By 141 the
Seleucid empire
had lost its land east
of the Euphrates and,
despite the attempts
of its kings, was still
disintegrating, as
seen in this map
of 129 BCE.*

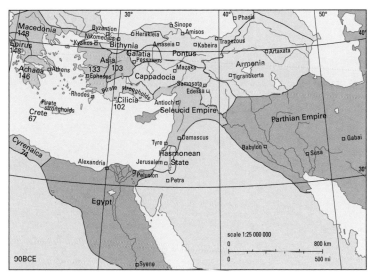

◀ *When it was finally
conquered by Rome
in 64 BCE the
Seleucid empire was
confined to the
provinces of Syria
and eastern Cilicia.
This map shows the
empire in 90 BCE.*

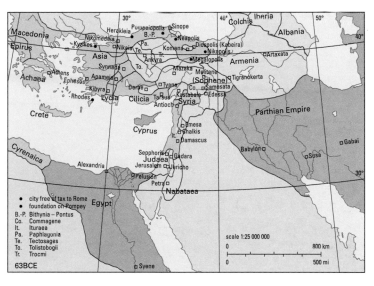

◀ *By 63 BCE the
Seleucid empire
was no more, while
the Parthian empire
had expanded still
further. A number of
minor kingdoms had
asserted themselves
in Asia Minor.*

Paestum

Poseidonia, later known as Paestum, was founded in the mid-7th century BCE by the existing Greek colony of Sybaris further south. It lies below Naples on the coast of Italy. Its defensive wall was about 16 feet (5 m) thick and nearly 3 miles (5 km) long. By a whim of the sea which first destroyed it and then retired from it, this city has the best-preserved archaic temples anywhere in the Greek world. At the end of the 5th century it was taken over by the local Lucanians, and in the 3rd it fell to Rome. We know that the Greeks in the Lucanian period lamented the decay of their way of life, but they did continue to produce a fine style of painting.

▶ Ancient Paestum had two sacred areas containing three temples. The town walls, built of travertine blocks, encircled a grid of intersecting streets.

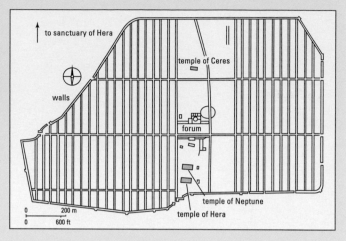

despair called in their old enemies, the Macedonians, and Sparta and Corinth fell.

During their first war in Greece, the Romans secured their first active allies there: the Aetolian league, a confederacy of cities on the northwestern side of the gulf of Corinth. If Philip V could not protect them against Roman interference, they must protect themselves; in 211 BCE, therefore, they entered the Roman alliance against the Macedonians, but made a separate peace with Philip after the Romans' withdrawal.

Now Philip turned east. He negotiated an alliance with the king of Syria, Antiochos the Great. Under Antiochos, Syria was perhaps the strongest kingdom in the Greek world. The Parthians were its tributaries and the king of Bactria ruled by license of Antiochos.

In 203 BCE, in another of the almost continuous wars of the great powers, Philip combined with Antiochos to menace the Egypt of the Ptolomies. Smaller powers rushed into the arms of Rome; at the same time they went to war with Philip. The Romans, whose diplomatic intelligence was by no means perfect, and whose suspicions were great, moved against Philip. The war was the policy not of the Roman people, who refused to fight it, but of the Senate, whose financial interests were international. There was an Italian presence at Delos, one of the greatest business centers in the region. The Roman ultimatum to Philip echoed the policy of protective interference; Philip must pay indemnities to Pergamon and Rhodes, and he must never again undertake military action against any Greek state.

Second Macedonian war

The inevitable war began in 200 BCE. The Roman plan was to free the Greek cities as protectorates, as a frontier power against Alexander's successors. The Aetolian cities joined the Romans in 198 BCE and Athens welcomed in Attalos of Pergamon; the Achaean cities at once reverted to their old

anti-Macedonian policy. Philip could muster only 26,000 men, including boys and old men. The Roman commander Flamininus defeated that army utterly at Kynoskephalai in Thessaly.

Philip was made to surrender what remained of his fleet, all his Asian cities, and strategic fortified cities in Greece, including Corinth; he had also to pay an indemnity, but by the terms of the treaty he became an ally of the Romans: the Aetolians gained little or nothing. In 196 BCE at the Isthmian games Flamininus proclaimed the nominal freedom of Greece, and many of the principal cities of the Peloponnese became Roman allies.

The Romans as a protecting power had now to try to settle the resentments of the Greek states. The Macedonians had ceded Argos to Sparta as a move in the war with Rome; Sparta had kept Argos and then negotiated a Roman alliance. Flamininus restored Argos to the Achaean league. Sparta revolted with an army of 15,000 men, so Flamininus invaded with 50,000. Sparta was not annexed, but it was crushed.

Rome defeats Antiochos of Syria

The Romans had now to play the other role of a protecting power; they had to protect the new frontiers. Antiochos the Great had taken in 197 BCE the whole coast of Asia Minor; he was now chewing his way westward along the coast of Thrace. But Rome negotiated with Antiochos for three years, and in 194 BCE the Roman army left Greece.

In 193 BCE Antiochos married his daughter to Ptolemy V of Egypt. The northern states of Greek Asia were his allies

▲ *The mid-5th century temple of Neptune and the temple of Hera (beyond), some 100 years older, stand in Hera's special sanctuary at Paestum; the small dedications that have been found are much the same.*

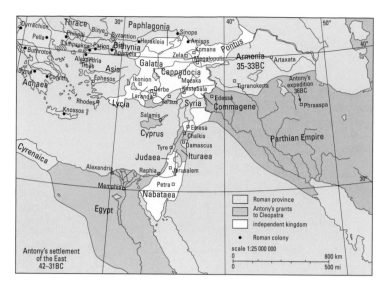

Antony's settlement
of the East
42–31BC

Roman province
Antony's grants
to Cleopatra
independent kingdom
Roman colony

scale 1:25 000 000

0   800 km
0   500 mi

▲ In 43 BCE Mark Antony was one of three men granted absolute athority for five years over the Roman empire. He took over the eastern provinces of the empire. Antony became the lover of Cleopatra, the queen of Egypt, granting her many of the lands once held by the first Ptolemies.

and Hannibal in exile was a refugee prince in his court. Antiochos' relations with Rome were bad, but without a state of war. At this point the Aetolians invited him into mainland Greece, with a promise of alliance with Philip and with Sparta. Trouble broke out at once, and old scores were settled. The Aetolians went to war, and the Achaeans extended their league to include Elis, Sparta, and Messenia. Antiochos entered mainland Greece with a small army, and the Romans were now bound to intervene again in Greece. In 191 BCE they destroyed his army at Thermopylai; Antiochos escaped almost alone. The next year the Romans under the Scipio brothers Africanus and Lucius recovered Thrace and marched on Asia. The Aetolians secured a truce with Rome.

The combined fleets of Rome, Rhodes, and Pergamon eventually destroyed the enemy. Roman naval power was a product of the first Carthaginian war; it is important to note the significance of naval power in the dominance of first the Athenians, then the Macedonians, the Carthaginians, and the Romans. It decided the control of much of the world.

A successful Roman land campaign in northwest Asia followed at once. Aetolia was

punished, but not annihilated. By the treaty of Apamea in Phrygia in 188 BCE, Antiochos lost most of Asia Minor, his ships, his elephants, and a large sum of money. Hannibal escaped inland. By overstepping its Greek protectorates, Rome had become in substance the governing power of mainland Greece. The whole Mediterranean was a Roman sea, and quarrel after quarrel was decided by Roman commissioners. In the Peloponnese the war between Sparta and the Achaean league blazed up again, until in 181 BCE the Romans stepped in to restore the integrity and the traditional institutions of Sparta.

Third Macedonian war

Not everyone was impotent against Roman power. Philip V's son Perseus made friends with the Rhodians, married the daughter of the successor to Antiochos, and found allies in Aetolia. The poor, democrats, and libertarians in every Greek city looked to Perseus. Eumenes of Pergamon appealed to Rome to destroy him; when Eumenes was nearly assassinated, Perseus was blamed, and Rome acted. Rome declared war in 171 BCE. In three years' time a Roman army of 100,000 was in Greece. Perseus had fewer than half that number; he failed to get help from the lower Danube because he could not afford to pay for it. In 168 BCE at Pydna his army was massacred, and he died in a Roman prison. There were no more Macedonian kings of significance, and Macedonia was split into four republics.

After Pydna, Rhodes was stripped, Delos handed to Athens as a free port, the Aetolian league dismembered, Pergamon deliberately weakened, and in Epirus so many were sold as slaves that the countryside was depopulated. When a new Antiochos of Syria (the fifth) invaded Egypt in 169–168 BCE, the Romans were already so strong that they simply told him to go away—and he went.

The destruction of Corinth

The final catastrophe for the Greeks was in the forties of the 2nd century BCE. It is easier to understand in terms of Roman than of Greek history. Roman government had become heavy-handed, but it was successful: in Spain, where final victory was deferred until 133 BCE; in Africa, where Carthage was forced into a local war in 150 BCE before it was utterly destroyed by the Romans in 146; and in Greece. In 150 BCE the survivors of the Achaean hostages to Rome were sent home, a new quarrel with the Spartans, who left the Achaean league, was settled by Rome in favor of Sparta, and in the resulting climate of furious resentment

Roman envoys were attacked at Corinth, now chief city of the Achaean league. A Roman army advanced from Macedonia. The consul Mummius assembled his army at Corinth in 146 BCE. The Greeks were routed.

Most of the Corinthians were massacred, and the rest sold as slaves. Local government by property qualification was established all over Greece, and democracy abolished. The leagues of cities were disbanded. Macedonia was made a province of Rome. The history of Greece became the history of a province of the Roman empire, and then of the Byzantine empire, and then of the Turkish empire. It was to be nearly 2,000 years before Greece was politically independent, but it is astonishing to what degree national consciousness persisted, still more so how greatly the Greeks contributed to what we value in the history of the human race.

▼ *This map shows the eastern limits of the Roman empire in 117 CE and the inexorable Roman annexations of Greek territory.*

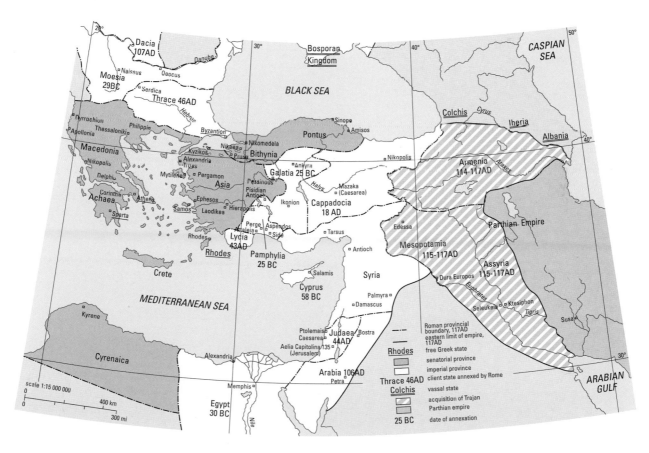

165

The Classical Impact of Hellenism

The influence of the Greeks—their arts, sciences, experience, language, and norms of decency, even their religion—by no means ceased at the establishment of the Roman province of Macedonia. In the shapes of pottery made until recently in Swat, in the pillars of wooden architecture still standing in Afghanistan, in elements of Buddhist art, even in the new realism of certain figurines as far a field as China, Greek influence is clear. Athenian tragedy and the poems of Homer were known in India, and in Egypt Aristophanes was still acted in the 5th century CE. These examples represent an inevitable diffusion. The place to look for depth of penetration is very well documented; it is the city of Rome. Veii, until it fell in 396 BCE, had been more Hellenized than Rome, and so had all Etruria and most of southern Italy. The Romans emerge into history fighting; civilization comes to them late.

Early Latin writers

At the celebration in 240 BCE, after their first victorious Carthaginian war, the Romans held public athletic contests, and a version of 5th-century Athenian tragedy was produced at Rome, in Latin. It was written by Livius Andronicus, a half-Greek ex-prisoner of war from Tarentum, who also translated Homer into Latin verse. The rhythms of Greek poetry did not take easily to the Latin language. But given this limitation, the Romans already had wonderful poets in Greek rhythms in the 2nd century BCE, and their own prose, by rubbing constantly against Greek models, refined itself just as quickly, ending in the abundance of Cicero, just before freedom of speech was lost and mannerism set in.

Naevius, one of the greatest of all Roman poets, was from Capua; he knew the Greeks and wrote tragedy, comedy, and some moving elegiac verses. His epic account of the Carthaginian war was written in an old Latin meter, but the shadow of Homer nourished it. Ennius, shortly after, chose a Latin adaptation of Greek hexameters. Lucilius, the first great Roman satirist, was an educated noble of the late 2nd century BCE to whom much that was Greek came naturally. He wrote sometimes in Greek rhythm, sometimes not, he mixed Greek words into Latin sentences and his philosophy was Greek.

We know much more about Plautus; he was an Umbrian who died about 184 BCE. His Latin comedies are adaptations of 4th-century Greek originals, with powerful injections of his own society, his own experience, and his own, very Roman jokes. In him what is Greek and what is Roman are interpenetrated, and something new has been created that the world had never seen before.

In the adaptations made by the comic poet Terence in the republican age from similar originals Greek elegance is supreme. The much later fragments of the mime-writer Laberius confirm the fluency and precision of language that the Roman stage commanded in the end. But Terence was exquisitely faithful to the Greekness of his originals. Terence was a slave from North Africa, born about 190 BCE. He slipped out of life, having been granted his freedom, at the age of 30, and is said to have died poor in the Peloponnese. It is reasonable to assume that the finest of all adapters into Latin had gone back to a language, and perhaps to places, that meant more to him.

◄ *(previous pages) This detail comes from the Ara Pacis, or Altar of Peace, built by Augustus in Rome. It combines Greek and Roman elements in a subtle yet brilliant way.*

▶ *The city was built on terraces that rise to a steep hill upon which was the temple of Athene Polias. The city was laid out on a grid plan, divided into even blocks. At the center of the town was the agora, another temple and the theater.*

Priene

Priene was an early Ionian city on the Asian coast, but never so grand or successful as Miletos, its neighbor. In the 4th century it transferred bodily to its own harbor town, which is the Priene we know today. Alexander built a temple of Athene there. But its river silted, and Priene is over 7 miles (12 km) from the sea. The site is spectacular, on the brow of a great cliff and at its foot. It had fine private houses and magnificent public buildings.

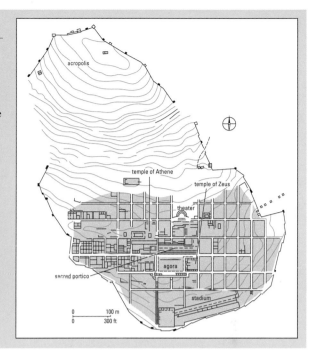

Literature involves philosophy and many elements of a tradition and a society; it involves what the Romans called *humanitas*. The measure of the importance of the Greeks is that *humanitas* is a Greek idea, one which came slowly into existence in the course of the painful history of the Greeks. Of that history the Roman writers of the late republic and the Augustan period are a continuation. They would have been the first to admit it.

Sculpture

One of the most striking of all the late achievements of the Greeks is the perfection of portrait sculpture. There is no doubt about its Greek origins; one need look only at the magnificent silver coinage of Greek Bactria. But the late republican portrait heads of the Romans have exactly the same quality. They are formidable faces, unashamed of their warts. There is something deeper than self-confidence about them, and at the same time an aggression, a scarred toughness, which speak of the cost of survival. They are the faces one might rely on to rule.

Where the Romans were most penetrated by the Greeks, they were most liberated, and most Roman. On the Campus Martius in Rome, the Altar of Peace of the Emperor Augustus dedicated in 9 BCE owed its origins to the Altar of Pity, the popular name for the altar of the 12 gods in the center of Athens. Everything about it is adaptation: Mother Earth has become Italy; Aeneas (a hero of Troy in the Iliad but now also considered the founder of Rome) is an Athenian elder; the Roman ceremonies in marble echo the representations of Athenian ceremonies. The moment that the friezes represent is not the climax of the ceremony, which took place in 13 BCE, but a moment of calm just before the climax. The atmosphere is serene, but a few human touches do service for the extraordinary liveliness of parts of the Parthenon frieze. Someone is being reproved for talking, a child wants to be picked up. The entire work has a gravity it would be hard to parallel at this date outside a Roman context. It is certainly Greek work, probably Asiatic

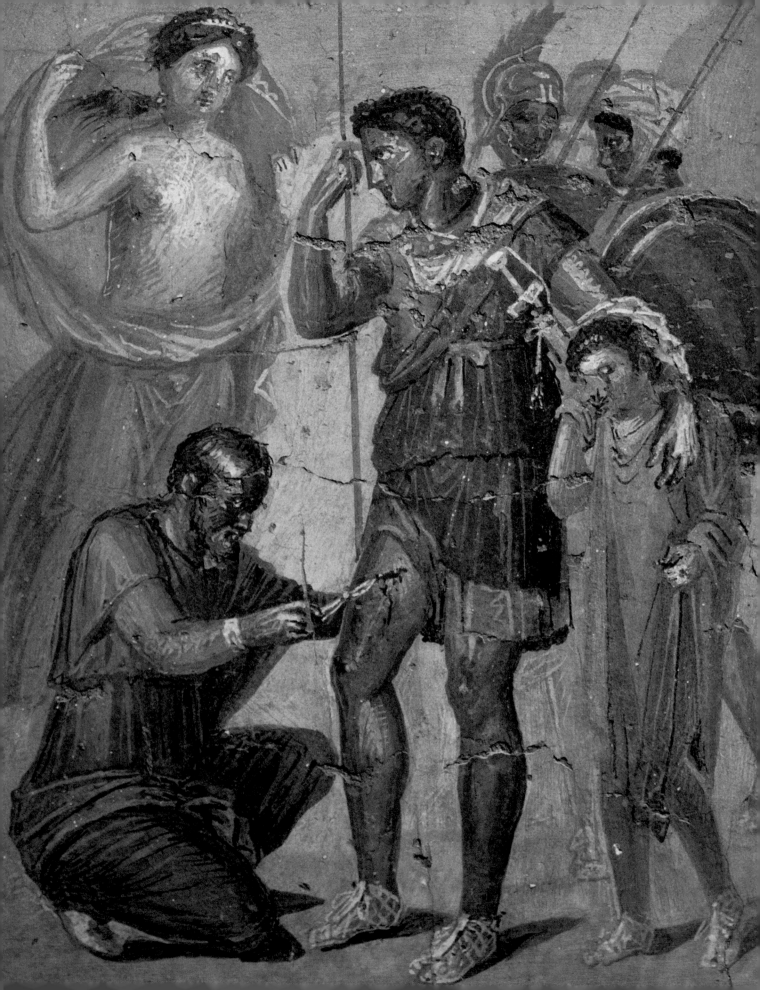

Greek. The relief carvings on the enclosure of the Altar of Pity in Athens were carved in the late 5th century, and imitated more than once later. But the Altar of Peace is not just a copy; although it includes adaptations from Greek work, it is profoundly original.

The Augustan poets

In the literature of the full Augustan period, it is sometimes almost as if Greeks were writing in Latin. The Eclogues of Vergil are steeped in a wide variety of late Greek poetry. In the Aeneid, Vergil is conscious not only of Homer, but of Alexandrian scholarly criticism of Homer. Some of his adaptations are failures, but even in his mistakes, Vergil was Hellenized to his finger tips.

Humanly perhaps the greatest of all Roman poets is Horace. He was also the most unregenerate Italian of the writers of the Augustan age. Perhaps for that reason, the boldness of his handling of Greek models was beyond anyone else's. He revived and transmitted to Europe the Greek art of lyric poetry. Where he differed from his contemporaries was in a preference, based on personal scholarship, for very early models, Archilochos, Alkaios and Sappho among them. His advice to young writers was "read the Greeks at night, and read the Greeks in the day."

Horace claimed as a spiritual ancestor Bion of Olbia. Bion lived from about 325 to 255 BCE, through the upheaval that followed Alexander's death. He studied under Aristotle's pupils as well as under Plato's, and also under hedonists and the Cynics, whose invective against the established world had so strong an influence on Jewish and early Christian invective against pagan gods.

The most complete literary statements we have of a philosophic position in this period were written in Latin. The most surprising example of a complete philosophy is the long Latin poem by Lucretius, who died about 55 BCE. In *On the Nature of Things* Roman verse is just in its early flower, and the philosophy, which is Epicurean, derives from the Athenian schoolmaster's son who lived when Bion of Olbia did.

The world in the late 1st century BCE was in many ways still the Alexandrian world. All over the Mediterranean, and in places as far afield as the silk road to China, Greek manners, architecture, and language existed. In Rome Augustus exploited the marble quarries of Italy, but Athenian marble and workmanship did not lose all their prestige.

Jewish literature

One area where the literature is preserved both in the native language and in Greek, is in Judea. In the centuries before Christ there was a huge Greek influence and presence. Judaea was part of the Greek east, and the last books of the Old Testament were composed in Greek. Josephus, a leader at the time of the revolt of the Jews under Nero, wrote his histories in Greek, not Aramaic. Jewish settlements in Asia, Greece, and Alexandria—the center of Hellenistic Judaic literature—retained their identity and their religion; but it is clear from the evidence that they absorbed from the Greeks more than the Greeks absorbed from them. The Alexandrian *Acts of the Jewish Martyrs* recall Euripides, and the Jewish art of Palestine in the time of Christ is Greek in origin and form. Even the roots of the Book of Revelations, the Apocalypse of John, are entwined among those of other strange documents written in Greek Asia. Heaven may not be Greek, but according to John it contains Greek architecture.

◄ *In his masterpiece, the Aeneid, Virgil tells the story of Aeneas, the mythical hero of Troy—seen in this Roman mural being treated for a leg wound—who fled the burning city to found Lavinium, the parent town of Rome.*

Post-Classical Revivals

For close on 2,000 years Greece lost its political independence; but Greece was still a shrine of cultural pilgrimages, frequented by scholars and philosophers, looted by emperors. Athens became a university town. The last battle in which the Greek east might possibly have revived its independence was the battle of Actium (31BCE), where Antony and Cleopatra were defeated by the fleet of Octavian (Augustus).

The Romans in Greece

After Octavian's victory, the worst looting of Greece was for a huge series of squares and colonnades in central Rome. Some of what went was not much loss; some of the looting was more serious. The four horses of San Marco in Venice come from the capture of Constantinople by the Crusaders in 1204 CE, but they had already traveled east, probably from the immense treasury of art that Nero looted from Greek sanctuaries. The Peiraeus was destroyed by one Roman general and rebuilt by another; wonderful Classical bronze statues have been found which must have been in store awaiting shipment probably to Rome. The Romans genuinely loved what they looted. Famous temples from the countryside were reerected in central Athens, including the temple of Ares from Acharnai, which was rededicated to Gaius Caesar, the young heir of Augustus.

In Athens, as elsewhere, the Romans dedicated new buildings and constructed aqueducts for the urban population. The climax of Roman building was in the 2nd century CE, under Hadrian. At that time a Romanized Greek and a Hellenized Roman must have been hard to tell apart. The Romans were in Crete, in Athens, in the north, and in farms all over the Peloponnese. Hadrian himself had an antiquarian and comprehensive taste for all the arts, but his passion was Greek. He was in love with a youth called Antinous, a Greek from Asia Minor, who was drowned in 130 CE. Hadrian commissioned more statues of Antinous, in a variety of classic poses, than would seem credible if so many did not still survive. He was worshiped as a god.

The Greeks and Constantinople

In 330, when Constantine refounded Byzantion (with the name Constantinople) as the second capital city of the Roman empire, the Greek world reemerged with at least its language intact. There is an important sense in which the Roman empire did not fall until 1453, when Constantinople yielded to the Turks. In a more important sense what survived the collapse of the west was a Greek empire. The architects of Hagia Sophia (built 532–37) did not just happen to be Greeks; their scientific knowledge, aesthetic brilliance, and originality are qualities that we recognize in this meeting of Rome, Greece, and the Hellenized east. The history of Greek architecture and of mathematics was continuous down to the Byzantine or Eastern Roman Empire.

This was a different world from that of Perikles and Pheidias, above all because Asia penetrated the Greeks as Greece penetrated the Romans. It would be hard to exaggerate the degree to which the ways in which the Byzantine Greeks saw reality were embedded in the Alexandrian age. The art of mosaic began when patterns of Egyptian

colored glass drove out shell-encrusted grottoes in the reign of Tiberius. Saint and emperor no longer look at all Roman; they look like Greeks in an Asian atmosphere.

There is very little striking about mainland Greece between the earthquake at Kenchreai and the Renaissance. Greece was invaded in the 4th to 9th centuries by Vizigoths, Huns, Avars, Slavs, and Bulgars. The Macedonian dynasty of Byzantine emperors (867–1025) was followed by the attacks of the Seljuk Turks from the east and the Normans from the west, and by interventions into the Byzantine world by the Crusades from the 11th to the 13th century. Italian princes built their palace in the buildings of the Athenian acropolis. The Ottoman Turks took Athens in 1458, five years after Constantinople. The Parthenon, then a church, became a mosque.

The rediscovery of ancient Greece

The Renaissance came to Greece from the east, with the last Byzantine princes. The Venetians held other parts of Greece, and a number of islands. But in the 15th century Gemistos Plethon, from Constantinople, had founded a society of humanists at Mistra, near the ruins of Sparta. It was by visiting him that the Italian Cyriaco of Ancona brought back to the west the first knowledge of the archaeological riches of Greece.

We have Cyriaco's manuscript of the Augustan geographer Strabo. From the east Cyriaco took his book by way of Mistra, where he copied out a missing page of the text. From the moment that he stayed with Gemistos Plethon, all his identifications are correct, and some of them were difficult to make. He visited and correctly identified site

▲ *The great 16th-century architect Andrea Palladio based his design for the Villa Capra on that of a classical Greek temple.*

after site, often noting down inscriptions. This was Byzantine knowledge before it was Italian. Almost the same list of identifications survives in the margins of manuscripts of Ptolemy. But when Cyriaco stayed with Italian princes still ruling in northern Greece, he identified nearly all his ruins wrongly.

Now the Turks controlled almost all of the eastern and southern Mediterranean, and the reawakening of Greece was slow. The center of the Parthenon was destroyed in 1687 by an explosion in a battle between Turks and Venetians. The Venetians made matters worse in an attempt to detach the pedimental sculptures by lowering them with ropes which snapped. The Turks returned, a smaller mosque was bult in the ruins and the stones of this and of numerous other buildings began to be destroyed, sold or given away. The agent to Lord Elgin took whatever of the Parthenon he was technically capable of removing, in the first years of the 19th century.

After independence

By the 1800s serious archaeological exploration had begun and the freedom of Greece was in sight (the European powers recognized Greek independence in 1832). Even poor and simple Greeks respected their marble inheritance. They were horrified by Elgin, even at the time, and more so by his contemporary Edward Clarke, who removed a statue from Eleusis which they believed was responsible for the earth's fertility. The peasant captain Makriyannis during the war of independence seriously upbraided one of his Greeks for selling ancient sculpture to foreigners. There was, admittedly, a plan of the first Greek parliament to restore the Parthenon in what would have been the style of the 1820s; there was even a plan to convert it into a royal palace; happily, money ran out.

▶ *Many of the pots made by Josiah Wedgwood's factory in the18th century were based on Greek vases.*

It was not easy 160 years ago to define a Greek. Had the plan which ended in the war of independence not failed in many places, it may have produced a Christian insurrection of the entire Balkans. When the war ended, the Duke of Wellington wanted the new state limited to the Peloponnese. As late as the Crimean war, most of Crete spoke Turkish just as most of Cyprus spoke Greek. The language had not died out, but it was revived in the late 18th century in many villages, and revived in a missionary spirit.

In all this time Greek communities of Asia Minor played an important part. Already before independence the Greeks were expanding. They were strong in southern Russia. In Egypt in the 19th century they ran the vast cotton industry and the tobacco industry until they were broken by the British. The area of Cairo called Garden City was largely built for them. It is astonishing how far the Greeks, without establishing a colony, spread in 19th-century Africa. There were once sponge-diving villages in the United States where the signposts were in Greek as well as English.

The modern history of Greece as an independent nation has been plagued by poverty until almost yesterday, by the still-unfinished story of struggles with Turkey, and by constant foreign interference. The west has played a part curiously close to Roman policy, and the Turks are not the first Asiatic power against which the Greeks have defined themselves. Physically, Athens has expanded to a terrifying size. Its distinguished modern buildings are neoclassic, in the Bavarian taste, or else the gift of rich Greeks from the provinces or from Egypt, as they might have been in the late 4th century. The arts however are in no way nostalgic, although things made for tourists are another matter.

Language: The Principal Inheritance

What there was to hold on to in the long foreign domination was the Greek language, which has survived in continuous use 4,000 years. At no time has so much of so great a merit and so permanent an interest to human beings been written in so many styles in one language as in the heyday of the Athenians. It is hard to pick on any later generation when nothing at all one would now wish to read was written in Greek.

Holy books

The only writings in Greek written under the Romans that are as valuable to us as Homeric poetry are as mixed in their origins as Shakespeare's adaptations of the neoclassic Greek Plutarch. The Gospels are also a holy book, but that is another matter. As Greek writings, on whatever traditional wisdom of this world or the next they draw, they can be considered as books among other books. They need more learned interpretation than they have ever had, but they are too important and too subtle to be left to the theologians. The hands of historians are at least more delicate. One of the winning qualities of these documents is that they translate almost perfectly into simple and moving language. Luther's German version or the English Geneva Bible of 1560 and the Authorized Version of 1611 convey clearly what the original quality is.

There is something moving about the end of the *Golden Ass* of the Latin writer Apuleius; it has a gravity and purity. But his his hunger for purity and illumination sits so oddly on the rest of his book and on its Greek origins, that only the thin shadow of the goddess Isis emerges, and we are left merely wondering

about that apparently compelling cult. The *Poimandres*, the first treatise of the *Corpus Hermeticum*, is an Egyptian mystical work written in Greek. It belongs with a library of such works now recovered that express at their best a personal, mystical religion. However, they all lack the concrete, precise quality of the Gospels; they lack the directness, the simple seriousness, the fatal climax. They are simply not as interesting.

The same and worse can be said of the Gospel of Thomas, and of the mass of apocryphal writings that continued to be produced in Greek in the Middle Ages. These are wild, undirected, sometimes absurd. Medieval Alexander romances are better written. These works represent an appalling decadence; yet the Gospels are still as powerful and as fresh and as invigorating as when they were written. They are alone.

But the witness of Paul to the quality of life in the Greek world of his day is fascinating. It is not only a matter of the great cities where he traveled, and of their interconnection, but also of the social organization of Hellenized Jews, and of the smaller Christian offshoots. Every religious group had a social basis, just as it had in Classical Greek cities. The interconnection of guild with guild and community with community was loose, but strong, and Christianity was by no means the only religion to spread in the same way. The religion of the Oriental, half-Hellenized god Mithras spread at the same time, largely through the Roman army. The victory of these universal religions was by no means immediate, although they were almost indestructible. Parts of Europe were still

pagan in the 9th and 10th centuries, and the most serious religious developments took place on the remote edges of the Hellenized world, in the Egyptian desert, in Irish and Northumbrian monasticism, and in northern Indian Buddhism.

Philosophers and poets

Until the collapse of Classical civilization, the Greeks had something intellectually serious to contribute both inside and outside Christianity. In the religious philosophy of Plato, the local basis of the Greek gods was already quite unimportant, and under the Romans the world was sufficiently visibly one place to make the victory of personal and universal religion inevitable. The greatest of all Greek religious philosophers, Plotinus, lived in the 3rd century CE. He was born in Egypt, his name was Roman, and his language Greek. He taught in Rome, visited Persia, and died in Campania. The metaphysical system he invented was complex and paradoxical, as most

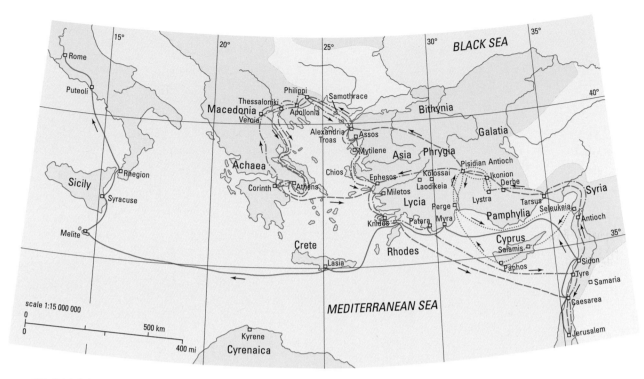

St Paul's 1st missionary journey

St Paul's 2nd missionary journey

St Paul's 3rd missionary journey

St Paul's journey to Rome

extent of the Roman empire

▲ *Between 46 and 62 CE, St Paul undertook a number of missionary journeys to Asia Minor and Europe. He spoke and wrote fluent Greek.*

metaphysical systems are, but his writings are also most moving, and utterly original in their tone. His writings were edited in the early 4th century CE by a much less original pupil, Pophyry, a Greek-speaking Syrian from Palestine who had studied in Athens.

Nor did Greek poetry cease to be written. One of the greatest of all Christian medieval poets was a Greek hymn writer, Romanos, who wrote in the 6th century CE. He was born in Syria, probably to Jewish parents. He was a deacon in Beirut until he moved to Constantinople, was famous in that city, but never held any great official position. There are dramatic and compassionate qualities in his work which go far back in Greek literary tradition, but Homer and Plato were no more than names to him. The richness and intensity of his work are of a quite new kind; they are a new force in Greek poetry.

Yet Mousaios, who wrote *Hew and Leander*, was his contemporary, and Ausonius, the last Classical poet in Latin, had already been dead for 100 years. The Greeks in fact had

emerged from Roman domination with an empire of their own, governed by Greeks in Greek, with all the wealth and flair, and all the inherited weaknesses of the age of Alexander's successors. As a political unity the Byzantine empire was ungovernable, but as a social reality it survived and revived many times, simply because the Greeks refused to give up their identity, either as Christians or as Greeks.

Modern writers

In 1453, when the last old Greek historian rode around the walls of Constantinople with the last emperor a few hours before the city fell to the Turks, and in full consciousness of that inevitable event, he thought of the whole weight of Greece and of Rome as too heavy a burden for one man's shoulders.

This historian was George Phrantzes; he wrote in old age, as a monk in Corfu, where sculpture of the 6th century BCE lay in the fields. We know that on the night on which the city fell Cyriaco of Ancona was reading from Livy to the sultan in his tent below the walls. But it was not of course the whole of Greece and Rome that fell on one night. Greek in verse and in prose persisted. The *Erotokritos*, the Cretan national poem, was written around the turn of the 16th and 17th centuries. It shows heavy Venetian influence, but in its verse, in its dialect and spirit, is purely Cretan Greek. Until the present generation, Cretan shepherds knew it by heart and sang it in the mountains. In prose, at the end of the reign of Henry VIII of England, a refugee from Corfu, who was known as Nicander Nucius and fought in a Greek regiment for Henry against the Scots, wrote an account of Britain, Ireland and much of Europe which does not disgrace its lineage among Greek histories. It records a speech before battle in some dynastic war, by a Greek to Greeks fighting in France, that would not have displeased Thucydides.

Not unnaturally, the best written Greek under the Turks was composed in a popular, direct style, a salted and expressive peasant language. The memoirs of Makriyannis are the supreme example of how impressive a peasant language can be; his writings are the first immense achievement of independent Greece. The naive but fresh and very talented paintings of Theophilos of Mytilene in Lesbos, who was still at work in this century, belong spiritually to the same world. But not all Greeks were peasants; an official, classicizing language had survived at Constantinople and through the Church. Its stranglehold on the official life of the country and on its refined literature has only recently been broken. It was a stiff officialese, but in its more sinuous and subtle spoken form it had its triumphs. In prose it was capable of ironies, and the anonymous, humorous 19th-century memoirs of an Asian Greek called

The Military Life could not have been written as effectively in any other style.

In verse, this style is an element in the startling originality of Constantine Kavafis (1863–1933), the Alexandrian poet. His family came from Constantinople and it had been rich, but Kavafis worked as a clerk in the irrigation department of the British administration in Egypt. His poetry is often a commentary on stories taken from the late Classical history of the Greeks. He was widely read, homosexual, passionate, and politically very bitter. Among his favorite writings were Oscar Wilde's book on socialism and Gibbon's *Decline and Fall*. As a writer and as a personality he was Greek to the bone; he was also utterly modern. The texture of his language may be untranslatable. His rhythms are impossible to imitate and his bite is hard to forget.

But the greatest of modern Greek writers is certainly George Seferis (1900–71), one of the most powerful and most moving and also one of the wisest poets of the 20th century, who ranks with Pasternak. He was born in Smyrna, and came to Athens as a refugee at the time of the Turkish destruction of Greek Asia. His education and reading were immensely wide even for a professional diplomat who was also a great poet. His understanding of the modern Greek language in all its behavior and history was deeper than anyone else's has ever been, but his writing embodied that understanding in ways that are not obvious; it can be sensed only in a complete rightness, an inevitability of words and phrases. In his writings the modern Greek language came of age. It is as strong as it ever was, as capable of discussing anything whatever, as it was in the time of Aristophanes, as fine in its texture, as modern.

Glossary

Academy A training ground for naked exercise outside Athens, a pleasant place with grass, trees and decorative and sacred buildings. It was made famous by Sokrates and above all by Plato, whose school of philosophy was centered there. The site has been identified, but is now built over.

Achaemenid empire The classical Persian empire.

agora The central area of a city or small town, usually a square or rectangle, with colonnades, and public and sacred buildings. Under the Romans one side was a vast official "basilica" and the rest colonnades. Hence monastic cloisters, college quadrangles, the squares of provincial towns.

akroterion Terracotta or marble ornament on the pinnacle or the edge of the roof of a building.

amphora Two-handled ("two-eared") pot for transporting oil, wine etc. Usually long, often with a sharp end, ideal for tying on a mule's or donkey's back, and easy to handle. The same word is used for smaller, finer vessels of similar shape.

beehive tomb Like a dome or bubble of stone with an alley or approach and great door, in which the rich or noble Bronze Age dead were buried. Sometimes enormous, perfectly proportioned, strangely echoing.

black-figure Pottery with black figures on a tan ground.

caryatid Column to support a porch or a colonnade, in the form of a free-standing woman bearing it on her head.

cavea The semicircle of stone benches rising in tiers in which the audience of an ancient theater sat in the open air.

celia The inner room of a temple where the principal statue stood.

centaur Creature with a human head and arms and upper body and the four legs and lower body of a horse.

city-state A sovereign state with a unified government based on one single town or city, and controlling its surrounding territories, great or small. Such a city or state might be artificially created (Megalopolis in Arcadia or Messene in Messenia) and its territory might

be enormous (Attica or Laconia) or small (Plataiai in Greece or Megara Flyblaia in Sicily).

Corinthian column Its capital is carved with an elaborate cluster of stone foliage (Hellenistic). The column is fluted.

Cynics Philosophic deriders of worldly values who cultivated rough dress and poverty. The Christians adopted their arguments against the gods and some of their moral and social attitudes.

deme A community, a village, or small town in Attica, was called a deme. *Demos* means people with a capital *P*. The local communities retained a basic political and social importance well into the 5th century.

Dioskouroi The twin brothers Kastor the athlete and Polydeukes the boxer (the Roman Pollux). Their parentage was half-human, half-divine. They were worshiped particularly in Sparta and its African colonies. The name means the youths who are sons of Zeus.

Doric column The plainest of plain capitals, and a simple column.

Eleusinian mysteries A symbolic or sacramental initiation that brought the Athenians, and all Greeks if they underwent it, into a special relation with the gods, and which offered mysterious happiness in the afterlife. The physical fact at the center of the mysteries was the growth of wheat. Eleusis was a sanctuary of the earth mother as corn goddess. It had a cave which led to the Underworld.

Epicureans The followers of Epicurus, cultivating a philosophy of pleasure, withdrawal from the world, friendship, and privacy. By limiting fear, hope, and desire a man attains to peace. Christianity owes something to this philosophy.

frieze A long band of relief sculpture decorating the upper stonework of a temple.

geometric A style of decoration with repeated geometric motifs, flourishing in Greece in the 8th century BCE and earlier. Horse, bird, and man, scenes of burial, processions, and battles and shipwrecks were introduced little by little in the centuries of this style, but purely geometric art at its best was almost more impressive. We treat it as a style of decorated pottery,

but it was used also for wall-painting and for textiles.

Gorgon A grotesque female figure with snake hair, so horrid that the sight of her might turn a man to stone. Most representations of her are rather jollier than this legend suggests.

Hellespont The narrow sea channel that divides Europe from Asia Minor at the northeast corner of the Mediterranean. Both Troy and Byzantion owed their importance to their situation here at the entrance to the Black Sea.

hems A tall block of stone with the head of a god and an erect sexual organ as its only features.

hydria Water-pot.

Indo-European This word was used in the 19th century of an original common language from which Indian and European languages were descended; then of the people who must have spoken it, and of their "folkwanderings." Some enthusiastic racialists believed that the Germans and the Afghan Pathans were its purest descendants. Today we are still forced to speak of an Indo-European family of languages, but the historical foundation for their development and separation remains obscure.

Ionic column Elegantly designed column of east Greek origin with capital like a pair of formalized ram's horns.

Isthmus The neck of land that joins southern Greece to the mass of Europe, cut today by the Corinth canal.

kalyx–krater A mixing bowl shaped like a deep cup.

koine The simplified Greek speech, without literary ambition or special dialect, spoken and written all over the ancient world in which Greek became a universal language.

kore The female equivalent of a kouros.

kouros A youth; a male nude statue of a youth, of a formal archaic shape which developed in Greece from the 7th century BCE to the 5th. It may represent a god, an athlete, a dead man, or it may be simply an offering to a god.

krater A mixing bowl for wine and water, sometimes fitted with a strainer.

Lapith Member of a mythical tribe of persons, superhuman only by being legendary. They fought a famous fight with the centaurs, who became drunken and lecherous at a Lapith wedding.

lekythos A small Athenian oil-pot used by athletes.

Levant The eastern end of the Mediterranean, where the sun rises; the coast from Byzantion (Istanbul) to Jaffa.

Linear A The earlier of the two Bronze Age Greek scripts, not yet decoded but in some ways similar to Linear B.

Linear B The script of the Mycenaeans in the Bronze Age. It has been decoded and can be read as an early form of the Greek language. The script is not alphabetical but syllabic: that is, each sign denotes not a single sound but a syllable.

metope A single slab of relief sculpture. Used in a series, separated from each other by plainer slabs with a design of vertical lines, around a temple just below its roof.

odeion A concert hall like a covered theater. It always has a roof.

omphalos The navel of the earth, the center of the world, marked by a stone shaped like a Christmas pudding, decorated by a network of woolen ribbons. It was at Delphi.

orchestra The dancing area or the chorus between the stage and the audience in an ancient theater.

Orientalizing The style of Greek art in the early archaic period that adopted innumerable decorative and animal motifs from the east.

ostracism An Athenian system for taking the heat out of politics by a vote of the people whether an exile should take place, and if so, then a second vote of the people to decide who should be exiled.

palaestra An open-air courtyard, surrounded by a colonnade, used as a wrestling school.

palmette A flat, formalized sprouting plant or bud in the shape of a heart upside down.

Panathenaic festival A state festival of Athene celebrated at Athens, publicly and lavishly celebrated with a procession, games and prizes, and a huge animal sacrifice with the distribution of the meat to the citizens.

paraskenia The side wings of the stone embellishments of the stage in a theater.

parodos Actors' entrance in an ancient theater used by the chorus.

peristyle The screen of pillars surrounding a temple, forming colonnades along its sides.

red-figure Pottery with tan figures on a black ground.

satrap The local ruler of a province of the classical Persian empire.

satyr Half-human, half-animal figure with divine powers, from the wilderness at the edges of the world. Satyrs had snub-noses, pricked ears, strong instincts, tails, a pair of legs, and nearly perpetual erections.

Seleucid empire The empire in Asia of the family of Seleukos, one of the generals of Alexander the Great and his principal successor in the east.

shaft grave A burial place in a deep narrow pit, used in the early Bronze Age. At Mycenae there was a circle of these graves, marked probably by stone markers.

silk road The overland route to China from the west, following roughly what are now the southern borders of the Soviet Union.

sophists The teachers of persuasive oratory and of paradoxical philosophy who shocked and excited the Athenians during the last 40 years of the 5th century BCE and in the 4th.

stoa A colonnade for any civil or commercial purpose, usually with rooms behind it, sometimes with two stories.

Stoics Philosophers of the stiff upper lip and the paradoxical extremes of virtuous atheism. Their logic and their moral arguments are of inspiring interest, but they were irritating people, as Horace makes clear.

temenos The enclosure of a sanctuary, the holy ground belonging to the god and governed by special rules.

Further Reading

Part One: The Land in Context

Albersmeier, Sabine, et al. *Heroes: Mortals and Myths in Ancient Greece.* Baltimore: Walters Art Museum, 2009.

Amemiya, Takeshi. *Economy and Economics of Ancient Greece.* New York: Routledge, 2007.

Barringer, Judith M. *Art, Myth, and Ritual in Classical Greece.* Cambridge: Cambridge University Press, 2008.

Calame, Claude. *Greek Mythology: Poetics, Pragmatics, and Fiction.* New York: Cambridge University Press, 2009

Connelly, Joan Breton. *Portrait of a Priestess: Women and Ritual in Ancient Greece.* Princeton: Princeton University Press, 2007.

Csapo, Eric, and Margaret C. Miller (eds). *The Origins of Theater in Ancient Greece and Beyond: From Ritual to Drama.* Cambridge: Cambridge University Press, 2007.

Cyrino, Monica Silveira. *A Journey Through Greek Mythology.* Dubuque, Iowa: Kendall/Hunt Pub. Co., 2008.

Errington, R. M. *A History of the Hellenistic World.* Malden, MA: Blackwell Pub. Ltd, 2008.

Gunter, Ann C. *Greek Art and the Orient.* Cambridge: Cambridge University Press, 2009.

Hard, Robin (translator). *The Library of Greek Mythology.* Oxford: Oxford University Press, 2008.

Johnston, Sarah Iles. *Ancient Greek Divination.* Oxford: Wiley-Blackwell Pub., 2008.

Neils, Jennifer. *The British Museum Concise Introduction to Ancient Greece.* Ann Arbor: University of Michigan Press, 2008.

Ostwald, Martin. *Language and History in Ancient Greek Culture.* Philadelphia: University of Pennsylvania Press, 2008.

Pomeroy, Sarah B. et al. *A Brief History of Ancient Greece: Politics, Society, and Culture.* New York: Oxford University Press, 2009.

Pritchett, W. Kendrick. *Ancient Greek Battle Speeches and a Palfrey.* Amsterdam: J.C. Gieben, 2002.

Sansone, David. *Ancient Greek Civilization.* Malden, MA: Wiley-Blackwell, 2009.

Tanner, Jeremy. *The Invention of Art History in Ancient Greece: Religion, Society and Artistic Rationalisation.* Cambridge: Cambridge University Press, 2006

Van Nortwick, Thomas. *Imagining Men: Ideals of Masculinity in Ancient Greek Culture.* Westport, CT: Praeger, 2008.

Warner, Rex. *Men and Gods: Myths and Legends of the Ancient Greeks.* New York: New York Review Books, 2008.

Part Two: The Age of Bronze

Alexander, Caroline. *The War that Killed Achilles: The True Story of Homer's Iliad.* New York: Viking, 2009.

Campbell-Dunn, G. J. K. *Who Were the Minoans?: An African Answer.* Christchurch, N.Z.: Penny Farthing Press, 2006.

Castleden, Rodney. *Mycenaeans.* New York, NY: Routledge, 2005.

Cromarty, Robert James. *Burning Bulls, Broken Bones: Sacrificial Ritual in Context of Palace Period Minoan Religion.* Oxford, England: Archaeopress, 2008.

Druitt, Tobias. *Corydon and the Siege of Troy.* New York: Alfred A. Knopf, 2009.

Due, Casey, *Recapturing a Homeric Legacy: Images and Insights from the Venetus, A Manuscript of the Iliad.* Washington, D.C.: Center for Hellenic Studies, 2009.

Euripides. *The Trojan Women.* Oxford: Oxford University Press, 2009.

Gemmell, David. *Troy: Fall of Kings.* New York: Ballantine Books, 2007.

Gesell, Geraldine Cornelia. *Town, Palace, and House Cult in Minoan Crete.* Göthenborg: P. Åströms Förlag, 1985.

Hall, Edith. *The Return of Ulysses: A Cultural History of Homer's Odyssey.* Baltimore: Johns Hopkins University Press, 2008.

Homer. *Homer's Odyssey.* Oxford: Oxford University Press, 2009.

Homer. *Homer's The Iliad.* New York: Chelsea House, 2007.

Johnsen, Linda. *Lost Masters: Sages of Ancient Greece.* Honesdale, PA: Himalayan Institute Press, 2006.

Louden, Bruce. *The Iliad: Structure, Myth, and Meaning.* Baltimore: Johns Hopkins University Press, 2006.

Marinatos, Nanno. *Minoan Kingship and the Solar Goddess: A Near Eastern Koine.* Urbana, IL: University of Illinois Press, 2009.

Moss, Marina L. *The Minoan Pantheon: Towards an Understanding of its Nature and Extent.* Oxford: John and Erica Hedges Ltd, 2005.

Osborne, Robin. *Greece in the Making, 1200-469 B.C..* New York,: Routledge, 2009.

Robbins, Michael W., *Bronze, Brains & Blood: The Battles, Weapons, Conquerors, Strategies & Heroes in Ancient Greece*

and Rome that Gave Us Civilization. Leesburg, VA: Weider History Group, 2008.

Schliemann, Heinrich. *Troy and its Remains: A Narrative of Researches and Discoveries Made on the Site of Ilium and in the Trojan Plain.* San Francisco, CA: Symbolon Press, 2009.

Schofield, Louise. *The Mycenaeans.* Los Angeles: J. Paul Getty Museum, 2007.

Shelmerdine, Cynthia (ed). *The Cambridge Companion to the Aegean Bronze Age.* Cambridge: Cambridge University Press, 2008.

Part Three: The Age of Tyranny

Abrams, Dennis. *Xerxes.* New York: Chelsea House Publishers, 2008.

Alston, Richard, and Onno M. van Nijf (eds). *Feeding the Ancient Greek City.* Dudley MA: Peeters Publishers, 2008.

Green, Peter. *The Greco-Persian Wars.* Berkeley: University of California Press, 1996.

Herodotus. *The History: An Account of the Persian War on Greece, including the Naval Battle at Salamis, the Battle with Athens at Marathon, and with Sparta at Thermopylae.* St. Petersburg, FL: Red and Black Publishers, 2009.

Kennell, Nigel M. *Spartans: A New History.* Malden, MA: Wiley-Blackwell, 2010.

Larson, Jennifer. *Ancient Greek Cults: A Guide.* New York: Routledge, 2007.

Lewis, Sian. *Ancient Tyranny.* Edinburgh: Edinburgh University Press, 2006

Mikalson, Jon D. *Ancient Greek Religion.* Malden, MA: Blackwell Pub., 2005.

Ogden, Daniel. *A Companion to Greek Religion.* Malden, MA: Blackwell Pub., 2007.

Shapiro, H. A. *Art and Cult Under the Tyrants in Athens.* Mainz am Rhein: P. von Zabern, 1989.

Shapiro, H. Alan. *Cambridge Companion to Archaic Greece.* Cambridge: Cambridge University Press, 2007.

Sweeney, Emmet John. *Gods, Heroes, and Tyrants: Greek Chronology in Chaos.* New York: Algora Pub., 2009.

Part Four: The Age of Perikles

Coulson, W. D. E. (ed). *The Archaeology of Athens and Attica under the Democracy: (*Proceedings of an International Conference Celebrating 2,500 Years Since the Birth of Democracy in Greece, held at the American School of Classical Studies at

Athens, December 4–6, 1992.) Oxford: Oxbow Books, 1994.

Davies, John Kenyon. *Democracy and Classical Greece.* Cambridge, MA: Harvard University Press, 1993.

Dynneson, Thomas L. *City-State Civism in Ancient Athens: Its Real and Ideal Expressions.* New York: Peter Lang, 2008.

Law, Polly. *The Athenian Empire.* Edinburgh: Edinburgh University Press, 2008.

Morris, Ian (ed). *Classical Greece: Ancient Histories and Modern Archaeologies.* Cambridge: Cambridge University Press, 1994.

Raaflaub, Kurt A. *Origins of Democracy in Ancient Greece.* Berkeley: University of California Press, 2007.

Stewart, Andrew F. *Classical Greece and the Birth of Western Art.* Cambridge: Cambridge University Press, 2008.

Taylor, Martha C. *Thucydides, Pericles, and the Idea of Athens in the Peloponnesian War.* Cambridge: Cambridge University Press, 2009.

Thucydides. *History of the Peloponnesian War.* New York: Barnes & Noble Classics, 2006.

Tracy, Stephen V. *Pericles: A Sourcebook and Reader.* Berkeley: University of California Press, 2009

Worman, Nancy Baker. *Abusive Mouths in Classical Athens.* Cambridge: Cambridge University Press, 2008.

Part Five: The Age of Alexander

Borza, Eugene N. *In the Shadow of Olympus: The Emergence of Macedon.* Princeton, N.J. : Princeton University Press, 1992.

Hammond, N.G.L. *Philip of Macedon.* Baltimore: Johns Hopkins University Press, 1994.

Heckel, Waldemar, and Lawrence A. Tritle (eds). *Alexander the Great: A New History.* Malden, MA: Wiley-Blackwell, 2009.

Sheppard, Ruth. *Alexander the Great at War: His Army, his Battles, his Enemies.* Oxford: Osprey, 2008.

Skelton, Debra. *Empire of Alexander the Great.* New York: Chelsea House, 2009.

Smith, Sir William. *A Smaller History of Greece from the Earliest Times to The Roman Conquest.* New York: Cosimo Classics, 2005.

Stoneman, Richard. *Alexander the Great: A Life in Legend.* New Haven, CT: Yale University Press, 2008.

The Hellenistic World from Alexander to the Roman Conquest: A Selection of Ancient Sources in Translation. Cambridge: Cambridge University Press, 2006.

Part Six: The Fate of Hellenism

Andricopoulos, Yannis. *The Greek Inheritance: Ancient Greek Wisdom for the Digital Era.* Charlottesville, VA: Imprint Academic, 2008.

Aske, Martin. *Keats and Hellenism: An Essay.* Cambridge: Cambridge University Press, 2004.

Bagnall, Roger, and Peter Derow. *The Hellenistic Period: Historical Sources in Translation.* Oxford: Blackwell, 2004.

Bingen, Jean. *Hellenistic Egypt: Monarchy, Society, Economy, Culture.* Berkeley: University of California Press, 2007.

Cotton, Hannah M. *From Hellenism to Islam: Cultural and Linguistic Change in the Roman Near East.* Cambridge: Cambridge University Press, 2009.

Kaldellis, Anthony. *Hellenism in Byzantium: The Transformations of Greek Identity and the Reception of the Classical Tradition.* Cambridge: Cambridge University Press, 2007.

Littlewood, Antony Robert. *Byzantium: The Guardian of Hellenism.* Montréal: 3Dmt Research and Information Centre of Concordia University, 2004.

Ma Asgeirsson, Jon, and Nancy Van Deusen (eds). *Alexander's Revenge: Hellenistic Culture through the Centuries.* Reykjavik: University of Iceland Press, 2002.

Makrides, Vasilios. *Hellenic Temples and Christian Churches: A Concise History of the Religious Cultures of Greece from Antiquity to the Present.* New York: New York University Press, 2009.

Manning, Joseph Gilbert. *The Last Pharaohs: Egypt Under the Ptolemies, 305–30 BC.* Princeton: Princeton University Press, 2009.

Mueller, Katja. *Settlements of the Ptolemies: City Foundations and New Settlement in the Hellenistic World.* Dudley, MA: Peeters, 2006.

Rapatzikou, Tatiani G. *Anglo-American perceptions of Hellenism.* Newcastle, UK: Cambridge Scholars Pub., 2007.

Schork, R. J. *Greek and Hellenic Culture in Joyce.* Gainesville: University Press of Florida, 1998.

Original Bibliography

The bibliography compiled for the original edition of this book remains a valuable summary of Greek scholarship in the 20th century.

Part One: The Land in Context

A. Andrewes, *The Greeks*. London 1967.

J. B. Bury and R. Meiggs, *History of Greece to the Death of Alexander the Great*. 4th ed. London 1975.

Cambridge Ancient History. 3rd ed. Cambridge 1970.

J. K. Campbell, *Honour, Family and Patronage*. Oxford 1964.

M. Cary, *The Geographic Background of Greek and Roman History*. Oxford 1949.

E. Dodwell, *Cyclopean or Pelasgic Remains*. London 1834.

J. du Boulay, *Portrait of a Greek Mountain Village*. Oxford 1974.

N.G.L. Hammond, *History of Greece to 322 BC*. 2nd ed. Oxford 1967.

S.C. Humphreys, *Anthropology and the Greeks. London 1978.*

W.M. Leake, *Travels in the Morea. 3 vols.* London 1830.

——*Travels in Northern Greece*. 4 vols. London 1835.

A.D. Momigliano, *Alien Wisdom*. Cambridge 1975.

Oxford Classical Dictionary. 2nd ed. Oxford 1970.

Pitton de Tournefort, *Relation d'un voyage du Levant*. Lyon 1717.

H.J. Rose, *A Handbook of Greek Mythology*. 6th ed. London 1958.

R. Stillwell, W. L. MacDonald, and M. A. McAllister, *The Princeton Encyclopedia of Classical Sites*. Princeton, N.J. 1976.

J. Stuart and N. Revett, *The Antiquities of Athens. 4 vols.* London 1762-1816.

Part Two: The Age of Bronze

C.W. Blegen, *Troy and the Trojans*. London 1963.

K. Branigan, *The Foundations of Palatial Crete*. London 1970.

H.-G. Buchholz and V. Karageorghis, *Prehistoric Greece and Cyprus*. London 1973.

J. Chadwick, *The Decipherment of Linear B*. 2nd ed. Cambridge 1968.

——*The Mycenaean World*. Cambridge 1976.

V.R. d'A. Desborough, *The Last Mycenaeans and their Successors*. Oxford 1964.

——*The Greek Dark Ages*. London 1972.

Sir Arthur Evans, *The Palace of Minas at Knossos*. Vols. 1–4. Repr. New York 1963.

M. I. Finley, *The World of Odysseus*. 2nd ed. Harmondsworth 1962.

A. Furumark, *The Mycenaean Pottery. Analysis and Classification*. Repr. Stockholm 1972.

——*The Chronology of Mycenaean Pottery*. Repr. Stockholm 1972.

J. W. Graham, *The Palaces of Crete*. Princeton, N.J. Repr. 1969.

R. Higgins, *Minoan and Mycenaean Art*. London and New York 1967.

M. S. F. Hood, *The Home of the Heroes. The Aegean before the Greeks*. London 1967.

——*The Minoans*. London 1971.

R. W. Hutchinson, *Prehistoric Crete*. Harmondsworth Repr. 1968.

G. S. Kirk, *Homer and the Epic*. Cambridge 1965.

——*Myth, its Meaning and Function*. Cambridge 1970.

A. D. Lacy, *Greek Pottery in the Bronze Age*. London 1967.

J. V. Luce, *The End of Atlantis*. London 1969.

S. Marinatos and M. Hirmer, *Crete and Mycenae*. London 1960.

F. Matz, *Crete and Early Greece*. London 1962.

O. Murray, *Early Greece and the Near East*. London 1980.

G. Mylonas, *Ancient Mycenae*. London 1957.

——*Mycenae and the Mycenaean Age*. Princeton, N.J. 1966.

M.P. Nilsson, *The Minoan-Mycenaean Religion and its Survival in Greek Religion*. 2nd ed. Lund 1950.

D.L. Page, *The Homeric Odyssey*. Oxford 1955.

——*History and the Homeric Iliad*. Berkeley, Ca. 1959.

J.D.S. Pendlebury, *The Archaeology of Crete*. Repr. New York 1965.

C. Renfrew, *The Emergence of Civilization. The Cyclades and the Aegean in the Third Millennium BC*. London 1972.

A.E. Samuel, The *Mycenaeans in History*. Englewood Cliffs, NJ. 1966.

N.K. Sandars. *The Sea Peoples*. London 1978.

K. Schefold, *Myth and Legend in Early Greek Art*. London 1966.

H. Schliemann, *Mycenae*. London 1878.

——*Ilios*. London 1880.

A. M. Snodgrass, *Archaeology and the Rise of the Greek State*. Cambridge 1977.

——The *Dark Age of Greece*. Edinburgh 1971.

F. H. Stubbings, *Mycenaean Pottery from the Levant*. Cambridge 1951.

——*Prehistoric Greece*. London 1972.

Lord William Taylour, *Mycenaean Pottery in Italy and Adjacent Areas*. Cambridge 1958.

——*The Mycenaeans*. London 1964.

G. Thomson, *The Prehistoric Aegean*. London 1978.

M. Ventris and J. Chadwick, *Documents in Mycenaean Greek*. 2nd ed. by J. Chadwick. Cambridge 1973.

E. Vermeule, *Greece in the Bronze Age*. 5th impression. Chicago, Ill., and London 1972.

A.J.B. Wace, *Mycenae. An Archaeological History and Guide*. Princeton, N.J. 1949.

——and F. H. Stubbings (eds.). *A Companion to Homer*. London 1962.

P. Warren, *The Aegean Civilizations*. Oxford 1975.

C. Zervos, *L'Art de la Crete neolithique et minoenne*. Paris 1956.

——*L'Art des Cyclades*. Paris 1957.

——*La Naissance de la civilisation en Grèce*. Vols 1–2. Paris 1962.

Part Three: The Age of Tyranny

A. Andrewes, *Greek Tyrants*. London 1956.

J. Boardman, *The Greeks Overseas*. 3rd ed. London 1980.

——*Preclassical*. Harmondsworth 1967.

——*Athenian Black Figure Vases*. London 1974.

——*Athenian Red Figure Vases of the Archaic Period*. London 1975.

——*Greek Sculpture: the Archaic Period*. London 1978.

R.J. Bonner, *Aspects of Athenian Democracy*. Berkeley, Ca. 1933.

C.M. Bowra, *Greek Lyric Poetry*. 2nd ed. Oxford 1961.

——*Pindar*. Oxford 1964.

A.R. Burn, *Lyric Age of Greece*. London 1960.

——*Persia and the Greeks*. London 1962.

P. Cartledge, *Sparta and Lakonia*. London 1979.

M. and V. Charbonneaux, *Archaic Greek Art*. London and New York 1971.

J.N. Coldstream, *Greek Geometric Pottery*. London 1968.

——*Geometric Greece*. London 1977.

J.K. Davies, *Athenian Propertied Families*. Oxford 1971.

V.R. d'A. Desborough, *The Greek Dark Ages*. London 1972.

T.J. Dunbabin, *The Western Greeks*. Oxford 1948.

V. Ehrenberg, *From Solon to Socrates*. 2nd ed. London 1973.

B. Farrington, *Greek Science*. 2nd ed. Harmondsworth 1969.

M. I. Finley, *Ancient Sicily*. London 1968.

W. G. Forrest, *The Emergence of Greek Democracy*. London 1966.

—*A History of Sparta, 950–192 BC*. London 1968.

H. Fränkel, *Early Greek Poetry and Philosophy*. Oxford 1975.

E.N. Gardiner, *Athletics of the Ancient World*. Oxford 1930.

A.J. Graham, *Colony and Mother City in Ancient Greece*. Manchester 1964.

D. Harden, *The Phoenicians*. Harmondsworth 1971.

H.A. Harris, *Greek Athletes and Athletics*. London 1964.

—*Sport in Greece and Rome*. London 1972.

A.R.W. Harrison, *The Law of Athens:* vol. 1 *The Family and Property*. Oxford 1968; vol. 2 *Procedure*. 1971.

C. and S. Hawkes (eds.), *Greeks, Celts and Romans*. London 1973.

C. Hignett, *Xerxes' Invasion of Greece*. Oxford 1963.

E. Homann-Wedeking, *Archaic Greece*. London 1968.

E. Hussey. *The Presocratics*. London 1972.

G.L. Huxley, *The Early Ionians*. London 1966.

L.H. Jeffrey, *Archaic Greece*. London 1976.

G.K. Jenkins, *Ancient Greek Coins*. London 1972.

A. Johnston, *The Emergence of Greece*. Oxford 1976.

G.S. Kirk and J. E. Raven, *The Presocratic Philosophers*. Cambridge 1957.

C.M. Kraay. *Archaic and Classical Greek Coins*. London 1976.

—and M. Hirmer, *Greek Coins*. London 1966.

E. Langlotz and M. Hirmer, *The Art of Magna Graecia*. London 1965.

A. Lesky, *History of Greek Literature*. London 1966.

P. Maas, *Greek Metre*, trans H. Lloyd-Jones. Oxford 1962.

S. Moscati, *The World of the Phoenicians*. London 1968.

M. P. Nilsson, *A History of Greek Religion*. 2nd ed. Oxford 1949.

—*Greek Popular Religion*. New York 1940.

—*Greek Piety*. Oxford 1948.

H.W. Parke, *Greek Oracles*. London 1967.

S. Piggott. *Ancient Europe*. Edinburgh 1973.

M.J. Price and N. Waggoner, *Archaic Greek Coinage*. London 1976.

D.S. Raven, *Green Metre*. London 1969.

E. Rawson. *The Spartan Tradition in European Thought*. Oxford 1969.

P.J. Rhodes. *The Athenian Boule*. Oxford 1972.

G.M.A. Richter *Korai: Archaic Greek Maidens*. London 1968.

—*Kouroi: Archaic Greek Youths*. 3rd ed. London 1970.

S. Sambursky, *The Physical World of the Greeks*. London 1956.

B. Schweitzer, *Greek Geometric Art*. London and New York 1971.

E. Vanderpool, *Ostracism at Athens*. Cincinnati, Ohio 1970.

M. L. West, *Early Greek Philosophy and the Orient*. Oxford 1971.

A.G. Woodhead, *The Greeks in the West*. London 1962.

Part Four: The Age of Perikles

P.E. Arias and M. Hirmer, *A History of Greek Vase Painting*. London 1962.

B. Ashmole, *Architect and Sculptor in Classical Greece*. London 1972.

J.D. Beazley, *Potter and Painter in Ancient Athens*. Oxford 1946.

H. Berve, G. Gruben and M. Hirmer, *Greek Temples, Theatres and Shrines*. London 1963.

M. Bieber, *The History of the Greek and Roman Theater*. 2nd ed. Princeton, N.J. 1961.

C. Blümel, *Greek Sculptors at Work*. 2nd ed. London 1969.

J. Boardman, *Greek Art*. Revised ed. London 1973.

— *Greek Gems and Finger Rings*. London 1971.

R.S. Buck, *Plato's Phaedo*. London 1955.

R. Carpenter, *The Architects of the Parthenon*. Harmondsworth 1970.

M. Cary and E.H. Warmington. *The Ancient Explorers*. London revised ed. 1963.

L. Casson, *Ships and Seamanship in the Ancient World*. Princeton, N.J. 1971.

—*Travel in the Ancient World*. London 1974.

W.R. Connor, *The New Politicians of Fifth Century Athens*. Princeton, N.J. 1971.

R.M. Cook. *Greek Art. Its Development, Character and Influence*. London 1972.

F.M. Cornford, *Before and after Socrates*. Cambridge 1932.

J.J. Coulton, *Greek Architects at Work*. London 1977.

J.K. Davies, *Democracy and Classical Greece*. London 1978.

J. de Romilly, *Thucydides and Athenian Imperialism*. Oxford 1963.

G.B.M. de Ste. Croix, *The Origins of the Peloponnesian War*. London 1972.

W.B. Dinsmoor, *The Architecture of Ancient Greece*. 3rd ed. London and New York 1950.

E.R. Dodds, *The Ancient Concept of Progress*. Oxford 1973.

K.J. Dover, *Aristophanic Comedy*. London 1972.

—*Greek Popular Morality*. Berkeley, Ca. 1974.

—*Greek Homosexuality*. London 1978.

V. Ehrenberg, *Sophocles and Pericles*. Oxford 1954.

J. Ellis Jones et al., *An Attic Country House*. London 1974.

J.H. Finley, *Thucydides*. Cambridge, Mass. 1976.

M.I. Finley (ed.), *Slavery in Classical Antiquity*. Cambridge 1960.

R. Flacelie're, *Daily Life in Greece at the Time of Pericles*. London 1965.

R. J. Forbes, *Studies in Ancient Technology*. 9 vols. 2nd ed. Leiden 1964–72.

C. W. Fornara, *Herodotus*. Oxford 1971.

A. French, *The Growth of the Athenian Economy*. London 1964.

G. Glotz, *Ancient Greece at Work*. London 1926.

W.C.K. Guthrie, *History of Greek Philosophy*. 5 vols. Cambridge 1962–78.

I. Henderson, "Ancient Greek Music" in *The New Oxford History of Music*, vol. 1: *Ancient and Oriental Music*. Oxford 1957.

R.J. Hopper. *The Acropolis*. London 1971.

—*Trade and Industry in Classical Greece*. London 1979.

J. Jones. *On Aristotle and Greek Tragedy*. London 1962.

D. Kurtz, *Athenian White Lekythoi*. Oxford 1975.

—and J. Boardman, *Greek Burial Customs*. London 1971.

W. K. Lacey, *The Family in Classical Greece*. London 1968.

M.L.W. Laistner, *A History of the Greek World from 479 to 323 BC*. 3rd ed. London 1957; paperback ed. 1970.

A.W. Lawrence, *Greek and Roman Sculpture*. London 1972.

—*Greek Architecture*. 3rd ed. Harmondsworth 1973.

A. Lesky, *Greek Tragedy*. London 1965.

R. J. Ling. *The Greek World*. Oxford 1976.

K. Lullies and M. Hirmer, *Greek Sculpture*. Revised ed. London 1960.

H.-I. Marrou, *A History of Education in Antiquity*. London 1956.

R. Meiggs, *The Athenian Empire*. Oxford 1972.

—and D. M. Lewis, *Selection of Greek Historical Inscriptions*. Oxford 1969.

H. Michell, *The Economics of Ancient Greece*. Revised ed. Cambridge 1957.

N. R. Murphy, *The Interpretation of Plato's Republic*. Oxford 1951.

H. W. Parke, *Festivals of the Athenians*. London 1977.

—*Greek Mercenary Soldiers*. Oxford 1933. Repr. 1970.

A.W. Pickard-Cambridge. *The Dramatic Festivals of Athens*. 2nd ed. Oxford 1968.

J. E. Raven. *Plato's Thought in the Making*. Cambridge 1965.

G. M. A. Richter, *The Sculpture and Sculptors of the Greeks*. 4th ed. New Haven, Conn. 1970.

——*Handbook of Greek Art*. 7th ed. London and New York 1974.

——*Portraits of the Greeks*. London 1966.

D. S. Robertson, *Greek and Roman Architecture*. 2nd ed. Cambridge 1943. Paperback ed. 1969.

M. Robertson, *History of Greek Art*. Cambridge 1976.

D. Ross, *Plato's Theory of Ideas*. Oxford 1951.

A. M. Snodgrass, *Arms and Armour of the Greeks*. London 1967.

B.S. Staveley, *Greek and Roman Voting and Elections*. London 1972.

D.E. Strong, *The Classical World*. London 1965.

A.E. Taylor, *Plato*. London 1926.

J. Travlos, *Pictorial Dictionary of Ancient Athens*. London 1971.

A.D. Trendall and T.B.L. Webster, *Illustrations of Greek Drama*. London 1971.

B. Vickers, *Towards Greek Tragedy*. London 1974.

J. Vogt, *Ancient Slavery and the Ideal of Man*. Oxford 1974.

A.J.A. Waldock, *Sophocles the Dramatist*. Cambridge 1966.

T.B.L. Webster, *Athenian Culture and Society*. London 1973.

F. E. Winter, *Greek Fortifications*. London 1971.

A.G. Woodhead, *The Study of Greek Inscriptions*. Cambridge 1959.

R. F. Wycherley, *How the Greeks Built Cities*. 2nd ed. London 1962.

A. F. Zimmern, *The Greek Commonwealth*. 5th ed. Oxford 1947. Paperback ed. 1961.

Part Five: The Age of Alexander

M. Bieber, *The Sculpture of the Hellenistic Age*. New York 1955.

M. Cary, *A History of the Greek World from 323 to 146 BC*. 2nd ed. London 1951.

G. L. Cawkwell, *Philip of Macedon*. London 1978.

K. J. Dover, *Lysias and the Corpus Lysiacum*. Berkeley, Ca. 1968.

J. R. Ellis, *Philip II and Macedonian Imperialism*. London 1976.

P. M. Fraser, *Ptolemaic Alexandria*. 3 vols. Oxford 1972.

G. T. Griffith, *History of Macedonia*, vol. 2. Oxford 1972.

P. Grimal, *Hellenism and the Rise of Rome*. London 1968.

G. Kennedy, *The Art of Persuasion in Greece*. London and Princeton, N.J. 1963.

K. Lane Fox, *Alexander the Great*. London 1973.

J.A.O. Larsen, *Greek Federal States*. Oxford 1968.

N. Lewis, *Papyrus in Classical Antiquity*. Oxford 1974.

A.A. Long, *Hellenistic Philosophy*. London 1974.

K. Pfeiffer. *History of Classical Scholarship: from the Beginnings to the End of the Hellenistic Age*. Oxford 1968.

A.W. Pickard-Cambridge, *Demosthenes*. New York 1914.

H. Randall Jr., *Aristotle*. New York 1960.

L.D. Reynolds and N. G. Wilson. *Scribes and Scholars*. 2nd ed. Oxford 1974.

W.D. Ross. *Aristotle*. 5th ed. London 1960.

——*The Development of Aristotle's Thought*. London 1957.

M.I. Rostovtzeff, *Social and Economic History of the Hellenistic World*. 3 vols. Oxford 1941.

W.W. Tarn, *Hellenistic Military and Naval Developments*. Cambridge 1930.

——*Hellenistic Civilization*. 3rd ed. rev. G. T. Griffith. London 1952.

F. G. Turner, *Greek Papyri: An Introduction*. Oxford 1968.

——*Greek Manuscripts of the Ancient World*. Oxford 1971.

T.B.L. Webster, *Hellenistic Poetry and Art*. London 1964.

H.D. Westlake, *Thessaly in the Fourth Century*. London 1935.

Part Six: The Fate of Hellenism

P. Brown, *The World of Late Antiquity*. London 1971.

R. Browning. *Medieval and Modern Greek*. London 1969.

F. Fraenkel, *Horace*. Oxford 1957.

L. Politis, *A History of Modern Greek Literature*. Oxford 1973.

S. Runciman, *Mistra*. London 1980.

W. St. Clair, *That Greece might still be Free*. London 1972.

C. A. Trypanis (ed.), *Medieval and Modern Greek Poetry*. Oxford 1951.

G. Williams, *Tradition and Originality in Roman Poetry*. Oxford 1968.

Greek Literature in English Translation

Aischylos, *Oresteia*, tr. D. Young. Oklahoma 1975.

——*Prometheus and Other Plays*, tr. P. Vellacott. Harmondsworth 1970.

Apollodoros, *The Library*, tr. 3. G. Frazer. 2 vols. London 1921.

Apollonios Rhodios, *Argonautica*, tr. E. V. Rieu. Harniondsworth 1959.

Aristophanes, tr. B.B. Rogers. 3 vols. London 1924.

Aristotle, *Ethics*, tr. J.A.K. Thomson. Harmondsworth 1969.

——*Metaphysics*. tr. J. Warrington. London 1968.

——*Poetics*, tr. G.F. Else. Michigan 1970.

——*Politics and Athenian Constitution*, tr. J. Warrington. London 1959.

Demosthenes and Aischines, *Political Speeches*, tr. A. N. W. Saunders. Harmondsworth 1975.

Euripides, tr. G. Murray. London 1976.

Greek Anthology, tr. P. Jay. London 1973.

Herodotos, tr. A. de Sélincourt. Harmondsworth 1954.

Hesiod and Theognis, tr. D. Wender. Harmondsworth 1973.

Hippokrates, tr. W.H.S. Jones and F. T. Withington. 4 vols. London 1923–31.

Homer, tr. A. Pope. 4 vols. London 1967.

Kallimachos, tr. A. W. Mair. London 1955.

C. P. Kavafis, *Poems*, tr. J. Mavrogordato. London 1971.

Lucian, tr. A.M. Harmon, K. Kilburn and M.D. Macleod. 8 vols. London 1913–67.

Menander, *Girl from Samos*, tr. E.G. Turner. London 1972.

Pausanias, tr. P. Levi. 2 vols. Harmondsworth 1971.

Pindar, tr. R. Lattimore. 2nd ed. Chicago. Ill. 1976.

Plato, *Gorgias*, tr. W. Hamilton. Harmondsworth 1971.

——*Last Days of Socrates*, tr. H. Tredennick. Harmondsworth 1969.

——*Laws*, tr. T. Saunders. Harmondsworth 1970.

——*Protagoras and Meno*, tr. W.K.C. Guthrie. Harmondsworth 1970.

——*Republic*, tr. H. D. P. Lee. Harmondsworth 1970.

——*Symposium*, tr. W. Hamilton. Harmondsworth 1970.

Plutarch, *Age of Alexander*. tr. I.S. Kilvert. Harmondsworth 1973.

G. Seferis, *Collected Poems*, tr. F. Keeley and P. Sherrard. London 1973.

Sophokles, tr. F.F. Watling. 2 vols. Harmondsworth 1969.

Theokritos, *Greek Pastoral Poetry*, tr. A. Holden. Harmondsworth 1974.

Thucydides, tr. R. Warner. Harmondsworth 1954.

Xenophon, *Persian Expedition*, tr. R. Warner. Harmondsworth 1967.

Index